D0082855

Bariatric Surgery

Bariatric Surgery

A Guide for Mental Health Professionals

edited by
James E. Mitchell
Martina de Zwaan

Routledge
Taylor & Francis Group

NEW YORK AND HOVE

Published in 2005 by
Routledge
Taylor & Francis Group
270 Madison Avenue
New York, NY 10016

Published in Great Britain by
Routledge
Taylor & Francis Group
27 Church Road
Hove, East Sussex BN3 2FA

© 2005 by Taylor & Francis Group, LLC
Routledge is an imprint of Taylor & Francis Group
Formerly a Brunner-Routledge title.

Printed in the United States of America on acid-free paper
10 9 8 7 6 5 4 3 2 1

International Standard Book Number-10: 0-415-94966-1 (Hardcover)
International Standard Book Number-13: 978-0-415-94966-8 (Hardcover)
Library of Congress Card Number 2005001383

No part of this book may be reprinted, reproduced, transmitted, or utilized in any form by any electronic, mechanical, or other means, now known or hereafter invented, including photocopying, microfilming, and recording, or in any information storage or retrieval system, without written permission from the publishers.

Trademark Notice: Product or corporate names may be trademarks or registered trademarks, and are used only for identification and explanation without intent to infringe.

Library of Congress Cataloging-in-Publication Data

Bariatric surgery : a guide for mental health professionals / edited by James E. Mitchell and Martina de Zwann.
    p. cm.
Includes bibliographical references and index.
ISBN 0-415-94966-1 (hardback)
    1. Obesity--Surgery--Psychological aspects. 2. Obesity--Surgery--Patients--Mental health. I. Mitchell, James E., 1947- II. De Zwann, Martina.

RD540.B376 2005
617.4'3--dc22   2005001383

Taylor & Francis Group
is the Academic Division of T&F Informa plc.

Visit the Taylor & Francis Web site at
http://www.taylorandfrancis.com

and the Routledge Web site at
http://www.routledgementalhealth.com

To Mike Howell, MD, and Tim Monson, MD, two very talented bariatric surgeons who were kind enough to allow us to become involved in research with their patients.

Contents

About the Editors

James E. Mitchell, MD, is the NRI/Lee A. Christoferson MD Professor and Chair of the Department of Neuroscience at the University of North Dakota School of Medicine and Health Sciences, and president and scientific director of the Neuropsychiatric Research Institute. Dr. Mitchell completed his undergraduate education at Indiana University and medical school at Northwestern University. After an internship in internal medicine, he completed his residency in psychiatry and a fellowship in consultation/liaison psychiatry at the University of Minnesota. After entering academics, he focused his activities primarily on research in the area of eating disorders and obesity. He is past president of the Academy for Eating Disorders and past president of the Eating Disorders Research Society. He is on the Editorial Board of the *International Journal of Eating Disorders* and the *Eating Disorders Review.*

Martina de Zwaan, MD, is head of the Department of Psychosomatic Medicine and Psychotherapy at the University of Erlangen-Nuremberg in Germany. She received her MD degree from the University of Vienna where she also completed a residency in psychiatry and neurology. She spent a year doing a postdoctoral fellowship at the University of Minnesota in eating disorders research before returning to Vienna, where she was on the faculty at the University of Vienna Medical School between 1994 and 2002. She was a visiting scientist at the Neuropsychiatric Research Institute in Fargo, ND, during a sabbatical between 2001 and 2002 before taking her current position at the University of Erlangen-Nuremberg. She is well known for her research in eating disorders and obesity.

Contributors

Anita P. Courcoulas, MD, MPH, FACS, is the director of bariatric surgery at the University of Pittsburgh Medical Center at Shadyside and is an associate professor of surgery in the Division of Thoracic and Foregut Surgery at the University of Pittsburgh School of Medicine. Dr. Courcoulas has completed specialty training in general, trauma, pediatric, and minimally invasive surgery. She is board-certified by the American Board of Surgery and is a Fellow of the American College of Surgeons. Dr. Courcoulas is an active member of several professional and scientific societies, including the American College of Surgeons, the Society for Surgery of the Alimentary Tract, the American Society for Bariatric Surgery, The International Foundation for the Surgery of Obesity, the Central Surgical Association, and SAGES. She is also an active member in Sigma Xi and Alpha Omega Alpha scientific medical honor societies. She is a leader in the field of surgical outcomes and bariatric surgery.

Maureen Dymek-Valentine, PhD, is on faculty at the University of North Carolina at Chapel Hill and serves as the chief psychologist for the UNC Eating Disorders Program. She previously served on the faculty of the University of Chicago, where she was the coordinator of the Eating Disorders Clinic and the director of research for the Center of Surgical Treatment for Obesity. Dr. Dymek-Valentine received her PhD in medical (clinical) psychology from the University of Alabama at Birmingham, completed her clinical internship at the University of North Carolina at Chapel Hill, and her postdoctoral fellowship in eating disorders at the University of Chicago.

Marla J. Engelberg, PhD, is a clinical psychologist at the Eating Disorders Program at North York General Hospital in Toronto, Canada. She received her doctorate in clinical psychology at McGill University and completed a postdoctoral fellowship in eating disorders and bariatric surgery at the University of Chicago.

Jonathan Flom, MD, is a staff psychiatrist with Cape Fear Valley Health System in Fayetteville, NC. He completed his bachelor's degree at Concordia College in Moorhead, MN, before going on to complete medical school at the University of North Dakota. He then completed a psychiatry residency at the University of North Dakota program in Fargo, ND, where he did a part-time fellowship in eating disorders research. He resides in Fayetteville with his family.

Melissa A. Kalarchian, PhD, assistant professor of psychiatry, Western Psychiatric Institute and Clinic, University of Pittsburgh Medical Center, is a clinical psychologist who has worked extensively in adapting obesity and eating disorder treatments to the needs of special populations. She is the recipient of a patient-oriented training grant from the National Institute of Diabetes, Digestive, and Kidney Diseases (NIDDK) to work toward helping severely obese patients achieve maintenance of maximal weight loss and optimal psychosocial adjustment after bariatric surgery.

Marsha D. Marcus, PhD, professor of psychiatry and psychology, chief of Behavioral Medicine and Eating Disorders, Western Psychiatric Institute and Clinic, University of Pittsburgh Medical Center, is a clinical psychologist with more than 20 years of experience in the adaptation, delivery, and evaluation of treatments for obesity and eating disorders, with a particular interest in the relationship between psychiatric status and health-related behaviors. She has overseen the conduct of numerous randomized clinical trials of cognitive behavioral interventions in the treatment of health-related conditions including binge eating disorder, pediatric obesity, and smoking.

Tricia Cook Myers, PhD, is a licensed psychologist with the Neuropsychiatric Research Institute and Eating Disorder Institute in Fargo, ND, and clinical assistant professor, Department of Neuroscience, at the University of North Dakota School of Medicine and Health Sciences. In addition to her work on clinical research protocols at the Neuropsychiatric Research Institute, Dr. Myers provides evaluation and treatment services to children, adolescents, adults, and families affected by eating disorders at the Eating Disorders Institute. Dr. Myers received her doctoral degree in clinical psychology from the University of North Dakota and completed an American Psychological Association-accredited internship at the University of Chicago Medical Center with a special emphasis in behavioral medicine. She received her master's and undergraduate degrees from North Dakota State University. She is a member of the Academy for Eating Disorders, North Dakota Psychological Association, Association for Advancement of Behavior Therapy, American Psychological Association, and National Register of Health Service Providers in Psychology.

Renee Rienecke-Hoste, PhD, is a postdoctoral fellow at the University of Chicago, where she is involved in both the Eating Disorders Program and the Center for Surgical Treatment of Obesity. Dr. Rienecke-Hoste received her PhD from Northwestern University and completed her predoctoral clinical internship at the University of Chicago.

Lorraine A. Swan-Kremeier, PsyD, is a licensed psychologist with the Neuropsychiatric Research Institute in Fargo, ND, and clinical assistant professor, Department of Neuroscience at the University of North Dakota School of Medicine and Health Sciences. Dr. Swan-Kremeier is involved in clinically based, grant-funded research projects in the area of identification, evaluation, and treatment of eating disorders. At the Eating Disorders Institute, she provides evaluation and treatment services to children, adolescents, adults, and families affected by eating disorders. Originally from Minneapolis, MN, Dr. Swan-Kremeier graduated from Macalester College in St. Paul, MN, and earned a doctorate of clinical psychology with a core emphasis in child and family psychology from the Minnesota School of Professional Psychology. She is a member of the Academy for Eating Disorders, American Psychological Association, and National Register of Health Service Providers in Psychology.

Preface

Overweight and obesity are reaching epidemic proportions in the United States and much of the world. The reasons for this are complex, and although some of these reasons are to some extent understood, no clear plan has emerged to stop or reverse this trend. Accompanying this marked increase in the prevalence of overweight and obesity has been a growing acceptance of the fact that most available weight loss treatments—be they behavioral, psychotherapeutic, or pharmacological—offer only modest benefits, and, unfortunately, the benefits are all too often not maintained over time. Because of this, bariatric surgery procedures have become an increasingly accepted tool to deal with severe obesity. Part of this reflects the changing prevalence of weight control problems, but to some extent this also reflects that bariatric surgery procedures have evolved to a point where the benefit/risk ratio is far more acceptable than it was 20 to 30 years ago. Most patients now who undergo these procedures lose a significant amount of weight, experience significant improvement in various comorbidities such as diabetes and hypertension, and adjust quite well to the changes in lifestyle required.

In selecting candidates for bariatric surgery procedures, mental health practitioners are often involved. This may be mandated by third-party payers, or it may be done at the request of the surgical team, which not uncommonly requires a psychosocial assessment before accepting patients as surgery candidates. The purpose of this book is to address the needs of mental health professionals who evaluate and treat patients who are candidates for or who have undergone bariatric surgery. We hope this book will fill an important place in the available literature, in that a single volume addressing these issues in a succinct, practical, and databased way, has not previously been published. This text will attempt to fill that void.

We will begin with a descriptive overview of the various bariatric surgery procedures, including their risks and complications, then progress through psychosocial assessment of bariatric surgery candidates, including interviewing, the use of standardized databases, and the use of various psychometric instruments. We will discuss comorbid psychopathology as it is encountered in bariatric surgery patients and the effects of bariatric surgery on such comorbid psychopathology. We will also review both short- and long-term psychosocial outcomes and quality of life. We will also discuss the limited but growing literature on various sorts of interventions to improve outcome in patients undergoing bariatric surgery procedure, focusing on strategies to eliminate binge eating in binge eating disorder bariatric surgery candidates, because this may to some extent compromise the extent of weight loss at long-term follow-up. Throughout the book, we will attempt to be scholarly yet practical, providing clinicians with the most up-to-date information on these topics, yet also attempting to translate recent findings into specific clinical recommendations. We sincerely hope that this book will be of use to mental health practitioners who work with bariatric surgery patient during the process of evaluation in preparation for bariatric surgery, and during aftercare.

James E. Mitchell, MD
Chairman, Department of Neuroscience, University of North Dakota
School of Medicine and Health Sciences.
President, Neuropsychiatric Research Institute, Fargo, ND

Martina de Zwaan, MD
Chairman, Department of Psychosomatic Medicine and Psychotherapy,
University Hospital Erlangen, Erlangen, Germany

CHAPTER 1

Overview of Bariatric Surgery Procedures

JAMES E. MITCHELL AND ANITA P. COURCOULAS

As has been widely recognized by the media in the last few years, the percentage of Americans—and the percentage of individuals in most other countries as well—who are obese has been accelerating rapidly over the last twenty years (Ogden, Carroll, & Flegal, 2003). Although the category of overweight (body mass index [BMI] 25–29.9 kg/m²) has stayed relatively stable, the percentage of individuals with a BMI greater than 30 kg/m² (obese) and with a BMI greater than 40 kg/m² (extreme obesity) has increased dramatically. We know that as BMI increases, overall mortality increases, as does the risk for a variety of untoward medical and psychosocial outcomes (Bray, 2003). Given that most obesity treatments have modest effects at best and many times do not result in significant weight change over time, for individuals with severe obesity, bariatric surgery procedures offer a viable and cost-effective alternative (Colquitt, Clegg, Sidhu, & Royle, 2003; Craig & Tseng, 2002; Fang, 2003; Herron, 2004; Mattison & Jensen, 2004). The purpose of this chapter is to provide an overview of the various surgical treatments available and to discuss their relative benefits and risks.

Before turning to the specific procedures, it is worthwhile to review some of the health risks associated with obesity. Extreme obesity is associated with a variety of adverse medical outcomes, including metabolic complications such as diabetes mellitus; hypertension; elevated triglycerides

1

and cholesterol and other dyslipidemias; increased intra-abdominal pressure, which can result in the development of hernias, urinary incontinence, and gastroesophageal reflux; increased rates of cardiovascular disease, including coronary artery disease and heart failure; respiratory problems, including obstructive sleep apnea; hormonal dysfunction resulting in amenorrhea; osteoarthritis; increased risk for a variety of cancers, including cancers of the breast, uterus, prostate, and colon; elevated levels of certain proinflammatory cytokines, which are associated with an increased risk of cardiovascular disease; and progressive liver disease, with the risk of the eventual development of cirrhosis and liver failure (Coviello & Nystrom, 2003; Dandona, Aljada, Bandyopadhyay, 2004; El-Atat, Aneja, McFarlane, & Sowers, 2003; Gami, Caples, & Somers, 2003; Kushner & Roth, 2003; Maggio & Pi-Sunyer, 2003; Sowers, 2003).

Given these health concerns and the growing prevalence of this disorder, bariatric surgery is an important alternative for patients with a BMI greater than 40 kg/m² or those with a BMI greater than 35 kg/m² who have certain comorbid conditions such as type II diabetes, hypertension, or dyslipidemias. The rationale for bariatric surgery rests on the exponential rise in medical problems with BMIs higher than 35 to 40 and the poor long-term weight loss success in morbidly obese patients following the best available diets. According to the most recent Consensus conference statement, patients with BMIs greater than 40 and patients with BMIs between 35 and 40 with coexisting comorbid medical conditions are candidates for surgical weight loss procedures (Gastrointestinal Surgery for Severe Obesity: Consensus Development Panel, 1991). However, bariatric surgery procedures necessitate a dramatic change in eating behavior and lifestyle and therefore should only be considered in individuals who are carefully evaluated and give fully informed consent and who clearly understand the implications of the step they are taking (Kushner & Roth, 2003). Patients should be deemed ineligible for surgery if they cannot understand the dietary changes and lifestyle modifications necessary to complement the procedure. In addition, poor surgical risk status, very advanced age, untreated endocrine or other medical disorders, and active addiction behaviors are some of the contraindications to bariatric surgery.

The History of Bariatric Procedures

To illustrate the anatomic changes involved in these various procedures, we will first illustrate normal gastrointestinal anatomy. The small bowel is designated as three separate portions—duodenum, jejunum, and ileum—from proximal to mid to distal sections (Figure 1.1).

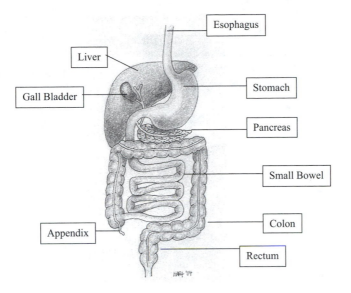

Figure 1.1 Normal anatomy.

The first procedure that generally gained wide popularity involved intestinal bypass, in which the proximal jejunum was bypassed into distal ileum, creating a long segment of blind intestine (Balsiger, Murr, Poggio, & Sarr, 2000). This was known as the jejunoileal bypass (JIB). Two variants of the JIB were developed: end-to-side (Payne) and end-to-end (Scott) (Figure 1.2), depending on how the proximal intestine was connected to the distal ileum.

This operation resulted in fairly profound malabsorption because a large part of the bowel surface had been bypassed and excluded from the alimentary stream. This procedure was associated with a variety of profound complications, including severe diarrhea and bile salt losses in the stool. Protein–calorie malnutrition was a common consequence, resulting in hair loss and edema. Specific vitamin and mineral deficiencies also occurred, including loss of vitamin B_{12}, vitamin K, vitamin A, magnesium, and the development of hypocalcemia with resulting bone thinning, osteoporosis, and bone pain. Additional complications were gallstones, arthritis, kidney stones, and some cases of long-term liver failure from cirrhosis (Balsiger, et al., 2000; Latifi, Kellum, DeMaria, & Sugerman, 2002).

The most favorable result after JIB was the excellent weight loss, but this was achieved as a result of extreme malabsorption, multiple deficiencies, and diarrhea. Many of these patients now have had the procedure reversed, although some follow-up work indicates that a subgroup of

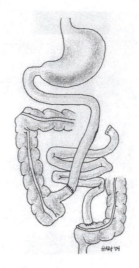

Figure 1.2 End-to-end (Scott) jejunoileal bypass.

patients do benefit from the procedure in the long term (Våge, Solhaug, Berstad, Svanes, & Viste, 2002). Because of the frequent and serious complications, JIB is no longer a recommended bariatric surgical procedure. Any of these patients encountered in clinical practice need to be followed carefully for metabolic complications and many, if not all, will have bypass reversal with conversion to an operation with a restrictive component.

At the other end of malabsorption to pure gastric restriction continuum was the horizontal gastroplasty and then vertical banded gastroplasty, which were introduced as a result of the development of surgical stapling devices after World War II. In a horizontal gastroplasty, a pouch was created in the upper stomach by introducing a horizontal suture line with several staples removed (the stoma) to allow for the passage of food substances (Figure 1.3). The idea was to create early satiety with horizontal gastric restriction. Unfortunately, both the stomach and the stoma enlarged with time, causing limited weight loss and subsequent weight regain. In the vertical banded gastroplasty, a vertical staple line parallel to the lesser curvature was placed with the proximal pouch draining into the distal pouch, with the outlet reinforced with a mesh collar to prevent enlargement of the stoma (Figure 1.4). This procedure was pursued and perfected by Dr. Edward Mason, who carefully measured a very small pouch volume fashioned along the lesser curvature of the stomach where it is less distensible with the concomitant use of a 5-cm restricting cuff.

The advantage to these purely restrictive procedures is that food is digested normally with no malabsorption or dumping, so there are almost

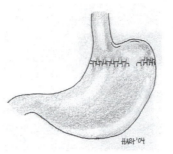

Figure 1.3 Horizontal gastroplasty.

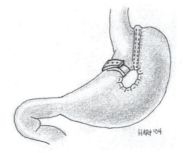

Figure 1.4 Vertical-banded gastroplasty.

no metabolic complications; conversely, however, the consumption and absorption of sweets is unlimited. Despite these improvements in surgical technique, purely restrictive procedures such as these are now rarely used because of inadequate long-term weight loss from staple line failures (Goldberg, Rivers, Smith, & Homan, 2000; Sugerman, 2001).

Gastric bypass, originally introduced in 1969 by Mason and Ito, was a hybrid procedure of gastric restriction and limited malabsorption. It involved creating a small proximal section of the stomach, a bypass of the larger gastric segment, and emptying of the proximal gastric pouch into a proximal intestinal loop (Schneider et al., 2003). Later this procedure was modified to configure a Roux-en-Y technique for drainage of the proximal gastric pouch to avoid bile reflux (Figure 1.5) (Colquitt et al., 2003). The Roux-en-Y configuration allows the biliopancreatic secretions or digestive juices to pass via the bile duct into the duodenum and then merge with the alimentary (food) stream, passing down from the stomach at the Y-type connection.

In later years, this operation has been further refined by a reduction in the size of the proximal gastric pouch to approximately 15 to 20 ml,

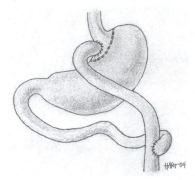

Figure 1.5 Roux-en-Y gastric bypass.

precise small gastric-to-intestinal-stoma size (with or without cuff/collar restriction), and complete staple line transection to avoid staple line failures (Figure 1.6). The length of the Roux-en-Y limb can also be varied, with a longer limb resulting in the more malabsorption and perhaps greater weight loss for patients with more severe "super obesity" (BMI > 50).

The Roux-en-Y gastric bypass is considered the gold standard bariatric surgical procedure in the United States and is the most common procedure of choice for most American bariatric surgeons. This procedure is a combination of gastric restriction and variable malabsorption and results in 60% to 80% excess weight loss over the first year in the majority of patients, with long-term weight stabilization at 50% to 60% loss of excess weight in nearly 80% of patients. Immediately after surgery, serious complication rates for gastric bypass range from 1% to 4% and include problems such as leak, infection, bleeding, and blood clots. Potential longer term complications and consequences are evident in as many as 12% to 26% of patients and are problems such as anemia from vitamin B_{12} and iron deficiency, calcium deficiency, intestinal ulcers, and dumping syndrome.

Roux-en-Y gastric bypass is increasingly being performed laparoscopically, which provides certain benefits compared with an open procedure, including more rapid discharge from the hospital, a quicker return to normal activities, and fewer incisional problems such as infection and hernias (Courcoulas, Perry, Buenaventura, & Luketich, 2003; Torsten, Lonröth, Fagevik-Olsen, & Lundell, 2003).

Other surgical approaches to both restriction and malabsorption have also evolved from this historical experience, and several of these procedures remain within the armamentarium of the bariatric surgeon. In 1983, Bø and Modalsli introduced gastric banding, a strictly restrictive procedure in which a band was used to section the stomach into proximal and

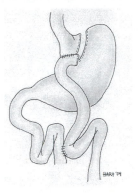

Figure 1.6 Transected Roux-en-Y gastric bypass.

Figure 1.7 Nonadjustable gastric banding.

distal segments (Figure 1.7). A similar but adjustable form of gastric banding was introduced by Kuzmak in 1992. This device has a balloon in the lining of the cuff that is inflatable and can be attached to a reservoir that is placed under the skin for access to adjust the cuff size. This technique has been modified for placement through a laparoscope (Favretti, O'Brien, & Dixon, 2002; Weiner, Blanco-Engert, Weiner, Matkowitz, Schaefer, & Pomhoff, 2003). Postoperative management then requires frequent follow-up visits so that the band can be adjusted to optimize food variety and weight loss (Favretti et al., 2002). Adjustable gastric banding has grown increasingly popular worldwide, particularly outside of the United States, where weight loss results are excellent (Figure 1.8) (O'Brien, et al., 2002; Steffen, Biertho, Ricklin, Piec, & Horber, 2003), and was recently approved for use in the United States. The weight loss results in this country have not been as favorable as those in Europe, however (DeMaria et al., 2001).

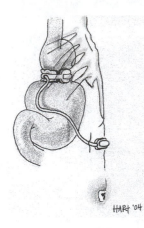

Figure 1.8 Adjustable gastric band.

The favorable results of this procedure are the absence of dumping, malabsorption, and other metabolic complications common to bypass and purely malabsorptive procedures. Band patients must adhere strictly to dietary guidelines and avoid high-calorie liquids and soft snack foods. There are possible significant complications of band placement, including slippage of the band, erosion of the band into the stomach, and tubing breakage problems (Busetto et al., 2002; DeMaria et al., 2001, O'Brien et al., 2002), which can occur in variable numbers of patients ranging from 3% to 27%.

The final area of surgical innovation has been in the use of more extreme malabsorptive procedures for treatment of "super obese" patients. Most recently, biliopancreatic diversion (BPD) and BPD with duodenal switch operations have been introduced into common bariatric surgical practice (Baltasar et al., 2002; Paiva, Bernardes, & Suretti, 2002; Scopinaro, Marinari, & Camerini, 2002). BPD is an improved intestinal bypass procedure that combines a partial, subtotal gastrectomy (smaller stomach capacity) and a very long Roux-en-Y anastomosis with a short common channel for nutrient absorption (Figure 1.9).

The long-term results of this procedure show the best excess body weight loss with maintenance at 70% to 75% in the majority of patients. Patients can eat much larger quantities of food and still achieve and maintain weight loss. The disadvantages are loose and foul-smelling stools, intestinal ulcers, anemia, vitamin and mineral deficiencies, and possible protein–calorie malnutrition in as many as 5% to 12% of patients. Because of these potential, lifelong problems, BPD patients require lifelong supplementation and follow-up.

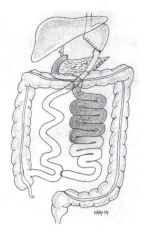

Figure 1.9 Biliopancreatic diversion (BPD).

BPD with duodenal switch is a hybrid operation that combines a gastric sleeve resection (70% greater curve gastrectomy) with long intestinal bypass in Roux-en-Y configuration (Figure 1.10). By leaving the first portion of the intestine in the food stream, the ulcer rate is reduced and dumping syndrome is eliminated.

These operations are clearly the most major and technically difficult procedures performed for weight loss and should be offered only by experienced surgeons with lifelong follow-up programs. The short-term serious complication rate with these highly malabsorptive procedures range from 4% to 12% (Gagner, Steffen, Biertho, & Horber, 2003). BPD and BPD with duodenal switch can also be approached successfully with the laparoscopic technique (Paiva et al., 2002; Scopinaro et al., 2002). Further variation and innovation has been recently introduced, including laparoscopic adjustable gastric band with a duodenal switch (Gagner et al., 2003).

It is important to note that, despite a fairly substantive body of case series' literature, debate continues as to the selection of the best procedure for any given patient. Some general guidelines are increasingly being accepted with the recognition that percent excess weight loss varies with the choice of procedure (Figure 1.11); therefore, "superobese" patients more often are being guided to the more malabsorptive procedures.

In addition, there is growing evidence that a proximal intestinal bypass procedure is necessary and perhaps more beneficial for patients with diabetes.

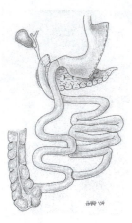

Figure 1.10 Biliopancreatic diversion with duodenal switch.

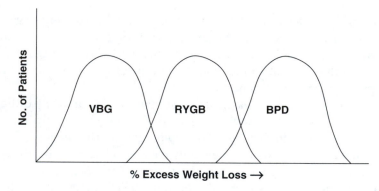

Figure 1.11 Procedure and excess weight loss.

Complications

In general, complications can be grouped into those that occur during surgery (intraoperative), those that occur shortly after surgery, and those that develop over time (Byrne, 2001; Elliot, 2003). Intraoperative problems include bleeding, possible trauma to other organs such as the spleen, and anesthetic complications. Short-term complications include bleeding, blood clot, lung collapse, bowel obstruction, and distension of the bypassed section of the stomach, which can result in gastric perforation. Postoperative intestinal leaks from the gastric to intestinal connection are the most serious acute complications (Latifi et al., 2002). Significant intestinal leakage is a medical emergency and requires prompt recognition, diagnosis, and treatment. Treatment is either drainage with percutaneous catheter or operation for repair of the disruption. After gastric bypass, some patients will develop a marginal ulcer at the area of anastomosis from stomach to intestine that usually can be managed with acid blockade. Other possible complications include wound infection, persistent nausea and vomiting from gastric outlet scarring (stricture), and other possible nutritional deficiencies including those specific to B_1 (thiamine) deficiency such as Wernicke's encephalopathy (Loh et al., 2004) and others.

In terms of late complications, an incisional hernia can develop in patients having undergone open procedures, which usually require reoperation (Latifi et al., 2002). Bowel obstruction from adhesions presents a small lifetime risk for all patients after abdominal surgery. Because of the rapid weight loss after various procedures, gall bladder disease may develop; because of this, some surgeons routinely perform a cholecystectomy as part of the bariatric procedure, particularly if stones are present at the time of the original surgery (Byrne, 2001). Nutritionally, some patients can develop B_{12} deficiency after gastric bypass; this should be addressed prophalactically with either intranasal or intramuscular B_{12} (Elliot, 2003). Magnesium and calcium deficiencies can also develop, as can iron deficiency anemia, particularly in women who are menstruating (Byrne, 2001; Elliot, 2003). Some patients will fail to lose an adequate amount of weight and should be considered for alternative procedures, but reoperation in such patients can be quite difficult, with an elevated risk of morbidity and mortality.

On a more positive note, many medical comorbidities improve substantially or remit completely, including a decrease in levels of circulating proinflammatory cytokines, improved cardiac functioning, improvement in hypertension, remission of sleep apnea syndrome, and remission of diabetes mellitus (which, surprisingly, corrects very early in the course of weight loss, suggesting that variables other than weight loss are involved) (Deitel, 2002).

Increasingly, reports are appearing of the use of bariatric surgeries in patients younger than age 18 (Garcia, Langford, & Inge, 2003). Much of this is attributable to the increase in adolescent obesity and the development of complications of type II diabetes, which traditionally were rarely seen in adolescents but now are fairly common (Garcia et al., 2003). Because of this, part of chapter 9 in this text is devoted to special issues regarding the use of this surgery in adolescents.

References

Balsiger, B. M., Murr, M. M., Poggio, J. L., & Sarr, M. G. (2000). Surgery for weight control in patients with morbid obesity. *Medical Clinics of North America, 84,* 477–489.

Baltasar, A., Bou, R., Miró, J., Bengochea, M., Serra, C., & Pérez, N. (2002). Laparoscopic biliopancreatic diversion with duodenal switch: Technique and initial experience. *Obesity Surgery, 12,* 245–248.

Bray, G. A. (2003). Risks of obesity. *Endocrinology and Metabolism Clinics of North America, 32,* 787–804.

Busetto, L., Segato, G., De Marchi, F., Foletto, M., De Luca, M., Caniato, D., et al. (2002). Outcome predictors in morbidly obese recipients of an adjustable gastric band. *Obesity Surgery, 12,* 83–92.

Byrne, T. K. (2001). Complications of surgery for obesity. *Surgical Clinics of North America, 81,* 1181–1993.

Colquitt, J., Clegg, A., Sidhu, M., & Royle, P. (2003). Surgery for morbid obesity. *Cochrane Database System Review,* 2003.

Courcoulas, A., Perry, Y., Buenaventura, P., & Luketich, J. (2003). Comparing the outcomes after laparoscopic versus open gastric bypass: A matched paired analysis. *Obesity Surgery, 13,* 341–346.

Coviello, J. S., & Nystrom, K. V. (2003). Obesity and heart failure. *Journal of Cardiovascular Nursing, 18,* 360–366.

Craig, B. M., & Tseng, D. S. (2002). Cost-effectiveness of gastric bypass for severe obesity. *The American Journal of Medicine, 113,* 491–498.

Dandona P, Aljada A, Bandyopadhyay A. (2004). Inflammation: the link between insulin resistance, obesity, and diabetes. Trends Immunology. 25, (1):4–7.

Deitel, M. (2002). The early effect of the bariatric operations on diabetes. *Obesity Surgery, 12,* 349.

DeMaria, E. J., Sugerman, H. J., Meador, J. G., Doty, J. M., et al. (2001). High failure rate after laparoscopic adjustable silicone gastric banding for treatment of morbid obesity. *Annals of Surgery, 233,* 809–818.

Elliot, K. (2003). Nutritional considerations after bariatric surgery. *Critical Care Nursing Quarterly, 26,* 133–138.

El-Atat, F., Aneja, A., McFarlane, S., & Sowers, J. (2003). Obesity and hypertension. *Endocrinology and Metabolism Clinics of North America, 32,* 823–854.

Fang, J. (2003). The cost-effectiveness of bariatric surgery. *American Journal of Gastroenterology, 98,* 2097–2098.

Favretti, F., Cadière, G. B., Segato, G., Himpens, J., De Luca, M., Busetto, L., et al. (2002). Laparoscopic banding: Selection and technique in 830 patients. *Obesity Surgery, 12,* 385–390.

Favretti, F., O'Brien, P. E., & Dixon, J. B. (2002). Patient management after LAP-BAND placement. *American Journal of Surgery, 184,* 38S–41S.

Fobi, M., Lee, H., Igwe, D., Felahy, B., James, E., Stanczyk, M., et al. (2002). Prophylactic cholecystectomy with gastric bypass operation: Incidence of gallbladder disease. *Obesity Surgery, 12,* 350–353.

Gagner, M., Steffen, R., Biertho, L., & Horber, F. (2003). Modern surgery: Technical innovation. Laparoscopic adjustable gastric banding with duodenal switch for morbid obesity: Technique and preliminary results. *Obesity Surgery, 13,* 444–449.

Gami, A. S., Caples, S. M., & Somers, V. K. (2003). Obesity and obstructive sleep apnea. *Endocrinology and Metabolism Clinics of North America, 32,* 869–894.

Garcia, V. F., Langford, L., & Inge, T. H. (2003). Application of laparoscopy for bariatric surgery in adolescents. *Current Opinion in Pediatrics, 15,* 248–255.

Gastrointestinal surgery for severe obesity: Consensus Development Panel. (1991). *Annals of Internal Medicine,* 115, 956–960.

Goldberg, S., Rivers, P., Smith, K., & Homan, W. (2000). Vertical banded gastroplasty: A treatment for morbid obesity. *AORN Journal, 72,* 988–1003.

Herron, D. M. (2004). The surgical management of severe obesity. *The Mount Sinai Journal of Medicine, New York, 71,* 63–71.

Kushner, R. F., & Roth, J. L. (2003). Assessment of the obese patient. Endocrinology and Metabolism Clinics of North America. 32 (4): 915–933.

Latifi, R., Kellum, J. M., DeMaria, E. J., & Sugerman, H. J. (2002). Surgical treatment of obesity. In T. Wadden and A. J. Stunkard (Eds.), *Handbook of Obesity Treatment* (pp. 339–356). New York: Guilford Press.

Loh, Y., Watson, W. D., Verma, A., Chang, S. T., Stocker, D. J., & Labutta, R. J. (2004). Acute Wernicke's encephalopathy following bariatric surgery: Clinical course and MRI correlation. *Obesity Surgery, 14,* 129–132.

Maggio, D. A., & Pi-Sunyer, F. X. (2003). Obesity and type 2 diabetes. *Endocrinology and Metabolism Clinics of North America, 32,* 805–822.

Mason, E. E., & Ito, C. (1969). Gastric bypass. *Annals of Surgery, 170,* 329–339.

Mattison, R., & Jensen, M. D. (2004). Bariatric surgery. For the right patient, procedure can be effective. *Postgraduate Medicine, 115,* 49–58.

O'Brien, P. E., Dixon, J. B., Brown, W., Schachter, L. M., Chapman, L., Burn, A. J., et al. (2002). The laparoscopic adjustable gastric band (Lap-Band®): A prospective study of medium-term effects on weight, health and quality of life. *Obesity Surgery, 12,* 652–660.

Ogden, C. L., Carroll, M. D., & Flegal, K. M. (2003). Epidemiologic trends in overweight and obesity. *Endocrinology and Metabolism Clinics of North America, 32,* 741–760.

Paiva, D., Bernardes, L., & Suretti, L. (2002). Laparoscpoic biliopancreatic diversion: Technique and initial results. *Obesity Surgery, 12,* 358–361.

Schneider, B. E., Villegas, L., Blackburn, G. L., Mun, E. C., Critchlow, J. F., & Jones, D. B. (2003). Laparoscopic gastric bypass surgery: outcomes. *Journal of Laparoendoscopic & Advanced Surgical techniques. Part A, 13,* 247–255.

Scopinaro, N., Marinari, B. M., & Camerini, G. (2002). Laparoscopic standard biliopancreatic diversion: Technique and preliminary results. *Obesity Surgery, 12,* 241–244.

Sowers, J. R. (2003) Obesity as a cardiovascular risk factor. *American Journal of Medicine, 115,* 37S–41S.

Steffen, R., Biertho, L., Ricklin, T., Piec, G., & Horber, F. F. (2003). Laparoscopic Swedish adjustable gastric banding: A five-year prospective study. *Obesity Surgery, 13,* 404–411.

Sugerman, H. J. (2001). Bariatric surgery for severe obesity. *Journal of the Associations for Academic Minority Physicians, 12,* 129–136.

Torsten, O., Lönroth, H., Fagevik-Olsén, M., & Lundell, L. (2003). Laparoscopic gastric bypass: Development of technique, respiratory function, and long-term outcome. *Obesity Surgery, 13,* 364–370.

Våge, V., Solhaug, J., Berstad, A., Svanes, K., & Viste, A. (2002). Jejunoileal bypass in the treatment of morbid obesity: A 25-year follow-up study of 36 patients. *Obesity Surgery, 12,* 312–318.

Weiner, R., Blanco-Engert, R., Weiner, S., Matkowitz, R., Schaefer, L., & Pomhoff, I. (2003). Outcome after laparoscopic adjustable gastric banding—8 years experience. *Obesity Surgery, 13,* 427–434.

CHAPTER 2

Psychosocial Assessment in Bariatric Surgery Candidates

MAUREEN DYMEK-VALENTINE, RENEE RIENECKE-HOSTE, AND MARLA J. ENGELBERG

With the explosion in rates of bariatric surgeries in recent years, increasing numbers of mental health professionals are being called on to assist the surgical team in selecting appropriate surgical candidates. However, many mental health professionals have limited knowledge of morbid obesity and bariatric surgery, and there are few published reports on psychosocial assessment of this population. This chapter seeks to provide information on the typical psychosocial presentation of individuals with morbid obesity, review the literature on psychosocial predictors of success in bariatric surgery to help the clinician make more informed suggestions about a patient's candidacy, present a structure for psychosocial assessments in this population, and discuss the process of making recommendations to the surgical team on a patient's candidacy.

Although the psychosocial functioning of bariatric surgery candidates has not been researched extensively, numerous studies have been conducted on psychosocial functioning in obese populations. Such studies have focused on assessing psychopathology, eating behavior, and quality of life.

Psychosocial Functioning in Obese Populations

Psychopathology

Research has generally found that most forms of gross psychopathology are not more prevalent in the obese than in the normal-weight population, although there are some notable exceptions (e.g., Bocchieri, Meana, & Fisher, 2002; Friedman & Brownell, 1995; Stunkard & Wadden, 1992). Depression and binge eating have significantly higher rates among individuals with obesity (Prather & Williamson, 1988; Smith, Marcus, Lewis, Fitzgibbon, & Schreiner, 1998; Spitzer et al., 1992; Spitzer et al., 1993). A recent population-based study of binge eating showed that 3% of obese individuals meet criteria for binge eating disorder (BED) compared with 1.5% of the overall cohort (Smith et al., 1999).

The relationship between mental health problems and obesity is moderated by gender, level of obesity, and treatment-seeking behavior. Although BED appears to occur more frequently in obese populations regardless of gender (Spitzer et al., 1993), a recent population-based study showed significantly higher rates of major depressive disorder and suicidality in overweight and obese women compared with normal-weight women, but lower rates of depressive disorder in overweight and obese men compared with their normal-weight counterparts (Carpenter, Hasin, Allison, & Faith, 2000). In addition, Sullivan et al. (1993) found that individuals with extreme obesity (body mass index [BMI] > 38 kg/m²) are at greater risk of poorer mental functioning than those with moderate obesity (BMI 34–37 kg/m²) in the Swedish Obese Subjects Study. In a smaller pilot study, Wadden et al. (2001) found that women presenting for bariatric surgery (BMI > 40 kg/m²) showed higher levels of depression than those presenting to medication clinic (BMI < 40 kg/m²). Rates of binge eating are also markedly higher among individuals seeking obesity treatment than among obese individuals in the general population, with 16% to 30% of those seeking weight-reduction treatment meeting criteria for BED (see de Zwaan et al., 2003).

Although certain subgroups of obese individuals are at increased risk for depression and psychological distress, the consensus among researchers and clinicians is that psychological symptomatology and distress is a result of obesity, rather than a cause (Friedman & Brownell, 1995; Stunkard & Wadden, 1992). This distress is likely secondary to the extreme discrimination and prejudice and limited physical functioning that obese individuals often experience.

Quality of Life

Numerous investigations have demonstrated a clear link between obesity and impaired quality of life (QOL). This relationship holds true regardless of age, gender, or race (Fontaine, Cheskin, & Barofsky, 1996; Ford, Moriarty, Zack, Mokdad, & Chapman, 2001; Kolotkin, Crosby, Williams, Hartley, & Nicol, 2001; Sullivan et al., 1993), but appears stronger as level of obesity increases (Doll, Petersen, & Stewart-Brown, 2000; Sullivan et al., 1993) and as treatment-seeking behavior increases (Fontaine et al., 1996; Kolotkin, Crosby, & Williams, 2002; Kolotkin, Crosby, Williams et al., 2001). Some studies have found an even stronger relationship between impaired QOL and obesity in women (Carpenter et al., 2000; Kolotkin et al., 2002; Larsson, Karlsson, & Sullivan, 2002; Mannucci et al., 1999). Quality of life refers to an individual's level of satisfaction with the physical, psychological, and social aspects of his or her life. The prejudice and discrimination experienced by obese individuals is widespread and can have a significant impact on their QOL. Studies have found that the obese are discriminated against in the workplace, in college admissions decisions, and by health care providers (Wadden & Stunkard, 1985). Obese individuals report having fewer social interactions than normal-weight individuals (Valtolina, 1996), and, compared with those with other chronic physical conditions such as diabetes or musculoskeletal deformities, chronic obesity can result in lower income and lower marriage rates (Gortmaker, Must, Perrin, Sobol, & Dietz, 1993).

Health-related quality of life (HRQOL) has recently received increased attention as an important construct in obesity and weight loss research. HRQOL refers to an individual's subjective evaluation of his or her health status and its impact on his or her general functioning. This construct is particularly relevant for obese individuals, who are at increased risk for a number of medical conditions, including hypertension, diabetes, coronary artery disease, and several types of cancer (Pi-Sunyer, 1993).

Several studies have found a relationship between obesity and impaired HRQOL. A study of obese individuals seeking outpatient treatment found that the obese patients reported significantly worse scores on a measure of HRQOL compared with the general population (Fontaine et al., 1996). HRQOL also varied according to severity of obesity; patients who were morbidly obese reported significantly worse levels of functioning, general health, and bodily pain than did mildly or moderately obese patients. In addition, the level of bodily pain experienced by obese patients was more severe than that experienced by patients with other chronic conditions, including patients with congestive heart failure and HIV-positive individuals, and was comparable with that of migraine sufferers.

Psychosocial Presentation of Bariatric Surgery Candidates

This section provides descriptive data for objective psychosocial measures of bariatric surgery candidates who presented for surgical evaluation at the Center for Surgical Treatment of Obesity at the University of Chicago between 2000 and 2002. All surgical candidates were given a packet of standardized psychosocial questionnaires assessing mood, self-esteem, eating pathology, and QOL as part of their presurgical assessment, resulting in a total of 221 participants. Ages ranged from 20 to 62 years, with a mean of 40.5 ± 10 years; BMIs ranged from 39 to 77 kg/m^2, with a mean of 54.1 ± 10 kg/m^2. The sample was 78% female, 68% Caucasian, and 24% African American. Patients reported an average of 13.9 ± 2 years of education. Most patients reported having been overweight for the majority of their lives, and the average age of obesity onset was reported as 12.2 ± 8.1 years. This section also contrasts the findings from the University of Chicago sample with those from other samples.

Mood and Self-Esteem

All patients were assessed with the Beck Depression Inventory (BDI; Beck, Ward, Mendelson, Mock, & Erbaugh, 1961), a standardized self-report questionnaire designed to assess the presence and severity of depressive symptomatology represented by scores from 0 to 63. The BDI scores in our samples ranged between 1 and 51, with a mean score of 17.1 ± 9.5, indicative of a mild to moderate, clinically significant level of depression (Groth-Marnat, 1999). Patients were also assessed with the Rosenberg Self-Esteem Scale (Rosenberg, 1965), a self-report measure that assesses overall self-esteem. The measure was scored such that higher scores indicated higher self-esteem. The Rosenberg Self-Esteem Scale scores in our sample ranged between 10 and 40, with a mean score of 28 ± 6.1. As displayed in Table 2.1, this score represents slightly lower-than-average self-esteem when compared with nonclinical college-age and adult samples (Twenge & Campbell, 2001). In addition, all patients were asked how important weight is in determining their self-esteem using a scale ranging from 1 (unimportant) to 4 (most important). Patients reported that weight and shape are "very important" in determining their self-concept, with an average score of $3.1 \pm .9$.

TABLE 2.1 Scores on Psychosocial Measures for Bariatric Surgery Candidates

	Bariatric Surgery Candidates	Normal Weight Comparison
Beck Depression Inventory	17.1 (9.5)	
Rosenberg Self-Esteem Scale[a]	28.0 (6.1)	32.9
Three-Factor Eating Questionnaire[b]		
Restraint	8.5 (4.2)	8.2 (5.7)
Disinhibition	10.5 (3.7)	6.0 (3.4)
Hunger	8.1 (3.5)	6.4 (3.5)
SF-36[c] (higher scores denote better functioning, scale 0–100)		
Physical functioning	35.6 (23.4)	85.2 (23.3)
Role-physical	31.4 (36.0)	81.0 (34.0)
Bodily pain	41.9 (20.6)	75.2 (23.7)
General health	36.7 (20.2)	72.0 (20.3)
Vitality	30.2 (20.2)	60.9 (21.0)
Social functioning	52.9 (28.9)	83.3 (22.7)
Role-emotional	55.8 (28.9)	81.3 (33.1)
Mental health	60.4 (21.0)	74.7 (18.1)
Impact of Weight on Quality of Life Questionnaire-Lite ($N = 97$)[d] (lower scores denote better functioning)		
Physical functioning	45.1 (8.2)	12.6 (2.4)
Self-esteem	26.6 (6.8)	9.7 (4.6)
Sexual life	13.0 (5.1)	4.5 (1.9)
Public distress	18.8 (4.3)	5.3 (1.4)
Work	12.3 (4.7)	4.2 (0.9)
Total	115.2 (21.8)	36.3 (8.4)

Note. Normal weight comparisons taken from [a]Twenge & Campbell, 2001; [b]Boerner et al., 2004; [c]Ware et al., 1993; [d]Kolotkin & Crosby, 2002.

Eating Behavior

To assess eating thoughts and behaviors, we used the Three-Factor Eating Questionnaire (TFEQ; Stunkard & Messick, 1985). The TFEQ is a self-report measure of dietary restraint, disinhibited eating, and hunger. In the sample of participants described in the section above, the mean score for dietary restraint was 8.5 ± 4.2 out of a possible 21, the mean score for disinhibited eating was 10.6 ± 3.7 out of possible 16, and the mean score for hunger was 8.1 ± 3.5 out of a possible 14. These data are similar to scores obtained in previous studies with bariatric surgery candidates (e.g., Kalarchian, Wilson, Brolin, & Bradley, 1998), but show elevated levels of disinhibition and hunger when compared to a large nonclinical female sample, as shown in Table 2.1 (Boerner, Spillane, Anderson, & Smith, 2004).

We also assessed the presence of BED using a second sample of bariatric surgery candidates (N = 168) that was consecutively evaluated between January and September 2002 (Dymek-Valentine, Rienecke-Hoste, & Alverdy, in press). Diagnoses were obtained using the Questionnaire of Eating and Weight Patterns-Revised (QEWP-R; Spitzer et al., 1993) and the eating disorders module of the Structured Clinical Interview for Diagnostic and Statistical Manual of mental disorders, 4th edition, Axis I Disorders (SCID; First, Spitzer, Gibbon, & Williams, 2001). In this study, 27% of the sample received a diagnosis of BED using the QEWP-R, compared with 14% using the SCID. An additional 17% of the sample reported subjective binges with the QEWP-R, compared with 16% using the SCID. Subjective binges are defined here as episodes of eating in which individuals experience a loss of control, but do not consume an objectively large amount of food. Agreement between the QEWP-R and SCID with regards to subjective binge episodes in the current sample was .39 using Cohen's kappa, indicating modest overlap between measures. While both methods of assessing BED were developed using the Diagnostic and Statistical Manual of mental disorders, 4th edition (DSM-IV; APA, 1994), diagnostic criteria, the methods yielded different results, indicating that diagnostic classification of BED in this population may be different depending on the methods used. However, the results indicate that a sizable portion (between 14% and 27%) met full criteria for BED and up to 44% of the population reported subjective binge eating. Rates of BED from other samples of bariatric surgery candidates vary considerably (between 1.4% and 49%), but average at around 27% (see de Zwaan et al., 2003; see chapter 5).

Health-Related Quality of Life

All individuals were assessed with the Medical Outcomes Study 36-Item Short-Form Health Survey (SF-36; Ware, Snow, Kosinski, & Gandek, 1993), a self-report survey containing eight subscales designed to assess general health-related quality of life. The SF-36 generates subscale scores in the areas of Physical Functioning, Role-Physical, Bodily Pain, General Health, Vitality, Social Functioning, Role-Emotional and Mental Health. Scores are transformed into a 100-point range, with higher scores indicating better quality of life. The mean transformed Physical Functioning score was 35.6 ± 23.4, the mean transformed Role-Physical score was 31.4 ± 36.0, the mean transformed Bodily Pain score was 41.8 ± 20.5, the mean transformed General Health score was 36.7 ± 20.2, the mean transformed Vitality score was 30.2 ± 20.2, the mean transformed Social Functioning score was 52.9 ± 28.9, the mean transformed Role-Emotional score was

55.8 ± 28.9, and the mean transformed Mental Health score was 60.5 ± 21.0. As displayed in Table 2.1, the bariatric surgery candidates showed a markedly lower level of quality of life on all subscales, as compared with normal weight controls from the SF-36 validity studies (Ware et al., 1993).

A subset of the sample assessed between 2001 and 2002 (N=98) was given the Impact of Weight on Quality of Life Questionnaire-Lite (IWQOL-Lite; Kolotkin, Crosby, Kosloski, & Williams, 2001), a self-report survey developed to assess HRQOL in obese populations. In addition to a total score, the IWQOL-Lite generates five subscale scores in the areas of physical functioning, self-esteem, sexual life, public distress, and work. On the IWQOL-Lite, higher scores indicate poorer QOL. The mean physical functioning subscale score was 45.1 ± 8.2, the mean self-esteem subscale score was 26.6 ± 6.8, the mean sexual life subscale score was 13.0 ± 5.1, the mean public distress subscale score was 18.8 ± 4.3, the mean work subscale score was 12.3 ± 4.5, and the mean total score was 115.2 ± 21.8. As displayed in Table 2.1, the bariatric surgery candidates showed a markedly lower level QOL on all subscales, as compared with a community sample of normal-weight controls (Kolotkin & Crosby, 2002). Notably, the bariatric surgery candidates also showed poorer IWQOL-Lite scores than a community sample of morbidly obese adults (Kolotkin & Crosby, 2002).

Other investigations into HRQOL among individuals seeking bariatric surgery have also shown markedly impaired levels of functioning in several different quality of life domains. Compared with the general population, bariatric surgery candidates report more difficulties in physical, social, and emotional functioning, more bodily pain, decreased vitality, and worse health overall (de Zwaan, Lancaster et al., 2002). They report fewer social interactions than other chronically ill individuals and report poor mental well-being, comparable with that of cancer survivors (Sullivan et al., 1993). Among individuals seeking bariatric surgery, HRQOL varies according to the presence of BED. Compared with patients without BED, those with BED show significantly more impairment in physical and mental functioning (de Zwaan, Mitchell et al., 2002). Impairment in several aspects of HRQOL also increases as the presence of comorbid medical conditions and comorbid depression increases (Kolotkin et al., 2003). In addition, Rand and Macgregor (1991) asked patients who had maintained weight loss for several years after bariatric surgery to choose between being morbidly obese or having another major physical disability. Patients said they would prefer to be at a normal weight with a serious disability such as deafness, blindness, dyslexia, diabetes, severe acne, heart disease, or an amputated leg rather than to be morbidly obese. Patients also said they would prefer to be at a normal weight than be an obese multimillionaire.

Psychosocial Predictors of Outcome

Past Hypotheses of Outcome Prediction

Traditional weight loss programs have relied primarily on behavioral and psychopharmacological approaches to treat obesity. These approaches can be successful in producing modest weight loss, but patients rarely maintain this weight loss over time. Efforts to improve these programs and to maintain long-term weight loss have included attempts to personalize the treatments by matching them to the patient, which has prompted the investigation of predictors of success and failure. Although accurate and reliable predictors of short- and long-term weight loss have largely eluded researchers, a few studies have found that BED, depression, and a history of sexual abuse may be negative prognostic indicators of successful weight loss in traditional weight loss programs. Because these same predictors have been hypothesized to relate to outcome in bariatric surgery, we will present a brief review of this literature.

Predictors of Outcome with Traditional Weight Loss Programs

Psychopathology

Despite the widely held belief that the presence of psychopathology predicts poor outcome in traditional weight loss programs, there is surprisingly little evidence to support this. However, a few studies have found that patients with a history of psychiatric problems, including depression, are more likely to drop out of weight loss treatment programs than are patients without such a history (Rabkin, 1983; Yass-Reed, Barry, & Dacey, 1993), and Eldredge and Agras (1997) found a strong association between poor outcome in a behavioral weight loss program and elevated scores on the Global Severity Index of the Symptom Checklist-90-Revised.

Eating Behavior

Combined with the higher rate of psychopathology among individuals with BED (Marcus et al., 1990; Spitzer et al., 1993; Yanovski, Nelson, Dubbert, & Spitzer, 1993) and their earlier onset of obesity and unstable weight history compared with overweight or obese non-binge eaters (Loro & Orleans, 1981; Spitzer et al., 1993), researchers hypothesized that those with BED would have a poorer outcome in traditional weight loss treatment programs compared with non-binge eaters. Indeed, studies have found that individuals with BED are more likely to drop out of weight loss treatment (Marcus, Wing, & Hopkins, 1988; Sherwood, Jeffery, & Wing, 1999) and are faster to regain weight after weight loss interventions than are obese non-binge eaters (Marcus et al., 1988; Wing & Greeno, 1994). Obese binge eaters have also been found to lose less weight in behavioral weight loss programs than obese non-binge eaters (Gormally, Rardin, & Black, 1980; Keefe, Wyshogrod, Weinberger, & Agras, 1984). In contrast, another study found that obese binge eaters in a weight reduction program were half as likely to drop out of treatment compared with obese non-binge eaters (Ho, Nichaman, Taylor, Lee, & Foreyt, 1995), and four studies have found little or no association between the frequency of pretreatment binge eating and posttreatment weight loss (Bonato & Boland, 1987; Gladis et al., 1998; Gormally et al., 1980; Teixeira et al., 2002).

Sexual Abuse

Some authors have postulated that in traditional weight loss programs, females with a history of sexual abuse lose less weight than those without such a history because of perceptions of increased vulnerability to future attacks while at a lower weight (Felitti, 1991; Felitti, 1993). King, Clark, and Pera (1996) found that patients in their weight loss program with a history of sexual abuse lost significantly less weight and were less compliant with treatment than patients without a history of sexual abuse. Furthermore, they found that individuals with a history of sexual abuse were significantly more likely to have experienced psychological distress and to have received psychiatric treatment. In addition, one study found that those who were sexually abused were less dissatisfied with their current overweight status (Wiederman, Sansone, & Sansone, 1999).

Based on the results of treatment outcome studies of traditional weight loss programs, researchers have hypothesized that the predictors of negative outcome in traditional weight loss programs would also predict poor outcome after bariatric surgery. The studies reviewed in the next section suggest that predictors of outcome differ for the two weight loss methods, and that the presence of psychopathology before bariatric surgery does not consistently predict poor outcome after surgery.

Research on Surgical Outcome Prediction

The available literature consistently shows that bariatric surgery is the most effective and lasting method of weight loss in the morbidly obese. However, although these results are promising, there appears to be a distinct subset of individuals who do not respond well to surgery and those who experience significant weight regain several years after surgery (e.g., Hsu et al., 1998; Kral, Sjostrom, & Sullivan, 1992). Identification of the variables that explain these differences in outcome is an important research and clinical goal. However, studies on psychosocial and demographic predictors of outcome have yielded conflicting and inconclusive results. Numerous studies have failed to find any relationship between presurgical demographics, psychiatric diagnosis, or psychological measures (e.g., Minnesota Multiphasic Personality Inventory, Millon Clinical Multi-axial Inventory) and surgical outcome (Chandarana, Conlon, Holliday, Deslippe, & Field, 1990; Davidson, Rohde, & Wastell, 1991; Dymek, le Grange, Neven, & Alverdy, 2001; Grana, Coolidge, & Merwin, 1989; Vallis & Ross, 1993). However, several studies have shown that presurgical age and weight predict postsurgical weight loss, with those of younger age and lower BMI benefiting the most from surgery (Barrash, Rodriguez, Scott, Mason, & Sines, 1987; Hafner, Rogers, & Watts, 1990; Vallis & Ross, 1993). Although these findings have been replicated several times, these factors do not explain all of the variance associated with outcome (Vallis & Ross, 1993).

Psychopathology

Other studies have demonstrated predictive value for certain psychological factors, but these have not been in the direction hypothesized and have not been consistently replicated. For example, in a study of 57 patients under-going gastroplasty, increased psychopathology, as measured by a history of inpatient or outpatient psychiatric treatment and Minnesota Multiphasic Personality Inventory scores, was not related to weight loss after surgery (Valley & Grace, 1987). Dymek and colleagues (2001) also found that the presence of depression before gastric bypass surgery did not predict weight loss or changes in quality of life after surgery. Other studies have demon-strated that increased psychological distress (e.g., SCL-90 inflations, increased depression) predicted *increased* postsurgical weight loss (Brolin et al., 1986; Dubovsky, Haddenhorst, Murphy, Liechty, & Coyle, 1985–86). These findings contradict previous hypotheses that increased psychiatric difficulty would be a predictor of poorer outcome. However, given research findings suggesting that the psychological distress commonly found among obese individuals is a result of obesity rather than a cause (van Gemert, Severeijns, Greve, Groenman, & Soeters, 1998), it may not be surprising to find that the presence of depression before surgery does not necessarily indicate poor outcome after surgery.

Although these studies suggest that the presence of psychopathology before surgery is not usually associated with weight loss postsurgery, it may be associated with medical complications postsurgery. Furthermore, medical complications may increase with the severity of presurgical psy-chopathology. Valley and Grace (1987) found that a history of inpatient psychiatric admissions was the single strongest predictor of both medical and psychological complications postsurgery. Seventy-five percent of patients with a history of inpatient psychiatric admissions had moderate to severe medical complications within the first year of surgery as compared with 12% of patients with no history of psychiatric admissions. A history of outpatient psychiatric treatment was not related to medical complications after surgery. In addition, 56% of the patients with a history of inpatient psychiatric admissions developed psychological problems after surgery for which they sought treatment, as compared with only 10% of patients with no history of psychiatric admissions. In another study of patients undergoing bariatric surgery, Powers, Boyd, Blair, Stevens, and Rosemurgy (1992) compared a group of patients who required psychiatric hospitalization after surgery with a group of patients who did not. The groups did not differ in the amount of weight lost after surgery. However, the hospitalized group had a much more extensive history of psychopathology, including several previous psychiatric admissions, than did the nonhospitalized group. These findings demonstrate the importance of defining success after weight loss surgery in multidimensional terms.

Eating Behavior

Similar to depression, the presence of binge eating before surgery has not consistently been found to negatively influence weight loss after surgery. One study of 116 patients undergoing bariatric surgery found no relationship between presurgical eating pathology and weight loss postsurgery (Powers, Perez, Boyd, & Rosemurgy, 1999). A smaller study of patients undergoing Roux-en-Y gastric bypass surgery found that binge eaters showed a significantly smaller percentage of excess weight loss after surgery than non-binge eaters (38.5% of excess weight compared with 53.9% of excess weight for non-binge eaters). However, they still lost a significant amount of weight, and binge eaters did not differ from non-binge eaters on any other domain assessed, including depression and QOL (Dymek et al., 2001). A prospective study of 82 patients undergoing vertical-banded gastroplasty found that neither binge eating nor psychological distress predicted weight loss after surgery, although both were negative predictors of HRQOL 2 years postsurgery (Sabbioni et al., 2002). Although most studies have found little or no association between presurgical binge eating and postsurgical weight loss, two studies have found that binge eaters are more likely to regain weight after surgery (Hsu, Betancourt, & Sullivan, 1996; Hsu, Sullivan, & Benotti, 1997; Hsu et al, 2002).

Because patients' food intake is so severely restricted after surgery, it is perhaps not surprising that binge eating decreases so dramatically and that binge eaters' weight loss is similar to that of non-binge eaters. However, studies have found that surgery also has a positive effect on other forms of eating pathology and on concerns about shape and weight (Dymek et al., 2001; Kalarchian et al., 1999).

Sexual Abuse

Very few studies have examined sexual abuse in the context of weight loss surgery. In a study of patients undergoing gastric bypass surgery, Ray, Nickels, Sayeed, and Sax (2003) found that patients with a history of sexual abuse lost significantly less of their excess weight at 1-year follow-up than those without such a history. However, these findings are complicated by the fact that 22% of the patients with a history of sexual abuse also had a history of inpatient psychiatric treatment, as compared with 4.6% of the nonabused patients. Another study showed patients with a history of sexual abuse were as successful with weight loss as those who had no history of sexual abuse 1 year after gastric bypass; however, those with a history of abuse did show higher levels of depressive symptoms postsurgically (Buser, Dymek-Valentine, Hilburger, & Alverdy, 2003).

These studies suggest that predictors of poor outcome in traditional weight loss programs do not predict poor outcome after weight loss surgery. It is noteworthy that past psychiatric diagnoses, including depression and binge eating, and psychological distress do not appear to be negative prognostic indicators for surgery. Furthermore, these findings are similar across different types of surgery and with different outcome measures. The reasons that predictors of outcome for behavioral or pharmacological weight loss approaches do not hold true for surgical approaches to weight loss are not clear. It is possible that the vastly different methods of each approach, as well as the vastly different success rates, preclude meaningful comparisons among them.

Although research does not provide consistent guidelines for clinicians in presurgical psychosocial assessment, it does suggest that the point of presurgical assessment is not to deny surgery to those people with psychiatric diagnoses or distress, but rather to identify possible areas of challenge and to make recommendations for further treatment. For example, it may be appropriate for patients with a history of psychiatric admissions to be referred for further psychological assessment or treatment to determine whether they are appropriate candidates for surgery (Valley & Grace, 1987). In addition to psychological functioning, the presurgical assessment should identify strengths and weaknesses of the patient's psychosocial functioning, so that the necessary presurgical and postsurgical interventions can be put into place (Glinski, Wetzler, & Goodman, 2001). The presurgical assessment can also serve as an opportunity to further educate the patient about the surgical process and the changes that will follow.

Suggested Psychosocial Assessment

At the Center for Surgical Treatment of Obesity at the University of Chicago, each surgical candidate undergoes a psychosocial assessment to determine readiness and suitability for surgery in addition to a nutritional and medical evaluation. The assessment consists of a 30- to 45-minute semistructured interview in addition to several self-report questionnaires that patients complete before the interview.

Interview

The psychosocial interview is often one of the most feared portions of the surgical evaluation. Many patients have never seen a mental health professional before the evaluation and present with numerous misconceptions about being analyzed or judged. As such, it is very common for patients to minimize psychosocial difficulties they may be experiencing from fears of "not passing" the evaluation and thus being denied surgery. For this reason, it is extremely important to spend time putting the patient at ease and providing a less threatening rationale for the evaluation. The following is an example of the rationale provided to patients for conducting a psychological evaluation at the University of Chicago:

> Assessor: I know that many people get a little nervous at the prospect of speaking with a psychologist. We are part of the surgery team because of the major effect this surgery has on people's lives. Surgery has drastic effects on the way you eat, your health, and your weight, and can also have a large impact on your relationships, self-esteem, vocational pursuits, and other areas. Most of the time, these changes feel very positive, but they can also be quite stressful. We are here to get to know you better prior to surgery, in order to plan the best care for you after surgery, should you go through it. Let me also say that some folks are reluctant to report things such as low mood or binge eating for fear that this will keep them from getting into the program. Many patients with obesity have these problems, and this doesn't necessarily preclude them from being accepted.

This explanation usually reassures patients and sets the tone for the evaluation to follow. The subsequent sections outline the main areas assessed during the evaluation and present the rationale for including each area in the assessment.

Psychiatric/Psychological Status

Current and past mental health functioning is assessed and patients are screened for all major psychiatric illnesses, including a detailed evaluation of eating disorder symptoms, affective disorders, and substance abuse. Although most forms of psychopathology are not more prevalent in this population, the effects of certain types of mental illness on surgical outcome are important to consider. For example, a patient with an uncontrolled psychosis or substance dependence may be at increased risk for postsurgical noncompliance.

In addition to assessing psychopathology, we assess the extent to which the psychopathology is being managed or is resolved. All patients are asked about current and past psychiatric hospitalizations and psychotherapy, and whether or not they have ever been prescribed psychotropic medication. They are also asked whether or not they believe that the treatments they have received have been effective in alleviating symptoms.

Stress and Coping Skills

The postoperative period is a time of significant stress and lifestyle changes. It follows that individuals will be best able to deal with these changes when other areas of their life are well managed. Each patient is asked about their current stress level, and is asked to think about potential stressors that may arise in the upcoming 6 to 12 months. If an individual is about to move or change jobs 2 months after the surgery, for example, surgery might be best postponed to a time of less chaos. Each patient is also asked about how he or she copes with stress and depressed mood. Many surgery candidates identify eating as a major coping mechanism. Many of them will be physically unable to self-soothe by eating after the surgery because food intake is limited, and may therefore need help identifying more adaptive coping mechanisms. Furthermore, eating as a stress response may potentially affect weight loss and outcome.

Social Support

Patients often need a significant amount of social support in the postoperative period. In the immediate postoperative period, patients will need assistance with transportation to clinic appointments, changing bandages, grocery shopping, and preparing meals. In the longer term, patients often need help with "moral support." Many patients come into the evaluation stating, "I don't want to bother or depend on others. I'd like to do this on my own." The psychosocial assessment is an excellent opportunity to educate individuals on the level of support they will need and to have the patient begin to identify specific support people.

Cognitive and Social Functioning

Cognitive and social functioning is assessed informally by interacting with the patient. Vocabulary, level of education, and understanding of the surgical process are all used to assess cognitive functioning. If there is a suspicion of low cognitive functioning, we conduct a mini-mental status exam developed by Folstein, Folstein, and McHugh (1975). Further neuropsychological testing may be warranted if the mini-mental status exam suggests extremely low functioning. The primary reason for assessing cognitive functioning is to be certain that patients are able to understand postsurgical instructions and comply with dietary requirements. For example, the postsurgical diet requires that patients consume a large quantity of protein, and patients have to be able to calculate and monitor their protein intake throughout the day and read food labels to assure that the foods they are eating contain enough protein.

Social skills are examined by evaluating the extent to which patients are friendly, pleasant, appropriately interactive, defensive, hostile, overly "chummy," or seem to have a problem with boundaries. Social skills are assessed to gauge how the patients will interact with the hospital staff during the hospital stay and during follow-up visits.

Motivation

Level of motivation is a key predictor of success with any behavior or lifestyle change. Motivation is assessed by directly asking patients to rate their desire to have surgery on a scale from 0 to 10, with 0 indicating that they do not really want to have the surgery and 10 indicating that they would have the surgery immediately if they could. Patients are also asked about their reasons for wanting the surgery. Although the vast majority of patients report a high level of internal motivation and cite health reasons for wanting the surgery, there is a small number of individuals who are considering surgery for external reasons, such as a spouse's or a parent's urging.

Appraisal of the Surgical Process

There is a considerable range of knowledge about the surgery. Although many patients have done exhaustive research, others know very little about the mechanics of the surgery or the necessary aftercare. All patients are asked about their understanding of the surgical process, the type of surgery they are having, and understanding of the postsurgical diet. Similarly, expectations of outcome are discussed, because some patients expect to lose unrealistically large amounts of weight (Rabner & Greenstein, 1994) and are not aware of the possible negative aspects of having surgery. The evaluation provides an opportunity to discuss the limitations of surgery and can potentially decrease dissatisfaction and disappointment with postsurgical outcome.

Objective Psychosocial Measures

At the University of Chicago, we supplement the clinical interview with several objective self-report measures to further assess mood, eating patterns, QOL, stress, and coping. Several measures have been briefly described in the Psychosocial Presentation of Bariatric Surgery Candidates section. The following section describes these measures in greater detail and includes descriptions of additional measures that can be used for assessment. Unless otherwise noted, we are not aware of relevant previously published norms or cutoff scores useful for interpreting these measures with this population. In interpreting these scores, it might be useful for the assessor to compare a patient's score with the University of Chicago sample outlined earlier in this chapter. Scores greater than 2 standard deviations from the mean were unusual in our sample and may warrant further investigation.

Mood

The BDI (Beck et al., 1961) is a widely used 21-item self-report measure designed to assess the presence and severity of depressive symptomatology. Although the presence of depression before surgery does not appear to be related to postsurgery weight loss, the stress and significant lifestyle changes that follow surgery suggest that active suicidality should be considered a contraindication for surgery, although patients with suicidal ideation may be reconsidered for surgery if their mood has stabilized after receiving psychological treatment. The BDI effectively discriminates between psychiatric and nonpsychiatric populations, and is significantly correlated with a variety of depression scales (see Beck, Steer, & Garbin, 1988). Commonly used interpretations of BDI scores are as follows: BDI scores from 10 to 18 indicate mild to moderate depression, scores from 19 to 29 indicate moderate to severe depression, and scores from 30 to 63 indicate severe depression (Groth-Marnat, 1999).

Eating Behavior

The TFEQ is a 51-item self-report measure that consists of three subscales: (1) Cognitive Restraint, which measures intentional restriction of food intake; (2) Disinhibition, which measures the inability to resist food stimuli; and (3) Hunger, which measures subjective sensations of hunger. Reliabilities for subscales obtained in mixed obese and normal-weight populations yield coefficient alphas between .85 and .93 (Stunkard & Messick, 1985). The Cognitive Restraint subscale exhibits high 2-week test-retest reliability ($r = .91$), good discriminant validity with respect to social desirability, and low susceptibility to dissimulation (Allison, Kalinsky, & Gorman, 1992).

Quality of Life

The IWQOL-Lite (Kolotkin et al., 2001) is a 31-item self-report measure that provides a total score and separate scores for five domains of functioning: (1) Physical Functioning measures the impact of weight on various physical activities ranging from self-care to mild exertion; (2) Self-Esteem assesses the impact of weight on self-consciousness and negative self-evaluation; (3) Sexual Life measures the extent to which weight interferes with sexual desire, performance, and enjoyment; (4) Public Distress measures the impact of weight on social and public activities; and (5) Work assesses the extent to which work performance and promotion are negatively influenced by weight. When QOL is assessed in clinical trials of interventions for specific diseases, the use of both generic quality of life measures and disease-specific QOL measures has been recommended, in part because disease-specific instruments are more sensitive to changes in QOL after clinical interventions than are generic measures (Kolotkin, Meter, & Williams, 2001). The IWQOL-Lite is a disease-specific instrument sensitive to the impact of obesity on a person's QOL. The IWQOL-Lite has also been shown to have sound psychometric properties. Internal consistency coefficients range from .82 to .94 for the subscale scores and .96 for the total score. Test-retest reliability over 2 weeks ranges from .84 to .91 for the subscale scores and .95 for the total score (Kolotkin & Crosby, 2002).

The SF-36 (Ware et al., 1993) is a 36-item self-report measure that assesses health-related quality of life in eight domains: (1) Physical Functioning measures the impact of physical health on various physical activities ranging from self-care to vigorous physical activity, (2) Role-Physical assesses the degree of functioning in work and other daily activities as a result of physical health, (3) Bodily Pain measures the degree of pain and pain-related functional limitations, (4) General Health assesses an individual's appraisal of his or her overall level of health, (5) Vitality measures energy level, (6) Social Functioning measures the impact of physical health on social functioning, (7) Role-Emotional assesses the degree of functioning in work and other daily activities as a result of emotional health, and (8) Mental Health measures the presence and degree of depression and anxiety. As opposed to the IWQOL-Lite, the SF-36 is a generic measure of QOL. It is a brief, comprehensive, and psychometrically sound measure that has been recommended for use in obesity research by the U.S. Task Force on Developing Obesity Outcomes and Learning Standards (Kolotkin et al., 2001).

Stress and Coping

Although not part of our assessment procedure, the Millon Behavioral Health Inventory (MBHI; Millon, Green, & Meagher, 1982) may be another helpful objective measure to include. The MBHI is a 150-item self-report instrument used to assess personality-based coping styles and psychosocial stressors that relate to the health care of medical patients (for a review, see Everly & Newman, 1997). It consists of 20 subscales that are divided into four categories: (1) Basic Coping Styles Scales, which assess the patient's style of coping with physical illness; (2) Psychogenic Attitudes Scales, which assess psychosocial stressors believed to affect physical illness; (3) Psychosomatic Correlates Scales, which assess similarities between the presenting illness and illnesses resulting primarily from psychological factors; and (4) Prognostic Indicators Scales, which assess pain treatment responsivity, life threat reactivity, and emotional vulnerability. The MBHI has demonstrated adequate test-retest reliability, internal consistency, and convergent and divergent validity when compared with other personality measures (for a review, see Everly & Newman, 1997). It was developed in a general medical population, but has since been used in the assessment of specific medical populations including bariatric surgery patients (Rowe, Downey, Faust, & Horn, 2000). The MBHI can be useful in evaluating patient communication, coping styles, and lifestyle behaviors, which may affect how patients cope with the stress of surgery and compliance with postsurgical follow-up care. Scores higher than 75 on any of the Millon clinical scales are unusual for medical populations and warrant further investigation (Millon et al., 1982).

Recommendations for the Surgical Team

The information obtained through the interview and self-report questionnaires is used to make recommendations that are shared with the surgical team at weekly meetings. Recommendations from the nutritional and medical teams are also discussed in the meetings. Although the decision to proceed with surgery is ultimately that of the surgeon, information from all sources is equally weighted during this process.

From a psychosocial perspective, the ideal candidate for surgery would be someone with no history of major psychopathology, few stressors, good coping skills, high internal motivation, good appraisal of the surgical process, and high cognitive and social functioning. Poor candidates would include individuals with severe, untreated psychopathology; poor coping and high stress; low cognitive and social functioning; low motivation; and poor appraisal of the surgical process.

Recommendations are decided on an individual case-by-case basis, although the following general guidelines are observed when making decisions (recommendations are not mutually exclusive):

1. Denying a patient: It is quite rare to outright deny a patient for psychosocial reasons alone. Given that there is very little evidence in the literature to suggest that certain psychological factors have a negative effect on surgical outcome, denying patients is only considered when extreme problems exist and there does not seem to be an apparent solution. For example, if someone suffers from severe mental retardation and does not have adequate social support, he or she may be denied, because he or she may not possess the cognitive abilities needed to comply with postsurgical follow-up, which can lead to severe problems such as vitamin deficiencies, hair loss, lack of weight loss, and poor recovery.

2. Requiring psychotherapy/medication management: Typically, patients presenting with moderate to severe psychopathology that is poorly managed are required to seek treatment before surgery. For example, someone with unmanaged moderate major depressive disorder and poor coping skills would be required to seek 3 to 6 months of psychotherapy. If suicidality (i.e., plans, gestures, or attempts) is present, psychological/psychiatric treatment and a 1-year period free of suicidal thoughts is required. The rationale for requiring treatment in individuals with major depressive disorder and poor coping is that some patients experience depression and suicidal ideation after obesity surgery (Kodama et al., 1998), which can exacerbate preexisting problems. Severe depression may also hinder patients' ability to make the necessary behavioral changes after surgery. Similarly, if a patient presents with substance abuse or dependence, he or she must seek treatment and be abstinent for 1 year before having surgery, because the use of certain substances is prohibited after surgery because it can interfere with recovery.

3. Recommending psychotherapy/medication management: We usually recommend, but do not require, treatment for patients experiencing milder psychopathology, such as BED or dysthymic disorder and who have adequate coping skills.

4. Requiring a letter from a treating clinician or psychiatrist: If a patient is in psychiatric treatment (psychotherapy or taking medication to manage psychological problems), we will require a letter from the clinician or psychiatrist commenting on the patient's

functioning and whether or not the patient seems prepared to undergo a major stressor such as surgery.

5. Requiring or recommending a stress management group: For individuals with poor coping skills, we will recommend that they attend a stress management group. Typical examples of such cases include patients who report that they eat in response to stress and experience subjective binge episodes. In the absence of more adaptive coping, we will *require* that they attend a stress management group, because adaptive coping techniques will likely help patients cope with the stress of surgery and help with postoperative adjustment.

6. Flagging: All patients who present with a history of significant psychopathology, poor coping, high stress, or any other significant psychosocial problems are "flagged." Flagging indicates that the patient should be observed more closely during the follow-up period.

Summary

With the increasing demand on mental health professionals to conduct psychosocial assessments of bariatric surgery candidates, research on psychosocial predictors of outcome has become critical. However, efforts to isolate predictors of outcome have yielded conflicting and inconclusive results and thus do not provide consistent guidelines for clinicians. Further research is certainly needed in this area. In the meantime, clinicians are advised to identify possible challenges and make recommendations for treatment rather than outright deny patients from surgery. Typical assessments include evaluation of psychological functioning, level of social support, coping skills, motivation for surgery, appraisal of the surgical process, and social and cognitive functioning.

References

Allison, D. B., Kalinsky, L. B., & Gorman, B. S. (1992). A comparison of the psychometric properties of three measures of dietary restraint. *Psychological Assessment, 4*, 391–398.

American Psychiatric Association (1994). Diagnostic and statistical manual of mental disorders (4th ed.). Washington, D.C.: Author.

Barrash, J., Rodriguez, E. M., Scott, D. H., Mason, E. E., & Sines, J. O. (1987). The utility of MMPI subtypes for the prediction of weight loss after bariatric surgery. *International Journal of Obesity, 11*, 115–128.

Beck, A. T., Steer, R. A., & Garbin, M. (1988). Psychometric properties of the Beck Depression Inventory: Twenty-five years of evaluation. *Clinical Psychology Review, 8*, 77–100.

Beck, A., Ward, C., Mendelson, M., Mock, J., & Erbaugh, J. (1961). An inventory for measuring depression. *Archives of General Psychiatry, 4*, 561–571.

Bocchieri, L. E., Meana, M., & Fisher, B. L. (2002). A review of psychosocial outcomes of surgery for morbid obesity. *Journal of Psychosomatic Research, 52*, 155–165.

Boerner, L., Spillane, N., Anderson, K., & Smith, G. (2004). Similarities and differences between women and men on eating disorder risk factors and symptom measures. *Eating Behaviors,* 5, 209–222.

Bonato, D. P., & Boland, F. J. (1987). Predictors of weight loss at the end of treatment and 1-year follow-up for a behavioral weight loss program. *International Journal of Eating Disorders,* 6, 573–577.

Brolin, R. E., Clemow, L. P., Kasnetz, K. A., Fynan, T. M., Silva, E. M., & Greenfield, D. P. (1986). Outcome predictors after gastroplasty for morbid obesity. *Nutrition International,* 2, 322–326.

Buser, A., Dymek-Valentine, M., Hilburger, J., & Alverdy, J. (2003). Outcome following gastric bypass surgery: Impact of past sexual abuse. *Obesity Surgery, 14,* 170–174.

Carpenter, K. M., Hasin, D. S., Allison, D. B., & Faith, M. S. (2000). Relationships between obesity and DSM-IV major depressive disorder, suicide ideation, and suicide attempts: Results from a general population study. *American Journal of Public Health, 90,* 251–257.

Chandarana, P. C., Conlon, P., Holliday, R. L., Deslippe, T., & Field, V. A. (1990). A prospective study of psychosocial aspects of gastric stapling surgery. *Psychiatric Journal of the University of Ottawa, 15,* 32–35.

Davidson, T., Rohde, P., & Wastell, C. (1991). Psychological profile and outcome in patients undergoing gastroplasty for morbid obesity. *Obesity Surgery, 1,* 177–180.

de Zwaan, M., Lancaster, K. L., Mitchell, J. E., Howell, L. M., Monson, N., Roerig, J. L., & Crosby, R. D. (2002). Health-related quality of life in morbidly obese patients: Effect of gastric bypass surgery. *Obesity Surgery, 12,* 773–780.

de Zwaan, M., Mitchell, J. E., Howell, L. M., Monson, N., Swan-Kremeier, L., Crosby, R., & Harold, C. S. (2003). Characteristics of morbidly obese patients before gastric bypass surgery. *Comprehensive Psychiatry, 44,* 428–434.

de Zwaan, M., Mitchell, J. E., Howell, M., Monson, N., Swan-Kremeier, L., Roerig, J. L, Kolotkin, R. L., & Crosby, R. D. (2002). Two measures of health-related quality of life in morbid obesity. *Obesity Research, 10,* 1143–1151.

Doll, H. A., Petersen, S. E. K., & Stewart-Brown, S. L. (2000). Obesity and physical and emotional well being: Associations between body mass index, chronic illness, and the physical and mental components of the SF-36 questionnaire. *Obesity Research, 8,* 160–170.

Dubovsky, S. L., Haddenhorst, A., Murphy, J., Liechty, R. D., & Coyle, D. A. (1985–86). A preliminary study of the relationship between preoperative depression and weight loss following surgery for morbid obesity. *International Journal of Psychiatry in Medicine, 15,* 185–196.

Dymek, M. P., le Grange, D., Neven, K., & Alverdy, J. (2001). Quality of life and psychosocial adjustment in patients after Roux-en-Y gastric bypass: A brief report. *Obesity Surgery, 11,* 32–39.

Dymek-Valentine, M., Rienecke-Hoste, R., & Alverdy, J. (2004). Assessment of binge eating disorder in morbidly obese patients evaluated for gastric bypass: SCID versus QEWP-R. *Eating and Weight Disorders, 9,* 211–216.

Eldredge, K. L., & Agras, W. S. (1997). The relationship between perceived evaluation of weight and treatment outcome among individuals with binge eating disorder. *International Journal of Eating Disorders, 22,* 43–49.

Everly, G. S., & Newman, E. C. (1997). The MBHI: Composition and clinical application. In T. Millon (Ed.), *The Millon inventories: clinical and personality assessment* (pp. 389–408). New York: Guilford.

Felitti, V. J. (1991). Long-term medical consequences of incest, rape, and molestation. *Southern Medical Journal, 84,* 328–331.

Felitti, V. J. (1993). Childhood sexual abuse, depression, and family dysfunction in adult obese patients: A case control study. *Southern Medical Journal, 86,* 732–736.

First, M., Spitzer, R., Gibbon, M., & Williams, J. (2001). *Structured clinical interview for DSM-IV axis I disorders.* New York: Biometrics Research, New York State Psychiatric Institute.

Folstein, M. F., Folstein, S. E., & McHugh, P. R. (1975). Mini-mental state: A practical method for grading the cognitive state of patients for the clinician. *Journal of Psychiatric Research, 12,* 189–198.

Fontaine, K. R., Cheskin, L. J., & Barofsky, I. (1996). Health-related quality of life in obese persons seeking treatment. *Journal of Family Practice, 43,* 265–270.

Ford, E. S., Moriarty, D. G., Zack, M. M., Mokdad, A. H., & Chapman, D. P. (2001). Self-reported body mass index and health-related quality of life: Findings from the Behavioral Risk Factor Surveillance System. *Obesity Research, 9,* 21–31.

Friedman, M. A., & Brownell, K. D. (1995). Psychological correlates of obesity: Moving to the next research generation. *Psychological Bulletin, 117,* 3–20.

Gladis, M. M., Wadden, T. A., Vogt, R., Foster, G., Kuehnel, R. H., & Bartlett, S. J. (1998). Behavioral treatment of obese binge eaters: Do they need different care? *Journal of Psychosomatic Research, 44,* 375–384.

Glinski, J., Wetzler, S., & Goodman, E. (2001). The psychology of gastric bypass surgery. *Obesity Surgery, 11,* 581–588.

Gortmaker, S. L., Must, A., Perrin, J. M., Sobol, A. M., & Dietz, W. H. (1993). Social and economic consequences of overweight in adolescence and young adulthood. *New England Journal of Medicine, 329,* 1008–1012.

Gormally, J., Rardin, D., & Black, S. (1980). Correlates of successful response to a behavioral weight control clinic. *Journal of Counseling Psychology, 27,* 179–191.

Grana, A. S., Coolidge, F. L., & Merwin, M. M. (1989). Personality profiles of the morbidly obese. *Journal of Clinical Psychology, 45,* 762–765.

Groth-Marnat, G. (1999). Handbook of psychological assessment (3rd ed.). New York: Wiley.

Hafner, R. J., Rogers, J., & Watts, J. McK. (1990). Psychological status before and after gastric restriction as predictors of weight loss in the morbidly obese. *Journal of Psychosomatic Research, 34,* 295–302.

Ho, K. S. I., Nichaman, M. Z., Taylor, W. C., Lee, E. S., & Foreyt, J. P. (1995). Binge eating disorder, retention, and dropout in an adult obesity program. *International Journal of Eating Disorders, 18,* 291–294.

Hsu, L. K. G., Benotti, P. N., Dwyer, J., Roberts, S. B., Saltzman, E., Shikora, S., Rolls, B. J., & Rand, W. (1998). Nonsurgical factors that influence the outcome of bariatric surgery: A review. *Psychosomatic Medicine, 60,* 338–346.

Hsu, L. K. G., Betancourt, S., & Sullivan, S. P. (1996). Eating disturbances before and after vertical banded gastroplasty: A pilot study. *International Journal of Eating Disorders, 19,* 23–34.

Hsu, L. K. G., Mulliken, B., McDonagh, B., Das, S. K., Rand, W., Fairburn, C. G., Rolls, B., McCrory, M. A., Saltzman, E., Shikora, S., Dwyer, J., & Roberts, S. (2002). Binge eating disorder in extreme obesity. *International Journal of Obesity, 26,* 1398–1403.

Hsu, L. K. G., Sullivan, S. P., & Benotti, P. N. (1997). Eating disturbances and outcome of gastric bypass surgery: A pilot study. *International Journal of Eating Disorders, 21,* 385–390.

Kalarchian, M. A., Wilson, G. T., Brolin, R. E., & Bradley, L. (1998). Binge eating in bariatric surgery patients. *International Journal of Eating Disorders, 23,* 89–92.

Keefe, P. H., Wyshogrod, D., Weinberger, E., & Agras, W. S. (1984). Binge eating and outcome of behavioral treatment of obesity: A preliminary report. *Behavior Research & Therapy, 22,* 319–321.

King, T. K., Clark, M. M., & Pera, V. (1996). History of sexual abuse and obesity treatment outcome. *Addictive Behaviors, 21,* 283–290.

Kodama, K., Noda, S., Murakami, A., Azuma, Y., Takeda, Yamanouchi, N., Okada, S., Komatsu, N., Sato, T., Miyazawa, Y., & Kawamura, I. (1998). Depressive disorders as psychiatric complications after obesity surgery. *Psychiatry and Clinical Neurosciences, 52,* 471–476.

Kolotkin, R. L., & Crosby, R. D. (2002). Psychometric evaluation of the impact of weight on quality of life-lite questionnaire (IWQOL-Lite) in a community sample. *Quality of Life Research, 11,* 157–171.

Kolotkin, R. L., Crosby, R. D., Kosloski, K. D., & Williams, G. R. (2001). Development of a brief measure to assess quality of life in obesity. *Obesity Research, 9,* 102–111.

Kolotkin, R. L., Crosby, R. D., Pendleton, R., Strong, M., Gress, R. E., & Adams, T. (2003). Health-related quality of life in patients seeking gastric bypass surgery vs. non-treatment-seeking controls. *Obesity Surgery, 13,* 371–377.

Kolotkin, R. L., Crosby, R. D., & Williams, G. R. (2002). Health-related quality of life varies among obese subgroups. *Obesity Research, 10,* 748–756.

Kolotkin, R. L., Crosby, R. D., Williams, G. R., Hartley, G. G., & Nicol, S. (2001). The relationship between health-related quality of life and weight loss. *Obesity Research, 9,* 564–571.

Kolotkin, R. L., Meter, K., & Williams, G. R. (2001). Quality of life and obesity. *Obesity Reviews, 2,* 219–229.

Kral, J. G., Sjostrom, L. V., & Sullivan, M. B. (1992). Assessment of quality of life before and after surgery for morbid obesity. *American Journal of Clinical Nutrition, 55,* 611S-4.

Larsson, U., Karlsson, J., & Sullivan, M. (2002). Impact of overweight and obesity on health-related quality of life—a Swedish population study. *International Journal of Obesity, 26,* 417–424.

Loro, A., & Orleans, C. (1981). Binge eating in obesity: Preliminary findings and guidelines for behavioral treatment. *Addictive Behaviors, 6,* 155–166.

Mannucci, E., Ricca, R., Barciulli, E., DiBernardo, M., Travaglini, R., Cabras, P. L., & Rotella, C. M. (1999). Quality of life and overweight: The obesity-related well-being (ORWELL 97) questionnaire. *Addictive Behaviors, 24,* 345–357.

Marcus, M. D., Wing, R. R., Ewing, L., Kern, E., Gooding, W., & McDermott, M. (1990). Psychiatric disorders among obese binge eaters. *International Journal of Eating Disorders, 9,* 69–77.

Marcus, M. D., Wing, R. R., & Hopkins, J., (1988). Obese binge eaters: Affect, cognitions, and response to behavioral weight control. *Journal of Consulting and Clinical Psychology, 55,* 433–439.

Millon, T., Green, C., & Meagher, R. (1982). *Millon Behavioral Health Inventory Manual* (3rd ed.) Minneapolis, MN: National Computer Systems.

Pi-Sunyer, F. X. (1993). Medical hazards of obesity. *Annals of Internal Medicine, 119,* 655–660.

Powers, P. S., Boyd, F., Blair, R. C., Stevens, B., & Rosemurgy, A. (1992). Psychiatric issues in bariatric surgery. *Obesity Surgery, 2,* 315–325.

Powers, P. S., Perez, A., Boyd, F., & Rosemurgy, A. (1999). Eating pathology before and after bariatric surgery: A prospective study. *International Journal of Eating Disorders, 25,* 293–300.

Prather, R. C., & Williamson, D. A. (1988). Psychopathology associated with bulimia, binge eating, and obesity. *International Journal of Eating Disorders, 7,* 177–184.

Rabkin, S. W. (1983). Psychosocial determinants of weight reduction in overweight individuals. *Journal of Obesity and Weight Regulation, 2,* 97–106.

Rabner, J. G., & Greenstein, R. J. (1994). Obesity surgery: Expectations and reality. *International Journal of Obesity and Related Metabolic Disorders, 15,* 841–845.

Rand, C. S. W., & Macgregor, A. M. C. (1991). Successful weight loss following obesity surgery and the perceived liability of morbid obesity. *International Journal of Obesity, 15,* 577–579.

Ray, E. C., Nickels, M. W., Sayeed, S., & Sax, H. C. (2003). Predicting success after gastric bypass: The role of psychosocial and behavioral factors. *Surgery, 134,* 555–564.

Rosenberg, M. (1965). *Society and the Adolescent Self Image.* Princeton, NJ: University Press.

Rowe, J. L., Downey, J. E., Faust, M., Horn, M. J. (2000). Psychological and demographic predictors of successful weight loss following silastic ring vertical stapled gastroplasty. *Psychological Reports, 86,* 1028–36.

Sabbioni, M. E. E., Dickson, M. H., Eychmuller, S., Franke, D., Goetz, S., Hurny, C., Naef, M., Balsiger, B., de Marco, D., Burgi, U., & Buchler, M. W. (2002). Intermediate results of health-related quality of life after vertical banded gastroplasty. *International Journal of Obesity, 26,* 277–280.

Sherwood, N. E., Jeffery, R. W., & Wing, R. R. (1999). Binge status as a predictor of weight loss treatment outcome. *International Journal of Obesity, 23,* 485–493.

Smith, D. E., Marcus, M. D., Lewis, C. E., Fitzgibbon, M., & Schreiner, P. (1998). Prevalence of binge eating disorder, obesity, and depression in a biracial cohort of young adults. *Annals of Behavioral Medicine, 20,* 227–232.

Spitzer, R. L., Devlin, M., Walsh, B. T., Hasin, D., Wing, R., Marcus, M., Stunkard, A., Wadden, T., Yanovski, S., Agras, S., Mitchell, J., & Nonas, C. (1992). Binge eating disorder: A multisite field trial of the diagnostic criteria. *International Journal of Eating Disorders, 11,* 191–203.

Spitzer, R. L., Yanovski, S., Wadden, T., Wing, R., Marcus, M. D., Stunkard, A., Devlin, M., Mitchell, J., Hasin, D., & Horne, R. L. (1993). Binge eating disorder: Its further validation in a multisite study. *International Journal of Eating Disorders, 13,* 137–153.

Stunkard, A., & Messick, S. (1985). The Three-Factor Eating Questionnaire to measure dietary restraint, disinhibition, and hunger. *Journal of Psychosomatic Research, 29,* 71–83.

Stunkard, A. J., & Wadden, T. A. (1992). Psychological aspects of severe obesity. *American Journal of Clinical Nutrition, 55 (Suppl),* 524–532.

Sullivan, M., Karlsson, J., Sjostrom, L., Backman, L., Bengtsson, C., Bouchard, C., Dahlgren, S., Jonsson, E., Larsson, B., Lindstedt, S., Naslund, I., Olbe, L., & Wedel, H. (1993). Swedish obese subjects (SOS)—an intervention study of obesity. Baseline evaluation of health and psychosocial functioning in the first 1743 subjects examined. *International Journal of Obesity & Related Metabolic Disorders: Journal of the International Association for the Study of Obesity, 17*, 503–512.

Teixeira, P. J., Going, S. B., Houtkooper, L. B., Cussler, E. C., Martin, C. J., Metcalfe, L. L., Finkenthal, N. R., Blew, R. M., Sardinha, L. B., & Lohman, T. G. (2002). Weight loss readiness in middle-aged women: Psychosocial predictors of success for behavioral weight reduction. *Journal of Behavioral Medicine, 25*, 499–523.

Twenge, J. M. & Campbell, W. K. (2001). Age and birth cohort differences in self-esteem: A cross-temporal meta-analysis. *Personality and Social Psychology Review, 5*, 321–344.

Valley, V., & Grace, D. M. (1987). Psychosocial risk factors in gastric surgery for obesity: Identifying guidelines for screening. *International Journal of Obesity, 11*, 105–113.

Vallis, T. M., & Ross, M. A. (1993). The role of psychological factors in bariatric surgery for morbid obesity: Identification of psychological predictors of success. *Obesity Surgery, 3*, 346–359.

Valtolina, G. (1996). Weight loss and psychopathology: A three-cluster MMPI typology. *Perceptual & Motor Skills, 82*, 275–281.

van Gemert, W. G., Severeijns, R. M., Greve, J. W. M., Groenman, N., & Soeters, P. B. (1998). Psychological functioning of morbidly obese patients after surgical treatment. *International Journal of Obesity, 22*, 393–398..

Wadden, T. A., Sarwer, D. B., Womble, L. G., Foster, G. D., McGuckin, B. G., & Schimmel, A. (2001). Psychosocial aspects of obesity and obesity surgery. *Surgical Clinics of North America, 81*, 1001–1024.

Wadden, T. A., & Stunkard, A. J. (1985). Social and psychological consequences of obesity. *Annals of Internal Medicine, 103*, 1062–1067.

Ware, J. E., Snow, K. K., Kosinski, M., & Gandek, B. (1993). *SF-36 Health Survey: Manual and Interpretation Guide.* Boston, MA: The Health Institute of New England Medical Center.

Wiederman, M. W., Sansone, R. A., & Sansone, L. A. (1999). Obesity among sexually abused women: An adaptive function for some? *Women & Health, 29*, 89–100.

Wing, R. R., & Greeno, C. G. (1994). Behavioural and psychosocial aspects of obesity and its treatment. *Baillieres Clinical Endocrinology & Metabolism, 8*, 689–703.

Yanovski, S. Z., Nelson, J. E., Dubbert, B. K., & Spitzer, R. L. (1993). Association of binge eating disorder and psychiatric comorbidity in obese subjects. *American Journal of Psychiatry, 150*, 1472–1479.

Yass-Reed, E. M., Barry, N. J., & Dacey, C. M. (1993). Examination of pretreatment predictors of attrition in a VLCD and behavior therapy weight-loss program. *Addictive Behaviors, 18*, 431–435.SSS

CHAPTER 3

The Use of a Standardized Database in Assessment

JAMES E. MITCHELL

As outlined elsewhere in this book, a variety of strategies can be used to gather information during the process of the psychosocial assessment of bariatric surgery candidates. An in-depth psychiatric or psychological evaluation obviously will be the mainstay of any assessment, as outlined in chapter 2. As discussed, certain psychometric instruments may also provide useful data both in assessing patients preoperatively and in charting their course after the procedure is completed. Other potential sources of information include interviewing family members and obtaining prior records, particularly those related to issues surrounding mental health.

Another strategy that perhaps is underused but that can provide a great deal of useful information is to use a standardized database system. An example of such a database is included in this chapter. Such a database can be provided to patients when they call for the evaluation. They can then be asked to complete it and bring it with them to the evaluation session, to send it in in advance, or to come early for the evaluation and complete it at the clinician's office. Having patients complete it at home has several advantages: it allows patients to discuss questions with other family members (e.g., establishing the dates of hospitalization), to check the names and dosages of medications, and, in certain situations, to contact previous health care providers for additional information. Although asking patients to complete such a database may seem to be assigning them an onerous task, in reality many patients see the utility of it from the beginning. First, it allows them an opportunity to organize their history in a way that they can be assured that the evaluating clinician has a relatively complete set of information about them. Second, as mentioned previously, it allows them to gather information that may not be easily recollected during the formal interview itself. Third, it assures the patient that information that cannot be covered during the interview because of time constraints still will find its way to the clinician's attention.

The time necessary to complete such an instrument will depend greatly on the number of medical and psychological problems the patient has experienced before. Most bariatric surgery patients will have fairly complicated histories, and, again, allowing them to complete the form in advance will often make it far easier for the clinician to disentangle the time course of various problems during the interview session.

The use of such a database has obvious benefits to clinicians as well. First, they are assured of having a reasonably complete data set on most points of history before seeing the patient, allowing them to focus their interview on areas where there is lack of clarity or where there are particular concerns. Second, if the technology is available, such a database can be presented on scannable forms or via computer interface. Such technologies allow patients to enter their own data and, if the proper software is available, the clinician can print a textual report that summarizes patients' responses on the items. The textual report generated can become part of the permanent record. Even if neither technology is available, having such a detailed history available to review immediately before seeing the patient can be reassuring to clinician and patient alike.

What follows is a database that has been used in the eating disorders program with various modifications, first at the University of Minnesota and then later at the Eating Disorders Institute in Fargo, ND. The version offered here is broad enough to target patients who are candidates for bariatric surgery, while also inquiring in some depth as to other problem eating disorder behaviors that may have been present previously, including anorexia nervosa and bulimia nervosa. Given their own needs, and other sources from which they may be receiving information, clinicians who wish to set up such a database may wish to make substantial modifications to this system.

Appendix

Note. The Eating Disorders Questionnaire that follows is also available for download from the publisher at www.routledgementalhealth.com. EDQ 9.0. Copyright © 2004, The Neuropsychiatric Research Institute. Permission to reproduce is granted.

EDQ
Version 9.0

INSTRUCTIONS: Please fill in the circle that best describes you for each item.

A. DEMOGRAPHIC INFORMATION

1. Sex: ○ Female ○ Male

2. Current Age: _____ years

   Date of Birth:

   ☐☐ / ☐☐ / ☐☐☐☐

3. Race (fill in only one):
   ○ White
   ○ African American
   ○ Native American
   ○ Hispanic
   ○ Asian
   ○ Other (please specify) _____

4. Marital Status (fill in only one):
   ○ Never married
   ○ Married (first marriage)
   ○ Divorced or widowed and presently remarried
   ○ Monogamous relationship, living with partner (but not married)
   ○ Monogamous relationship, not living with partner
   ○ Divorced and not presently married
   ○ Widowed and not presently remarried

5. What is your primary role? (fill in only one)
   ○ Wage earner, full-time
   ○ Wage earner, part-time
   ○ Student, full-time
   ○ Student, part-time
   ○ Homemaker
   ○ Unemployed
   ○ Other (specify) _____

B. WEIGHT HISTORY

1. Current Weight:

   ☐☐☐ lbs.

2. Current Height:

   ☐ ft. ☐☐ in.

3. I would like to weigh:

   ☐☐☐ lbs.

4. **Highest Weight** (non-pregnancy) since age 18:

   Weight ☐☐☐ lbs. **at** Age ☐☐ yrs.

5. **Lowest Weight** since age 18:

   Weight ☐☐☐ lbs. **at** Age ☐☐ yrs.

6. **Highest Weight between ages 12 and 18:**

   Weight ☐☐☐ lbs. **at** Height ☐ ft. ☐☐ in. **at age**
   ○ 12
   ○ 13
   ○ 14
   ○ 15
   ○ 16
   ○ 17

7. **Lowest Weight between ages 12 and 18:**

   Weight ☐☐☐ lbs. **at** Height ☐ ft. ☐☐ in. **at age**
   ○ 12
   ○ 13
   ○ 14
   ○ 15
   ○ 16
   ○ 17

8. At your current weight, do you feel that you are:
   ○ Extremely thin   ○ Slightly overweight
   ○ Moderately thin   ○ Moderately overweight
   ○ Slightly thin   ○ Extremely overweight
   ○ Normal weight

9. How much do you fear gaining weight?
   ○ Not at all
   ○ Slightly
   ○ Moderately
   ○ Very much
   ○ Extremely

EDQ 9.0. Copyright © 2004, The Neuropsychiatric Research Institute. Used with permission.

Continue on Next Page

EDQ - continued, pg. 2

10. How <u>dissatisfied</u> are you with the way your body is proportioned?

   ○ Not at all dissatisfied
   ○ Slightly dissatisfied
   ○ Moderately dissatisfied
   ○ Very dissatisfied
   ○ Extremely dissatisfied

11. How important is your weight and shape in affecting how you feel about yourself as a person?

   ○ Not at all important
   ○ Slightly important
   ○ Moderately important
   ○ Very important
   ○ Extremely important

12. How fat do you currently feel?

   ○ Not at all fat
   ○ Slightly fat
   ○ Fat
   ○ Very fat
   ○ Extremely fat

13. Please indicate on the scales below how you feel about different areas of your body. (Fill in the circle of best response for each body part.)

	(a) Face	(b) Arms	(c) Shoulders	(d) Breasts	(e) Stomach	(f) Waist	(g) Hips	(h) Buttocks	(i) Thighs
Extremely positive	○	○	○	○	○	○	○	○	○
Moderately positive	○	○	○	○	○	○	○	○	○
Slightly positive	○	○	○	○	○	○	○	○	○
Neutral	○	○	○	○	○	○	○	○	○
Slightly negative	○	○	○	○	○	○	○	○	○
Moderately negative	○	○	○	○	○	○	○	○	○
Extremely negative	○	○	○	○	○	○	○	○	○

14. On the average, how often do you weigh yourself?

   ○ Never
   ○ Less than monthly
   ○ Monthly
   ○ Several times/month
   ○ Weekly
   ○ Several times/week
   ○ Daily
   ○ 2 or 3 times/day
   ○ 4 or 5 times/day
   ○ More than 5 times/day

C. DIETING BEHAVIOR

1. On the average, how many main meals do you eat each day?

2. On the average, how many snacks do you eat each day?

3. On the average, how many days a week do you eat the following meals?

   <u>Breakfast:</u> [ ] days a week   <u>Lunch:</u> [ ] days a week   <u>Dinner:</u> [ ] days a week

4. Do you try to avoid certain foods in order to influence your shape or weight?

   ○ Yes (If Yes, what?) _____
   ○ No

5. Have you ever been on a diet, restricted your food intake, and/or reduced the amounts or types of food eaten to control your weight?

   ○ Yes
   ○ No (If No, go to section D, "BINGE EATING BEHAVIOR.")

6. At what age did you first begin to diet, restrict your food intake, and/or reduce the amount or types of food eaten to <u>control</u> your weight?

   [ ] years old

7. At what age did you first begin to diet, restrict your food intake, and/or reduce the amount or types of food eaten to <u>lose</u> weight?

   [ ] years old

EDQ 9.0. Copyright © 2004, The Neuropsychiatric Research Institute. Used with permission.

Continue on Next Page

EDQ - continued, pg. 3

8. Over the last year, how often have you begun a diet that lasted for more than 3 days?

☐☐☐ times

9. Over the last year, how often have you begun a diet that lasted for 3 days or less?

☐☐☐ times

10. Indicate your preferred ways of dieting (fill in all that apply).

○ Skip meals
○ Completely fast for 24 hours or more
○ Restrict carbohydrates
○ Restrict sweets/sugar
○ Reduce fats

○ Reduce portion size
○ Exercise more
○ Reduce calories
○ Other: _____

11. In which of the following treatments or types of treatment for eating or weight problems have you participated?

(a) Supervised Diets:	Yes	No	If Yes, ages used	Weight at Start	Weight at End
Weight Watchers ®	○	○			
Jenny Craig ®	○	○			
Nutrasystems ®	○	○			
Optifast ®	○	○			
Procal ®	○	○			
Nutramed ®	○	○			
Liquid protein diet	○	○			
Others: _____	○	○			

(b) Medication for Obesity:	Yes	No	If Yes, ages used	Weight at Start	Weight at End
Phentermine	○	○			
Fenfluramine	○	○			
Xenical (Orlistat ®)	○	○			
Sibutramine (Meridia ®)	○	○			
Topiramate (Topomax ®)	○	○			
Wellbutrin (Buproprion ®)	○	○			
Over-the-counter diet pills (specify): _____	○	○			
Other medication treatment (specify): _____	○	○			
Human Chorionic Gonadotropin (HCG)	○	○			
Others: _____	○	○			

(c) Psychotherapy for Eating Problems, Weight Loss, or Weight Gain:	Yes	No	If Yes, ages used	Weight at Start	Weight at End
Behavior Modification	○	○			
Individual Psychotherapy	○	○			
Group Psychotherapy	○	○			
Hypnosis	○	○			
Others: _____	○	○			

(d) Psychotherapy for Eating Disorder:	Yes	No	If Yes, ages used	Weight at Start	Weight at End
Individual Cognitive Behavioral	○	○			
Group Cognitive Behavioral	○	○			
Interpersonal Psychotherapy	○	○			
Nutritional Counseling	○	○			
Others: _____	○	○			

EDQ 9.0. Copyright © 2004, The Neuropsychiatric Research Institute. Used with permission.

Continue on Next Page

EDQ - continued, pg. 4

(e) Medication for Eating Problems/Weight Problems:	Yes	No	If Yes, ages used	If Yes, maximum dosage
Fluoxetine (Prozac ®)	O	O		
Desipramine (Norpramin ®)	O	O		
Paroxetine HCl (Paxil ®)	O	O		
Sertraline HCl (Zoloft ®)	O	O		
Citalopram (Celexa ®)	O	O		
Fluvoxamine (Luvox ®)	O	O		
Naltrexone (Trexan ®)	O	O		
Escitalopram (Lexapro ®)	O	O		
Quetiapine (Seroquel ®)	O	O		
Olanzapine (Zyprexa ®)	O	O		
Risperidone (Risperidol ®)	O	O		
Others: _____	O	O		

(f) Self-help groups:	Yes	No	If Yes, ages used
Bulimia Anonymous	O	O	
Overeaters Anonymous	O	O	
Anorexics Anonymous	O	O	
Others: _____	O	O	

(g) Surgical Procedures:	Yes	No	If Yes, at what age	Weight at Start	Weight at End
Liposuction	O	O			
Gastric bypass	O	O			
Gastric banding	O	O			
Other intestinal surgery (specify): _____	O	O			
Gastric balloon/"bubble"	O	O			
Others: _____	O	O			

12. Please record your major diets which resulted in a <u>weight loss of 10 pounds or more</u>.

	Age at time of diet	Weight at start of diet	# lbs. lost	Type of diet
(1)				
(2)				
(3)				
(4)				
(5)				
(6)				
(7)				
(8)				
(9)				
(10)				

13. Have you ever had any significant physical or emotional symptoms while attempting to lose weight or after losing weight?

O Yes   O No

If Yes, describe your symptoms, how long they lasted, if they made you stop your weight loss program, and if they made you seek professional help.

Problem	Year	Duration (weeks)	Stopped weight loss program? Yes / No	Type of professional help, if any
			O O	
			O O	
			O O	
			O O	
			O O	

EDQ 9.0. Copyright © 2004, The Neuropsychiatric Research Institute. Used with permission.

Continue on Next Page

EDQ - continued, pg. 5

D. BINGE EATING BEHAVIOR

1. Have you ever had an episode of binge eating characterized by:

   (a) eating, in a discrete period of time (e.g., within any two hour period), an amount of food that is definetely larger than most people eat in a similar period of time?

   ○ Yes   ○ No

   (b) a sense of lack of control over eating during the episode (e.g., a feeling that one cannot stop eating or control what or how much one is eating)?

   ○ Yes   ○ No

   If No to either a) or b), go to section E, "WEIGHT CONTROL BEHAVIOR."

2. Please indicate on the scales below how <u>characteristic</u> the following symptoms are or were of your <u>binge eating</u>.

	Never	Rarely	Sometimes	Often	Always
(a) feeling that I can't stop eating or control what or how much I eat	○	○	○	○	○
(b) eating much more rapidly than usual	○	○	○	○	○
(c) eating until I feel uncomfortably full	○	○	○	○	○
(d) eating large amounts of food when not feeling physically hungry	○	○	○	○	○
(e) eating alone because I am embarrassed by how much I am eating	○	○	○	○	○
(f) feeling disgusted with myself, depressed, or very guilty after overeating	○	○	○	○	○
(g) feeling very distressed about binge eating	○	○	○	○	○

3. How old were you when you began binge eating?

   ☐☐ years old

4. When did binge eating start to occur on a regular basis, on average at least 2 times each week?

   ☐☐ years old

5. What was your height and weight at that time?

   Weight   **Height**
   ☐☐☐ lbs. **at**   ☐ ft. ☐☐ in.

6. What is the total duration of time you had a problem with binge eating (whether or not you are binge eating now)?

   Days   **Months**   **Years**
   ☐☐   ☐☐   ☐☐

E. WEIGHT CONTROL BEHAVIOR

1. Have you ever self-induced vomiting after eating in order to get rid of the food eaten?

   ○ Yes   ○ No (If No, go to question 8.)

2. How old were you when you induced vomiting for the first time?

   ☐☐ years old

3. How old were you when you first induced vomiting on a regular basis (on average at least two times each week)?

   ☐☐ years old

4. How long did you self-induce vomiting?

   Days   **Months**   **Years**
   ☐☐   ☐☐   ☐☐

EDQ 9.0. Copyright © 2004, The Neuropsychiatric Research Institute. Used with permission.

Continue on Next Page

EDQ - continued, pg. 6

5. Have you ever taken syrup of Ipecac ® to control your weight?

   O Yes   O No

6. How old were you when you took Ipecac ® for the first time?

   ☐☐ years old

7. How long did you use Ipecac ® to control your weight?

Days	Months	Years
☐☐	☐☐	☐☐

---

8. Have you ever used laxatives to control your weight or "get rid of food?"

   O Yes   O No (If No, go to question 13.)

9. How old were you when you first took laxatives for weight control?

   ☐☐ years old

10. How old were you when you first took laxatives for weight control (on a regular basis on average at least two times each week)?

    ☐☐ years old

11. How long did you use laxatives for weight control?

Days	Months	Years
☐☐	☐☐	☐☐

12. What type and amounts of laxatives have you used? (Indicate all types that apply and the maximum number used per day.)

	Yes	No		Maximum Number per Day						
			1	2	3	4	5	6-10	11-20	>20
Ex-Lax ®	O	O	O	O	O	O	O	O	O	O
Correctol ®	O	O	O	O	O	O	O	O	O	O
Metamucil ®	O	O	O	O	O	O	O	O	O	O
Colace ®	O	O	O	O	O	O	O	O	O	O
Dulcolax ®	O	O	O	O	O	O	O	O	O	O
Phillips Milk of Magnesia ®	O	O	O	O	O	O	O	O	O	O
Senokot ®	O	O	O	O	O	O	O	O	O	O
Perdiem ®	O	O	O	O	O	O	O	O	O	O
Fleet ®	O	O	O	O	O	O	O	O	O	O
Other (specify):	O	O	O	O	O	O	O	O	O	O

---

13. Have you ever used diuretics (water pills) to control your weight?

    O Yes   O No (If No, go to question 18.)

14. How old were you when you first took diuretics for weight control?

    ☐☐ years old

15. How old were you when you first took diuretics for weight control (on a regular basis, on average at least two times each week)?

    ☐☐ years old

16. How long did you use diuretics for weight control?

Days	Months	Years
☐☐	☐☐	☐☐

17. What type and amount of diuretics have you used? (Indicate all that apply and the maximum number used per day.)

(a) Over-the-counter Diuretics:	Yes	No		Maximum Number per Day								
			1	2	3	4	5	6	7	8	9	10	>10
Aqua-Ban ®	O	O	O	O	O	O	O	O	O	O	O	O
Diurex ®	O	O	O	O	O	O	O	O	O	O	O	O
Midol ®	O	O	O	O	O	O	O	O	O	O	O	O
Pamprin ®	O	O	O	O	O	O	O	O	O	O	O	O
Others (specify):	O	O	O	O	O	O	O	O	O	O	O	O

EDQ 9.0. Copyright © 2004, The Neuropsychiatric Research Institute. Used with permission.

Continue on Next Page

EDQ - continued, pg. 7

(b) Prescription Diuretics:	Yes	No		1	2	3	4	5	6	7	8	9	10	>10
			Maximum Number per Day											
	O	O		O	O	O	O	O	O	O	O	O	O	O
	O	O		O	O	O	O	O	O	O	O	O	O	O

18. Have you ever used diet pills to control your weight?

    O Yes   O No (If No, please go to question 22.)

19. How old were you when you first used diet pills for weight control?

    ☐☐ years old

20. How long did you use diet pills to control your weight?

Days	Months	Years
☐☐	☐☐	☐☐

21. What types and amounts of diet pills have you used **within the last month**? (Indicate all that apply and the maximum number per day.)

(a) Over-the-counter:	Yes	No		1	2	3	4	5	6	7	8	9	10	>10
			Maximum Number per Day											
Dexatrim ®	O	O		O	O	O	O	O	O	O	O	O	O	O
Dietac ®	O	O		O	O	O	O	O	O	O	O	O	O	O
Acutrim ®	O	O		O	O	O	O	O	O	O	O	O	O	O
Protrim ®	O	O		O	O	O	O	O	O	O	O	O	O	O
Ma Huang	O	O		O	O	O	O	O	O	O	O	O	O	O
Ephedrine	O	O		O	O	O	O	O	O	O	O	O	O	O
Chromium	O	O		O	O	O	O	O	O	O	O	O	O	O
Guarana seed	O	O		O	O	O	O	O	O	O	O	O	O	O
Garcinia Cambogia	O	O		O	O	O	O	O	O	O	O	O	O	O
Caffeine	O	O		O	O	O	O	O	O	O	O	O	O	O
Other (specify): _____	O	O		O	O	O	O	O	O	O	O	O	O	O

(b) Prescription:	Yes	No		1	2	3	4	5	6	7	8	9	10	>10
			Maximum Number per Day											
	O	O		O	O	O	O	O	O	O	O	O	O	O
	O	O		O	O	O	O	O	O	O	O	O	O	O

22. During the entire LAST MONTH, what is the average frequency that you have engaged in the following behaviors? (Please fill in one circle for each behavior.)

	Never	Once a Month or Less	Several Times a Month	Once a Week	Twice a Week	Three to Six Times a Week	Once a Day	More Than Once a Day
Binge eating (as defined on pg. 5, D.1.)	O	O	O	O	O	O	O	O
Vomiting	O	O	O	O	O	O	O	O
Laxative use to control weight	O	O	O	O	O	O	O	O
Use of diet pills	O	O	O	O	O	O	O	O
Use of diuretics	O	O	O	O	O	O	O	O
Use of enemas	O	O	O	O	O	O	O	O
Use of Ipecac ® syrup	O	O	O	O	O	O	O	O
Exercise to control weight	O	O	O	O	O	O	O	O
Fasting (skipping meals for entire day)	O	O	O	O	O	O	O	O
Skipping meals	O	O	O	O	O	O	O	O
Eating very small meals	O	O	O	O	O	O	O	O
Eating meals low in calories and/or fat grams	O	O	O	O	O	O	O	O
Chewing and spitting out food	O	O	O	O	O	O	O	O
Rumination (vomit food into mouth, chew, and re-swallow)	O	O	O	O	O	O	O	O
Saunas to control weight	O	O	O	O	O	O	O	O
Herbal products ("fat burners")	O	O	O	O	O	O	O	O

EDQ 9.0. Copyright © 2004, The Neuropsychiatric Research Institute. Used with permission.

Continue on Next Page

EDQ - continued, pg. 8

23. During **any one month period**, what is the HIGHEST frequency that you have engaged in the following behaviors? (Please fill in one circle for each behavior.)

	Never	Once a Month or Less	Several Times a Month	Once a Week	Twice a Week	Three to Six Times a Week	Once a Day	More Than Once a Day
Binge eating (as defined on pg. 5, D.1.)	O	O	O	O	O	O	O	O
Vomiting	O	O	O	O	O	O	O	O
Laxative use to control weight	O	O	O	O	O	O	O	O
Use of diet pills	O	O	O	O	O	O	O	O
Use of diuretics	O	O	O	O	O	O	O	O
Use of enemas	O	O	O	O	O	O	O	O
Use of Ipecac ® syrup	O	O	O	O	O	O	O	O
Exercise to control weight	O	O	O	O	O	O	O	O
Fasting (skipping meals for entire day)	O	O	O	O	O	O	O	O
Skipping meals	O	O	O	O	O	O	O	O
Eating very small meals	O	O	O	O	O	O	O	O
Eating meals low in calories and/or fat grams	O	O	O	O	O	O	O	O
Chewing and spitting out food	O	O	O	O	O	O	O	O
Rumination (vomit food into mouth, chew, and re-swallow	O	O	O	O	O	O	O	O
Saunas to control weight	O	O	O	O	O	O	O	O
Herbal products ("fat burners")	O	O	O	O	O	O	O	O

F. EXERCISE

1. How frequently do you exercise?

   O Not at all   O Several times per week
   O Once per month or less   O Once per day
   O Several times per month   O Several times a day
   O Once per week

2. If you exercise, how long do you usually exercise each time?

   O Less than 15 minutes
   O 15 - 30 minutes
   O 31 - 60 minutes
   O 61 - 120 minutes
   O More than 120 minutes

3. If you exercise, please indicate the types of exercise you do (fill in all that apply).

   O Biking   O Walking
   O Running   O In-lineskating
   O Swimming   O Stairmaster
   O Weighttraining   O Treadmill
   O Aerobics   O Stationary bike
   O Calisthenics   O Other: _____

G. MENSTRUAL HISTORY

1. Age of onset of menses: [ ][ ] years

2. Have you ever had periods of time when you stopped menstruating for three months or more (which were unrelated to pregnancy)?

   O Yes   O No   If Yes, number of times: [ ][ ]

3. Did weight loss ever cause irregularities of your cycle?

   O Yes   O No   If Yes, describe:
   _____
   _____

4. Have you menstruated during the last three months?

   O Yes   O No

EDQ 9.0. Copyright © 2004, The Neuropsychiatric Research Institute. Used with permission.

Continue on Next Page

EDQ - continued, pg. 9

5. Are you on birth control pills?   O Yes   O No

6. Are you on hormone replacement?   O Yes   O No

7. Are you post menopausal?   O Yes   O No

8. Please indicate when during your cycle you feel most vulnerable to binge eating. Please fill in the single best response.

     O I do not binge eat during menstruation   O 1 - 2 days prior to menstruation
     O 11 - 14 days prior to menstruation   O After menstruation onset
     O 7 - 10 days prior to menstruation   O No particular time
     O 3 - 6 days prior to menstruation

9. Do you crave particular foods (have a desire or urge to consume a specific food item or drink) for the <u>few days prior to</u> menstruation?

     O Yes   O No   If Yes, what foods do you crave?
     _____
     _____

10. Do you crave particular foods (have a desire or urge to consume a specific food item or drink) <u>during</u> your menstruation?

     O Yes   O No   If Yes, what foods do you crave?
     _____
     _____

11. Marriage and pregnancy:

	Yes	No	Does Not Apply
(a) Did problems with weight and/or binge eating begin before you were married?	O	O	O
(b) Did problems with weight and/or binge eating begin after you were married?	O	O	O
(c) Did problems with weight and/or binge eating begin before your first pregnancy?	O	O	O
(d) Did problems with weight and/or binge eating begin after your first pregnancy?	O	O	O

12. Do you have children?

     O Yes   O No (If No, skip to section H, "HISTORY OF ABUSE.")

     (a) For your FIRST child, what was your...
         ...weight at the start of your pregnancy?   ...weight at delivery?   ...lowest weight in the first year after delivery?

     (b) For your SECOND child, what was your...
         ...weight at the start of your pregnancy?   ...weight at delivery?   ...lowest weight in the first year after delivery?

     (c) For your THIRD child, what was your...
         ...weight at the start of your pregnancy?   ...weight at delivery?   ...lowest weight in the first year after delivery?

     (d) For your FOURTH child, what was your...
         ...weight at the start of your pregnancy?   ...weight at delivery?   ...lowest weight in the first year after delivery?

EDQ 9.0. Copyright © 2004, The Neuropsychiatric Research Institute. Used with permission.

Continue on Next Page

EDQ - continued, pg. 10

H. HISTORY OF ABUSE

1. Before you were 18, did any of the following happen to you?

Yes	No	
O	O	Someone constantly criticized you and blamed you for minor things.
O	O	Someone physically beat you (hit you, slapped you, threw something at you, pushed you).
O	O	Someone threatened to hurt or kill you, or do something sexual to you.
O	O	Someone threatened to abandon or leave you.
O	O	You watched one parent physically beat (hit, slap) the other parent.
O	O	Someone from your family forced you to have sexual relations (unwanted touching, fondling, sexual kissing, sexual intercourse).
O	O	Someone outside your family forced you to have sexual relations (unwanted touching, fondling, sexual kissing, sexual intercourse).

2. After you were 18, did any of the following happen to you?

Yes	No	
O	O	Someone constantly criticized you and blamed you for minor things.
O	O	Someone physically beat you (hit you, slapped you, threw something at you, pushed you).
O	O	Someone threatened to hurt or kill you, or do something sexual to you.
O	O	Someone threatened to abandon or leave you.
O	O	You watched one parent physically beat (hit, slap) the other parent.
O	O	Someone from your family forced you to have sexual relations (unwanted touching, fondling, sexual kissing, sexual intercourse).
O	O	Someone outside your family forced you to have sexual relations (unwanted touching, fondling, sexual kissing, sexual intercourse).

I. PSYCHIATRIC HISTORY

1. Have you ever been hospitalized for psychiatric problems?

    O Yes (If Yes, please complete the section below.)
    O No

HOSPITAL NAME & ADDRESS (CITY, STATE)	WHAT YEAR	DIAGNOSIS (IF KNOWN) OR PROBLEMS YOU WERE HAVING	TREATMENT YOU RECEIVED	WAS THIS HELPFUL?	
				Yes	No
				O	O
				O	O
				O	O
				O	O
				O	O

EDQ 9.0. Copyright © 2004, The Neuropsychiatric Research Institute. Used with permission.

Continue on Next Page

EDQ - continued, pg. 11

2. Have you ever been treated out of the hospital for psychiatric problems?

   ○ Yes (If Yes, please complete the section below.)

   ○ No

YEAR(S) WHEN TREATED	DOCTOR OR THERAPIST'S NAME & ADDRESS (CITY, STATE)	DIAGNOSIS (IF KNOWN) OR PROBLEMS YOU WERE HAVING	TREATMENT YOU RECEIVED	WAS THIS HELPFUL? Yes	No
				○	○
				○	○
				○	○
				○	○
				○	○

3. Complete the following information for any of the following types of medications you are now taking or have ever taken:

		Took Previously	On Currently	Current Dosage	If taking currently, for what problem?
(a) ANTIDEPRESSANTS					
Prozac ®	(Fluoxetine)	○	○		
Zoloft ®	(Sertraline)	○	○		
Paxil ®	(Paroxetine)	○	○		
Luvox ®	(Fluvoxamine)	○	○		
Celexa ®	(Citalopram)	○	○		
Effexor ®	(Venlafaxine)	○	○		
Wellbutrin ®	(Bupropion)	○	○		
Elavil ®	(Amitriptyline)	○	○		
Tofranil ®	(Imipramine)	○	○		
Sinequan ®	(Doxepin)	○	○		
Norpramin ®	(Desipramine)	○	○		
Vivactil ®	(Protriptyline)	○	○		
Desyrel ®	(Trazodone)	○	○		
Parnate ®	(Tranylcypromine)	○	○		
Nardil ®	(Phenelzine)	○	○		
Anafranil ®	(Clomipramine)	○	○		
Remeron ®	(Mirtazapine)	○	○		
Serzone ®	(Nefazodone)	○	○		
St. John's Wort		○	○		
Lexapro ®	(Escitalopram)	○	○		

(b) MAJOR TRANQUILIZERS					
Clozaril ®	(Clozapine)	○	○		
Zyprexa ®	(Olanzepine)	○	○		
Risperdal ®	(Risperidone)	○	○		
Haldol ®	(Haloperidol)	○	○		
Navane ®	(Thiothixene)	○	○		
Trilafon ®	(Perphenazine)	○	○		
Thorazine ®	(Chlorpromazine)	○	○		
Stelazine ®	(Trifluoperazine)	○	○		
Prolixin ®	(Fluphenazine)	○	○		
Orap ®	(Pimozide)	○	○		
Moban ®	(Molindone)	○	○		
Loxitane ®	(Loxapine)	○	○		
Seroquil ®	(Quetiapine)	○	○		
Mellaril ®	(Thioridazine)	○	○		
Geodon ®	(Ziprasidone)	○	○		
Abilify ®	(Aripiprozole)	○	○		

EDQ 9.0. Copyright © 2004, The Neuropsychiatric Research Institute. Used with permission.

Continue on Next Page

EDQ - continued, pg. 12

		Took Previously	On Currently	Current Dosage	If taking currently, for what problem?
(c) MINOR TRANQUILIZERS					
Valium ®	(Diazepam)	O	O		
Librium ®	(Chlordiazepoxide)	O	O		
Serax ®	(Oxazepam)	O	O		
Halcion ®	(Triazolam)	O	O		
Tranxene ®	(Clorazepate)	O	O		
Ambien ®	(Zolpidem)	O	O		
Klonopin ®	(Clonazepam)	O	O		
Ativan ®	(Lorazepam)	O	O		
BuSpar ®	(Buspirone)	O	O		
Dalmane ®	(Flurazepam)	O	O		
Xanax ®	(Alprazolam)	O	O		
Sonata ®	(Zaleplon)	O	O		

		Took Previously	On Currently	Current Dosage	If taking currently, for what problem?
(d) MOOD STABILIZERS					
Lithobid ®	Lithium ®	O	O		
Depakote ®	Sodium Valproate ®	O	O		
Tegretol ®	(Carbamazepine)	O	O		
Topomax ®	(Topiramate)	O	O		
Lamictal ®	(Lamotrigine)	O	O		
OTHER:		O	O		
OTHER:		O	O		
OTHER:		O	O		
OTHER:		O	O		

J. MEDICAL HISTORY

1. Please list all medical hospitalizations:

WHEN? YEAR(S)	WHERE? (Hospital Name & City)	PROBLEM	DIAGNOSIS	TREATMENT YOU *RECEIVED*

2. Please list all other medical treatment you've received. (Include any significant problem, but do not include flu, colds, routine exams.)

WHEN? YEAR(S)	WHERE? (Doctor's Name & Address)	PROBLEM	DIAGNOSIS	TREATMENT YOU RECEIVED

EDQ 9.0. Copyright © 2004, The Neuropsychiatric Research Institute. Used with permission.

Continue on Next Page

EDQ - continued, pg. 13

K. CHEMICAL USE HISTORY

1. In the last six months, how often have you taken these drugs?

	Not At All	Less Than Monthly	About Once a Month	Several Times a Month	About Once a Week	Several Times a Week	Daily	Several Times a Day
ALCOHOL	O	O	O	O	O	O	O	O
STIMULANTS (Amphetamines, Uppers, Crank, Speed)	O	O	O	O	O	O	O	O
DIET PILLS	O	O	O	O	O	O	O	O
SEDATIVES (Barbiturates, Sleeping Pills, Valium ®, Librium ®, Downers)	O	O	O	O	O	O	O	O
MARIJUANA/HASHISH	O	O	O	O	O	O	O	O
HALLUCINOGENS (LSD, Mescaline, Mushrooms, Extasy)	O	O	O	O	O	O	O	O
OPIATES (Heroin, Morphine, Opium)	O	O	O	O	O	O	O	O
COCAINE/CRACK	O	O	O	O	O	O	O	O
PCP (Angel Dust, Phencyclidine)	O	O	O	O	O	O	O	O
INHALANTS (Glue, Gasoline, etc.)	O	O	O	O	O	O	O	O
CAFFEINE PILLS (No Doz ®, Vivarin ®, etc.)	O	O	O	O	O	O	O	O
OTHER: _____	O	O	O	O	O	O	O	O
_____	O	O	O	O	O	O	O	O

2. What is the most you have used any of these drugs during a one-month period (month of heaviest use)?

(Example: If you used sleeping pills about once a month many years ago, but not at all now, you would fill in the circle under "About Once a Month" on the line "Sedatives - Barbiturates...")

	Not At All	Less Than Monthly	About Once a Month	Several Times a Month	About Once a Week	Several Times a Week	Daily	Several Times a Day
ALCOHOL	O	O	O	O	O	O	O	O
STIMULANTS (Amphetamines, Uppers, Crank, Speed)	O	O	O	O	O	O	O	O
DIET PILLS	O	O	O	O	O	O	O	O
SEDATIVES (Barbiturates, Sleeping Pills, Valium ®, Librium ®, Downers)	O	O	O	O	O	O	O	O
MARIJUANA/HASHISH	O	O	O	O	O	O	O	O
HALLUCINOGENS (LSD, Mescaline, Mushrooms, Extasy)	O	O	O	O	O	O	O	O
OPIATES (Heroin, Morphine, Opium)	O	O	O	O	O	O	O	O
COCAINE/CRACK	O	O	O	O	O	O	O	O
PCP (Angel Dust, Phencyclidine)	O	O	O	O	O	O	O	O
INHALANTS (Glue, Gasoline, etc.)	O	O	O	O	O	O	O	O
CAFFEINE PILLS (No Doz ®, Vivarin ®, etc.)	O	O	O	O	O	O	O	O
OTHER: _____	O	O	O	O	O	O	O	O
_____	O	O	O	O	O	O	O	O

3. Assuming all the drugs mentioned above were readily available, which would you prefer? _____

Continue on Next Page

EDQ 9.0. Copyright © 2004, The Neuropsychiatric Research Institute. Used with permission.

EDQ - continued, pg. 14

Have you ever had any of the following problems because of your alcohol or drug use? (if Yes, please specify.)

4. Drinking and driving when unsafe?

    ○ Yes......When?   ○ More than 6 months ago
    ○ No   ○ During the past 6 months
    ○ Both

5. Medical problems?

    ○ Yes......When?   ○ More than 6 months ago
    ○ No   ○ During the past 6 months
    ○ Both

6. Problems at work or school?

    ○ Yes......When?   ○ More than 6 months ago
    ○ No   ○ During the past 6 months
    ○ Both

7. An arrest?

    ○ Yes......When?   ○ More than 6 months ago
    ○ No   ○ During the past 6 months
    ○ Both

8. Family trouble?

    ○ Yes......When?   ○ More than 6 months ago
    ○ No   ○ During the past 6 months
    ○ Both

---

9. Have you ever smoked cigarettes?

○ Yes
○ No (If No, go to question 10.)

What was the most you ever smoked?

○ Only occasionally
○ Less than one pack per day
○ About one pack per day
○ One to two packs per day
○ About two packs per day
○ More than two packs per day

If you are smoking now, how much do you smoke?

○ Only occasionally
○ Less than one pack per day
○ About one pack per day
○ One to two packs per day
○ About two packs per day
○ More than two packs per day

---

10. Do you drink coffee?

○ Yes
○ No (If No, go to question 11.)

On the average, how many cups of <u>caffeinated</u> coffee do you drink per day?

○ Less than 1	○ 4 cups
○ 1 cup per day	○ 5 cups
○ 2 cups	○ 6 - 10 cups
○ 3 cups	○ More than 10 cups

On the average, how many cups of <u>decaffeinated</u> coffee do you drink per day?

○ Less than 1	○ 4 cups
○ 1 cup per day	○ 5 cups
○ 2 cups	○ 6 - 10 cups
○ 3 cups	○ More than 10 cups

---

11. Do you drink tea?

○ Yes
○ No (If No, go to question 12.)

On the average, how many cups of <u>caffeinated</u> tea do you drink per day?

○ Less than 1	○ 4 cups
○ 1 cup per day	○ 5 cups
○ 2 cups	○ 6 - 10 cups
○ 3 cups	○ More than 10 cups

On the average, how many cups of <u>decaffeinated</u> tea do you drink per day?

○ Less than 1	○ 4 cups
○ 1 cup per day	○ 5 cups
○ 2 cups	○ 6 - 10 cups
○ 3 cups	○ More than 10 cups

---

12. Do you drink cola or soft drinks?

○ Yes
○ No (If No, go to next section.)

On the average, how many cans/glasses of <u>caffeinated</u> cola or soft drinks do you drink per day?

○ Less than 1	○ 4 cans
○ 1 can per day	○ 5 cans
○ 2 cans	○ 6 - 10 cans
○ 3 cans	○ More than 10 cans

On the average, how many cans/glasses of <u>decaffeinated</u> cola or soft drinks do you drink per day?

○ Less than 1	○ 4 cans
○ 1 can per day	○ 5 cans
○ 2 cans	○ 6 - 10 cans
○ 3 cans	○ More than 10 cans

EDQ 9.0. Copyright © 2004, The Neuropsychiatric Research Institute. Used with permission.

Continue on Next Page

EDQ - continued, pg. 15

L. FAMILY MEMBERS

1.

	NAME	AGE IF LIVING	CAUSE OF DEATH	AGE AT DEATH
FATHER				
MOTHER				
BROTHERS & SISTERS				
SPOUSE				
CHILD 1				
CHILD 2				
CHILD 3				
CHILD 4				

2. Are you a twin?   O Yes   O No

(If Yes, is your twin identical?   ___Yes   ___No)

3. Were you adopted?   O Yes   O No

(If Yes, at what age were you adopted? _____)

M. FAMILY MEDICAL AND PSYCHIATRIC HISTORY

1. Fill in the circle in the column of any of your *blood relatives* who has, or has had, the following conditions or problems:

   * Include half brothers/half sisters

Columns: MOTHER | FATHER | *BROTHERS | *SISTERS | UNCLE | AUNT | GRANDPARENTS | CHILDREN

CONDITIONS

Condition	M	F	B	S	U	A	G	C
Alcoholism or Drug Abuse	O	O	O	O	O	O	O	O
Anorexia Nervosa	O	O	O	O	O	O	O	O
Anxiety	O	O	O	O	O	O	O	O
Arthritis/Rheumatism	O	O	O	O	O	O	O	O
Asthma, Hay Fever, or Allergies	O	O	O	O	O	O	O	O
Binge-Eating	O	O	O	O	O	O	O	O
Birth Defects	O	O	O	O	O	O	O	O
Bleeding Problems	O	O	O	O	O	O	O	O
Bulimia Nervosa	O	O	O	O	O	O	O	O
Cataracts	O	O	O	O	O	O	O	O
Cancer or Leukemia	O	O	O	O	O	O	O	O
Colitis	O	O	O	O	O	O	O	O
Deafness	O	O	O	O	O	O	O	O
Depression	O	O	O	O	O	O	O	O
Diabetes	O	O	O	O	O	O	O	O
Drug Abuse	O	O	O	O	O	O	O	O
Epilepsy (seizures, fits)	O	O	O	O	O	O	O	O
Eczema	O	O	O	O	O	O	O	O
Gall Bladder Malfunction	O	O	O	O	O	O	O	O
Gambling	O	O	O	O	O	O	O	O
Glaucoma	O	O	O	O	O	O	O	O
Gout	O	O	O	O	O	O	O	O
Heart Attack	O	O	O	O	O	O	O	O
Heart Disease	O	O	O	O	O	O	O	O
Hyperlipidemia (excessive fat in blood)	O	O	O	O	O	O	O	O

CONDITIONS

Condition	M	F	B	S	U	A	G	C
Hypertension (high blood pressure)	O	O	O	O	O	O	O	O
Jail or Prison	O	O	O	O	O	O	O	O
Kidney Disease	O	O	O	O	O	O	O	O
Liver Cirrhosis	O	O	O	O	O	O	O	O
Manic Depression (Bipolar)	O	O	O	O	O	O	O	O
Mental Retardation	O	O	O	O	O	O	O	O
Migraine or Sick Headaches	O	O	O	O	O	O	O	O
Nerve Diseases (Parkinson's, MS, etc.)	O	O	O	O	O	O	O	O
Obesity (overweight)	O	O	O	O	O	O	O	O
Psychiatric Hospitalization	O	O	O	O	O	O	O	O
Thyroid Disease/Goiter	O	O	O	O	O	O	O	O
Pernicious Anemia	O	O	O	O	O	O	O	O
Psychosis	O	O	O	O	O	O	O	O
Rheumatic Fever	O	O	O	O	O	O	O	O
Schizophrenia	O	O	O	O	O	O	O	O
Sickle Cell Disease	O	O	O	O	O	O	O	O
Stroke	O	O	O	O	O	O	O	O
Suicide Attempt	O	O	O	O	O	O	O	O
Suicide (completed)	O	O	O	O	O	O	O	O
Syphilis	O	O	O	O	O	O	O	O
Tuberculosis (TB)	O	O	O	O	O	O	O	O
Other Glandular Diseases	O	O	O	O	O	O	O	O
Ulcers	O	O	O	O	O	O	O	O
Yellow Jaundice	O	O	O	O	O	O	O	O
Other: _____	O	O	O	O	O	O	O	O

EDQ 9.0. Copyright © 2004, The Neuropsychiatric Research Institute. Used with permission.

Continue on Next Page

EDQ - continued, pg. 16

2. If any of your *blood relatives* have not had ANY of the above conditions or problems, please indicate here:
   - O Mother
   - O Father
   - O Brothers
   - O Sisters
   - O Uncles
   - O Aunts
   - O Grandparents
   - O Children

N. MEDICATION HISTORY

1. What medications are you now taking?

MEDICATION NAME	DOSAGE	HOW LONG HAVE YOU BEEN TAKING THIS MEDICATION?

2. What drugs, medications, or shots are you allergic to?

MEDICATION/DRUG/SHOT NAME	REACTION

O. SOCIAL HISTORY

1. Highest level achieved in school (choose one):
   - O 8th grade or less
   - O Some high school
   - O High school graduate
   - O Trade or technical school
   - O Some college
   - O College graduate
   - O Graduate study
   - O Graduate degree
   - O Post-graduate degree

   Specify highest degree attained:
   - O M.D./D.O.
   - O Ph.D./Psy.D./Ed.D.
   - O Pharm.D.
   - O M.A. or M.S.
   - O B.A. or B.S.
   - O B.S.N.
   - O Other: _____

2. Are you now employed?   O Yes   O No   If No, when were you last employed? _____

3. Current occupation or last work if now unemployed: _____

4. Were you ever in the armed services?   O Yes   O No

   Years of service (from when to when?) _____   Highest rank achieved _____

5. Have you ever been arrested?   O Yes   O No

   Age(s) when arrested: Reason(s) for arrest: Did you spend time in jail?

   _____   _____   _____

   _____   _____   _____

Continue on Next Page

EDO 9.0. Copyright © 2004. The Neuropsychiatric Research Institute. Used with permission.

P. MEDICAL CHECKLIST

Fill in the circle of any of the following that you have experienced during the last four weeks. You should indicate items which are very noticeable to you and not those things which, even if present, are minor.

GENERAL:
- O Severe loss of appetite
- O Severe weakness
- O Fever
- O Chills
- O Heavy sweats
- O Heavy night sweats - bed linens wet
- O Fatigue
- O Sudden change in sleep

SKIN:
- O Itching
- O Easy bruising that represents a change in the way you normally bruise
- O Sores
- O Marked dryness
- O Hair fragile - comes out in comb
- O Hair has become fine and silky
- O Hair has become coarse and brittle

HEAD:
- O Struck on head - knocked out
- O Frequent dizziness that makes you stop your normal activity and lasts at least 5 minutes
- O Headaches that are different from those you normally have
- O Headaches that awaken you
- O Headaches with vomiting

EYES:
- O Pain in your eyes
- O Need new glasses
- O Seeing double
- O Loss of part of your vision
- O Seeing flashing lights or forms
- O Seeing halos around lights

EARS:
- O Pain in your ears
- O Ringing in your ears
- O Change in hearing
- O Room spins around you

NOSE:
- O Bleeding
- O Pain
- O Cannot breathe well
- O Unusual smells

MOUTH:
- O Toothache
- Soreness or bleeding of:
  - O Lips
  - O Tongue
  - O Gums
- O Unusual tastes
- O Hoarseness

NECK:
- O Pain
- O Cannot move well
- O Lumps
- O Difficulty swallowing
- O Pain on swallowing

NODES:
- O Swollen or tender lymph nodes (Kernals)

BREASTS:
- O Pain
- O New lumps
- O Discharge from nipples

LUNGS:
- O Pain in chest
- O Pain when you take a deep breath
- O New cough
- O Coughing up blood
- O Green, white, or yellow phlegm
- O Wheezing
- O Short of breath (sudden)
- O Wake up at night - can't catch breath
- O Unable to climb stairs

HEART:
- O Pain behind breastbone
- O Pain behind left nipple
- O Pain on left side of neck or jaw
- O Heart racing
- O Heart thumps and misses beats
- O Short of breath when walking
- O Need 2 or more pillows to sleep
- O Legs and ankles swelling (not with menstrual period)
- O Blue lips/fingers/toes when indoors and warm

GASTRO-INTESTINAL:
- O Have lost all desire to eat
- O Food makes me ill
- O Cannot swallow normally
- O Pain on swallowing
- O Food comes halfway up again
- O Sudden persistent heartburn
- O Pain or discomfort after eating
- O Bloating
- O Sharp, stabbing pains in side or shoulder after eating

EDQ 9.0. Copyright © 2004, The Neuropsychiatric Research Institute. Used with permission.

Continue on Next Page

GENITO-URINARY:
- ○ Stabbing pain in back by lower ribs
- ○ Urinating much more frequently
- ○ Sudden awakening at night to urinate
- ○ Passing much more urine
- ○ Not making much urine
- ○ Unable to start to urinate
- ○ Must go to urinate quickly or afraid of losing urine
- ○ Pain on urination
- ○ Wetting yourself
- ○ Blood in urine
- ○ Pus in urine

NEUROLOGICAL:
- ○ Fainting
- ○ Fits
- ○ Weakness in arms or legs
- ○ Change in speech
- ○ Loss of coordination
- ○ Sudden periods or onset of confusion
- ○ Sudden changes in personality (suddenly not the same person)
- ○ Loss of ability to concentrate
- ○ Seeing things
- ○ Loss of touch
- ○ Tingling in arms or legs
- ○ Unable to chew properly
- ○ Memory loss
- ○ Tremulous or shaky

MALE:
- ○ Pain in testicles
- ○ Swelling of testicles
- ○ Swelling of scrotum

FEMALE:
- ○ Sudden change in periods
- ○ Between periods bleeding

LIST ANY OTHERS NOT MENTIONED ABOVE:

_____

_____

_____

EDQ 9.0. Copyright © 2004, The Neuropsychiatric Research Institute. Used with permission.

CHAPTER 4

Bariatric Surgery and Psychopathology

MELISSA A. KALARCHIAN AND MARSHA D. MARCUS

The goals of this chapter are to synthesize what is known about psychopathology among bariatric surgery patients and to highlight research on the relationship of psychopathology to postoperative outcomes. For comprehensive reviews of psychosocial factors in bariatric surgery, we refer readers to recent publications on this topic (Bocchieri, Meana, & Fisher, 2002; Herpertz et al., 2003).

Obesity and Psychopathology

There have been numerous studies on the relationship of obesity to psychopathology. Earlier investigations found few or no differences between normal weight and obese individuals in psychological functioning (Friedman & Brownell, 1995; Stunkard & Wadden, 1992; Wadden, Womble, Stunkard, & Anderson, 2002). However, many of the earlier studies had methodological limitations, such as cross-sectional designs, small sample size, or use of nonstandardized assessment instruments. Furthermore, many studies were conducted before widespread acceptance of the body mass index (BMI) [(weight in kg)/(height in m^2)] as the preferred index of adiposity. Finally, studies reporting on overall mental health among obese individuals may have obscured relationships between obesity and certain aspects of psychological functioning or among particular subgroups of the obese population.

Results from two large, nationwide surveys suggest links between obesity and psychological functioning, even after controlling for numerous covariates. In the Behavioral Risk Factor Surveillance Study, individuals with BMIs greater than 30 reported worse mental health than did individuals with a BMI of 30 or less (Ford, Moriarty, Zack, Mokdad, & Chapman, 2001). In particular, there was a significant association between BMI and the risk of having 14 or more days of poor mental health during the last 30 days. Data from the Third National Health and Nutrition Examination Survey (1988–1994) also suggested a relationship between obesity and psychopathology (Onyike, Crum, Lee, Lyketsos, & Eaton, 2003). Specifically, obesity was associated with past-month depression in women, but not men. Further analyses suggested that obesity was associated with depression mainly among severely obese individuals.

Obesity and Specific Forms of Psychopathology

Recent studies using newer research designs also suggest links between obesity and specific forms of psychopathology, especially depression and binge eating (Faith, Calamaro, Dolan, & Pietrobelli, 2004). For example, in a large community study, Roberts, Kaplan, Shema, and Strawbridge (2000) examined the relationship between obesity and depression after controlling for numerous covariates, including sociodemographic factors, social support, chronic medical conditions, functional impairment, and life events. Cross-sectional analyses documented that 15.5% of obese individuals were depressed compared with 7.4% of normal-weight individuals. Moreover, when participants who were depressed at the initial evaluation were excluded, prospective analyses documented a relationship between obesity at baseline and depression 1 year later.

Numerous studies have shown that binge eating is associated with weight gain, obesity onset, and severity of obesity (Yanovski, 2003). Binge eating is also associated with psychiatric comorbidity. In one of the first studies to examine psychopathology among obese binge eaters, interviewers blind to patients' binge status documented that 60% of obese binge eaters met criteria for one or more psychiatric disorders compared with 28% of non-binge eaters of similar age and weight (Marcus, Wing, Ewing, & Kern, 1990). Differences were most apparent with respect to mood disorder: 32% of binge eaters reported a history of affective disorder versus 8% of non-binge eaters. Binge eaters also reported significantly more psychiatric symptoms, especially symptoms of depression, anxiety, and sexual dysfunction.

Night eating syndrome (NES), a clinical syndrome marked by morning anorexia, evening hyperphagia, and insomnia, is also associated with obesity (Stunkard & Allison, 2003). NES has been further characterized as a stress-related, eating, sleeping, and mood disorder with a coherent pattern of behavioral and neuroendocrine characteristics (Birketvedt et al., 1999). Rand, Macgregor, and Stunkard (1997) reported on the prevalence of NES in the general population (1.5%) and in bariatric surgery patients (27%). It has been suggested that binge eating and night eating are frequently co-occurring, but are distinct syndromes among surgery patients (Adami, Meneghelli, & Scopinaro, 1999). However, further research is needed to fully understand the clinical significance of night eating among obese individuals and its relationship to binge eating and mood.

Risk Factors for Psychopathology Among Obese Individuals

Friedman and Brownell (1995) reviewed the literature and concluded that the effects of obesity on psychological functioning vary across individuals. That is, certain subgroups of the obese population exhibit increased psychopathology. For example, demographic factors such as being female and weight-related behavior patterns such as dieting and binge eating have been related to the development of psychopathology. Additionally, individuals presenting for treatment of obesity display a higher prevalence of psychopathology than do obese individuals in the community (see meta-analysis by Friedman & Brownell, 1995). Furthermore, the type of obesity treatment sought has been related to the degree of psychological distress. In one study, individuals seeking treatment at a hospital-based obesity clinic offering pharmacotherapy or bariatric surgery were significantly more distressed as indicated by scores on the Symptom Checklist-90-Revised (Derogatis, 1983) than was a community group seeking behavioral treatment (Higgs et al., 1997).

The co-occurrence of obesity and chronic illness can also have an adverse effect on health. A population-based study by Doll, Petersen, and Stewart-Brown (2000) explored associations among BMI, chronic illness, and health-related quality of life. They demonstrated marked differences between obese and nonobese individuals in physical functioning, but few differences in emotional well-being on the Medical Outcomes Study 36-Item Short-Form Health Survey (McHorney, Ware, & Raczek, 1993), even after adjusting for the frequency of health service utilization. However, the subgroup of individuals with both obesity and chronic illness reported particularly poor physical and emotional health.

Finally, childhood adversity may represent a common risk factor for the development of both obesity and psychopathology. For example, several studies have linked childhood adversity to the development of obesity later in life (Felitti et al., 1998; Lissau & Sorensen, 1994; Williamson, Thompson,

Anda, Dietz, & Felitti, 2002). Childhood adversity has also been linked to the development of depression and eating disorders. For example, Wonderlich and colleagues (2001) found that childhood sexual abuse was associated with the presence of binge eating and several other forms of impulsive, self-destructive behavior in a controlled study. Further research is needed to identify subgroups of the obese population at increased risk for psychiatric morbidity and the mechanisms for these effects. Available findings suggest that severely obese patients seeking bariatric surgery may represent one such vulnerable subgroup.

Psychopathology Among Bariatric Surgery Patients

After bariatric surgery, patients enter a phase of rapid weight loss that requires many physical and emotional adjustments. Body weight typically reaches a plateau 18 to 24 months after surgery (e.g., Brolin, Robertson, Kenler, & Cody, 1994). Overall failure rates, defined as "either failure to lose significant weight or weight regain after significant weight loss," have been estimated at 20% (Benotti & Forse, 1995). However, little is known about how psychosocial factors relate to longer term outcomes after bariatric surgery.

In the sections that follow, we synthesize findings regarding psychological functioning in general, and eating disorders in particular, among bariatric surgery patients. Additionally, we examine factors related to outcome during the initial weight loss phase and the subsequent period of longer term weight stabilization. We use *Diagnostic and statistical manual of mental disorders*, 4th edition (DSM-IV; American Psychiatric Association, 1994), terminology in which Axis I is used to diagnose clinical disorders or those that are likely to be a focus of clinical attention. Axis II is used for diagnosis of personality disorders and mental retardation, which are regarded as more enduring conditions. Binge eating disorder (BED) is included in the DSM-IV as a proposed diagnostic category requiring further study. The core feature of this disorder is persistent and recurrent episodes of binge eating in the absence of inappropriate compensatory behavior such as self-induced vomiting.

Psychological Functioning Before Surgery

Black, Goldstein, and Mason (1992) conducted one of the earlier examinations of psychopathology among bariatric surgery candidates. They compared 88 patients seeking vertical banded gastroplasty to 76 "psychiatrically normal" subjects, matched on age and gender. On the Diagnostic Interview Schedule (Robins, Helzer, Croughan, & Ratcliff, 1981), 84% of patients met criteria for at least one disorder compared with 59% of the comparison group. Surgery patients were significantly more likely than were individuals in the comparison group to have had a lifetime history of mood disorders (especially major depression, 19.3% versus 5.3%), anxiety disorders (especially agoraphobia, 11.4% versus 2.6%; simple phobia, 22.7% versus 5.3%; and posttraumatic stress disorder, 10.2% versus 1.3%), bulimia nervosa (8.0% versus 1.3%), and tobacco dependence (40.9% versus 21.1%). Of note, all participants meeting diagnostic criteria for posttraumatic stress disorder were women. Patients were also more likely than those in the comparison group to exhibit personality disorder symptoms and disorders or to meet diagnostic criteria for more than one disorder.

Black, Goldstein, Mason, Bell, and Blum (1992) found evidence that the relatives of bariatric surgery patients might also have increased psychopathology. That is, patients were more likely to report having first-degree relatives with a history of depression, bipolar disorder, antisocial personality, and other psychiatric disorders than were the comparison individuals. These results suggest that psychiatric disorders among surgery patients may be attributable to familial and perhaps genetic factors.

The Swedish Obese Subjects study, a multidisciplinary project involving both a cross-sectional registry and a longitudinal intervention study, has also yielded data on the psychological profile of bariatric surgery patients. The study was designed to document whether a large, intentional weight loss reduces mortality over a 20-year period. A secondary aim was to look at specific morbidity, mortality, and quality of life in patients receiving bariatric surgery (most of whom received vertical banded gastroplasty) compared with a group of patients receiving nonsurgical, conventional treatment. The two groups were matched on 18 variables. Baseline results indicated that clinically significant depression, anxiety, and impaired social interaction were three to four times higher in severely obese individuals than in matched nonobese individuals (Sullivan et al., 1993). Furthermore, mental health in severely obese women was significantly poorer than in severely obese men, and women perceived more psychosocial difficulties.

Glinski, Wetzler, and Goodman (2001) reported a high degree of psychopathology among gastric bypass candidates, with 70% meeting criteria for a current or past Axis I disorder based on a semistructured clinical interview. At the time of assessment, 50% met criteria for a current disorder, and 23% were taking psychotropic medication. Depressive disorders were the most common current disorder (19%), and anxiety disorders were the second most prevalent (17%). Available research suggests psychopathology is relatively common among patients seeking bariatric surgery, and women may be particularly vulnerable. However, it remains unclear whether psychiatric morbidity is a cause, consequence, or correlate of severe obesity.

Psychological Functioning After Surgery

Most studies have shown that bariatric surgery has a positive impact on psychosocial functioning. Solow, Silberfarb, and Swift (1974) reported on the psychosocial effects of the original surgical procedure for weight loss, intestinal (jejunoileal) bypass, a procedure that caused significant morbidity and mortality that was eliminated by about 1980 (Benotti & Forse, 1995). A semistructured psychiatric interview and questionnaire were administered to 29 patients before surgery and again at 6-month intervals afterward. The investigators documented improvements in mood, self-esteem, interpersonal and vocational effectiveness, and body image.

More recently, a wealth of information has come from the Swedish Obese Subjects intervention study described earlier. Among the first 487 patients treated, poor health-related quality of life before intervention, documented on a battery of generic instruments supplemented with obesity-specific modules, was dramatically improved after bariatric surgery; scores were relatively stable among individuals in the comparison group (Karlsson, Sjostrom, & Sullivan, 1998). Positive changes peaked at 6 or 12 months after surgery, with a slight to moderate decrement in scores at the 24-month follow-up. Improvements in psychosocial functioning were related to the degree of weight loss. A similar pattern of changes in mental health was documented among 157 patients receiving the Greenville gastric bypass (Waters et al., 1991). All scores on a mental health battery covering four specific constructs (anxiety, depression, positive well being, and self-control) and two general ones (vitality and general health) improved significantly at 6 and 12 months after surgery, but most returned to baseline by 24 and 36 months.

In summary, available research suggests that bariatric surgery has a positive short-term impact on psychological functioning that may dissipate over time. Although surgery has a positive impact overall, some patients do experience the onset or recurrence of psychiatric disorders such as depression after bariatric surgery (e.g., Kodama et al., 1998), and some investigators have noted instances of suicide (e.g., Hsu et al., 1998). Thus optimal multidisciplinary care of the bariatric surgery patient should include ongoing monitoring of psychosocial functioning. Patients meeting criteria for clinical disorders can be referred for appropriate treatment, individuals with a history can be monitored for recurrence of psychopathology, and those with subclinical symptoms can be taught more adaptive ways of coping, all of which would be expected to minimize the impact of mental health problems on adjustment after operation (see chapter 8).

Eating Disorders Before Surgery

Several groups of researchers have conducted focused assessments of eating pathology among patients seeking bariatric surgery. Kalarchian, Wilson, Brolin, and Bradley (1998) administered an assessment battery including the Eating Disorder Examination (Fairburn & Cooper, 1993), considered the "gold standard" for the assessment of eating disorder behaviors and psychopathology. Thirty-nine percent of participants reported at least one binge episode per week over the previous 3 months, and 25% reported at least two episodes per week. Binge eaters reported more eating disorder psychopathology, including increased eating, shape and weight concerns, and more disinhibition and hunger, than did non-binge eaters.

Similar rates of binge eating have been documented utilizing alternate assessment methods in other patient samples. For example, Saunders, Johnson, and Teschner (1998) assessed 125 patients presenting for bariatric surgery and found that the prevalence of severe binge eating on the Binge Eating Scale (Gormally, Black, Daston, & Rardin, 1982) was 33.3% and was associated with depressive symptoms. Sanchez-Johnsen, Dymek, Alverdy, and Le Grange (2003) studied an ethnically diverse sample of women seeking bariatric surgery (62 African Americans, 18 Latinas, and 130 Whites) and found that rates of BED did not differ between minority individuals and White individuals, with an overall rate of 26%.

Investigators have also examined the relationship of binge eating to eating behavior and overall psychopathology among surgery patients. For example, Hsu and colleagues (2002) administered an assessment battery including the Structured Clinical Interview for DSM-IV (First, Spitzer, Gibbon, & Williams, 1995) to 37 bariatric surgery candidates who also participated in a 24-hour laboratory feeding paradigm. Twenty-five percent of participants reported clinically significant binge eating (11% met full BED criteria, and 14% met partial criteria). Binge eaters not only had higher eating concern, shape concern, and disinhibition scores, but also ate more in the feeding laboratory. However, no differences were found between BED and non-BED patients on other psychopathology. In another study, de Zwaan et al. (2003) found that bariatric surgery patients with BED (17.3% of the sample) exhibited increased general psychopathology and reduced quality of life relative to patients without BED (82.7%). (For more detailed discussion of eating disorders among weight loss surgery patients, see chapter 5.)

Onset of Eating Disorders After Surgery

Diagnoses of eating disorders after bariatric surgery appear to be most common among patients who had eating disturbances before surgery (Hsu, Betancourt, & Sullivan, 1996; Hsu, Sullivan, & Benotti, 1997); the onset of anorexia nervosa is rare (Atchison, Wade, Higgins, & Slavotinek, 1998; Bonne, Bashi, & Berry, 1996; Guisado et al., 2002; Scioscia, Bulik, Levenson, & Kirby, 1999). It is important to recognize that eating disorders, especially BED, may manifest differently in patients who have undergone bariatric surgery. Although there is agreement that binge eating is characterized by a sense of "loss of control," or the subjective feeling that one cannot control where, when, or how much is consumed, there has been debate as to whether consumption of an "objectively large" amount of food is a clinically useful parameter (Niego, Pratt, & Agras, 1997). Therefore, in our own research (Kalarchian et al., 2002) and that of others (Hsu et al., 1997), binge eating has been defined by a sense of loss of control over eating, independent of the amount consumed, among patients who have a reduced gastric capacity after surgery.

After bariatric surgery, patients experience vomiting if they do not eat slowly, chew their food well, and stop eating as soon as they feel full. Powers, Perez, Boyd, and Rosemurgy (1999) found that 79% of patients reported occasional vomiting, with one third reporting weekly vomiting at follow-up 5 years after operation. On interview, various explanations were given for vomiting, with most patients reporting "...they knew they shouldn't eat certain foods or certain amounts of foods, but did anyway...." (p. 299). Mitchell et al. (2001) documented that at follow-up 13 to 15 years after surgery, 68.8% of patients reported problems with vomiting and 42.7% with "plugging," defined as the subjective experience of ingested food becoming lodged in the stomach. An eating pattern of frequent snacking may also emerge in lieu of binge eating after surgery and can contribute to inadequate weight loss or weight regain (Saunders, 2004).

Aberrant eating patterns may develop after surgery that do not meet full diagnostic criteria for eating disorders, but can be associated with clinically significant distress and impaired weight management. For example, a new eating disorder has been proposed, postsurgical eating avoidance disorder, based on the observed coexistence of eating disorder symptoms, such as inappropriate compensatory behavior and body image disturbance, and anxiety symptoms, such as fear of weight gain (Segal, Kussunoki, & Larino, 2004). (See chapter 5 for a complete discussion of these issues.)

Impact of Surgery on Eating Disorders

Research suggests that bariatric surgery has a positive short-term impact on binge eating and related psychopathology. For example, Kalarchian, Wilson, Brolin, and Bradley (1999) administered the Eating Disorder Examination interview to 50 patients before and about 4 months after gastric bypass surgery. No subjects reported recurrent binge eating, loss of control over eating, or use of inappropriate compensatory behaviors, such as self-induced vomiting to influence shape and weight, at follow-up. Depressive symptoms decreased markedly after surgery. Dietary restraint increased, and disinhibition and hunger scores decreased in patients classified as non-binge eaters before operation, and increased in binge eaters such that the groups were virtually indistinguishable at follow-up.

Adami, Gandolfo, Meneghelli, and Scopinaro (1996) administered clinical interviews to (BPD) surgery patients before and again 2 years after biliopancreatic diversion. Binge eating fell sharply after surgery, with only a few patients starting to binge eat, and overall psychological status improved. In a subsequent study, there was nearly complete disappearance of binge eating and no changes in night eating in the 3 years after BPD (Adami, Meneghelli, Bressani, & Scopinaro, 1999).

Malone and Alger-Mayer (2004) classified bariatric surgery patients as non- ($n = 52$; 48%), moderate ($n = 31$; 28%), or severe ($n = 26$; 24%) binge eaters before undergoing surgery. These three groups of patients had similar outcomes in terms of improved depression scores, binge eating, and health-related quality of life at 12-month follow-up after vertical banded gastroplasty, gastric banding, or gastric bypass. Thus surgery appears to have a positive short-term impact regardless of severity of binge eating before surgery.

Relationship of Psychopathology to Bariatric Surgery Outcomes

Few studies have tested a priori predictors of weight loss in bariatric surgery patents. Many of the examinations of psychosocial factors related to outcomes have been based on post hoc analyses of data sets, which can lack conceptual clarity and statistical power. Below, we highlight studies on psychological factors associated with short-term outcomes, as well as data on factors related to longer term weight management.

Factors Related to Short-Term Outcomes (Up to 2 Years)

Studies on the relationship of psychiatric symptomatology to early postoperative outcomes have yielded equivocal findings, and results can be difficult to compare across studies because of methodological issues and differences in patient samples. The number of preoperative inpatient psychiatric admissions (Valley & Grace, 1987) and diagnoses of depression and anxiety (Powers, Rosemurgy, Coovert, & Boyd, 1988) have been associated with a variety of medical and psychiatric complications after surgery. Binge eating has also been associated with vomiting and band-related complications after adjustable silicone gastric banding (Busetto et al., 1997).

Findings on the relationship of psychiatric symptoms to early weight loss are mixed. Latner and colleagues (2004) administered a semistructured psychiatric interview to a predominantly low-income, inner-city group of women before surgery and found that the prevalence of psychiatric diagnoses was unaffected by surgery, and psychiatric conditions were unrelated to surgical outcome at follow-up (mean 16.4 months after surgery). However, more frequent preoperative binge eating, along with greater initial BMI, follow-up length, and postoperative exercise predicted greater decreases in BMI. In another study, patients who had higher scores on the BES, indicating more severe binge eating, also lost *more* weight than did those with lower scores at follow-up 6 months after gastric bypass (Boan, Kolotkin, Westman, McMahon, & Grant, 2004). However, binge eating has also been associated with a smaller percentage of excess weight loss at 6 months after gastric bypass (Dymek, le Grange, Neven, & Alverdy, 2001) and 18 months after vertical banded gastroplasty (Macias & Vaz Leal, 2003). Similarly, Averbukh and colleagues (2003) found that severity of depressive symptoms before surgery, as measured by scores on the Beck Depression Inventory, was associated with higher degree of excess weight loss at 1 year after surgery, but other investigators have not found a relationship between preoperative Beck Depression Inventory scores and weight loss (e.g., Dixon, Dixon, & O'Brien, 2003). Thus the relationship of depressive symptoms or binge eating to early postoperative weight loss is not well understood.

Factors Related to Longer Term Outcomes (2 Years or More After Surgery)

Studies of Overall Psychopathology

Very few studies have examined the impact of psychopathology before surgery on longer term outcomes. Larsen (1990) found that 41% of patients had a diagnosis on Axis I before surgery, dropping to 22% at 3-year follow-up. On Axis II, 22% had a diagnosis, remaining relatively stable at 19% at follow-up. When degree of weight loss (less than 20 kg/greater than 20 kg) and Axis II diagnosis (yes/no) were dichotomized, personality disorder was associated with poorer weight loss. With respect to psychopathology, social functioning, quality of life, and sexual functioning, all questionnaire scores improved after operation and were correlated with their preoperative levels.

Powers, Rosemurgy, Boyd, and Perez (1997) administered a presurgical psychiatric assessment to 131 bariatric surgery patients. Before surgery, 44% of patients had an Axis I psychiatric diagnosis, and 24% had an Axis II diagnosis. Affective disorders were the most common, reported by 37% of patients. At follow-up at a mean of 5.7 years after operation, almost half of the patients reported an improvement in their mental health. Preoperative psychiatric diagnosis was not related to weight loss or overall mental health after surgery.

Studies of Binge Eating

Several cross-sectional and retrospective studies have linked binge eating to longer term weight management after bariatric surgery. Hsu and colleagues (1996, 1997) have conducted two retrospective studies examining the relationship of both preoperative and postoperative eating disturbances to weight loss after bariatric surgery. In a pilot study (1996), 24 from a sample of 120 patients who underwent vertical banded gastroplasty within the previous 3.5 years were interviewed concerning their eating behaviors and psychiatric status. Thirty-seven percent had BED, 21% had bulimia nervosa, 42% had NES, and 33% had excessive fluid intake before surgery, and these eating disturbances tended to persist after surgery. Patients diagnosed with an eating disturbance postoperatively were more likely to exhibit a weight regain of at least 5 pounds over the 3 months before interview than did individuals without these disturbances. However, preoperative eating disturbances and psychopathology did not predict regain.

In a separate study, Hsu et al. (1997) interviewed 27 patients 20.8 months after gastric bypass. By recall, 81.5% of subjects reported a presurgical eating disturbance (as defined in the previous study). At follow-up, 25.9% of subjects had at least one eating disturbance. As hypothesized, both weight regain and current eating disturbances were predicted by the interaction between presurgical eating disturbance and length of time since surgery. Specifically, presurgical eating disturbances were unrelated to postsurgical eating disturbances and weight regain up to 2 years after surgery. However, presurgical eating disturbances were significantly related to current eating disturbances and weight regain 2 years or more after surgery.

In a questionnaire-based study, Kalarchian et al. (2002) examined factors related to longer term weight control among a cross-section of

99 patients assessed 2 through 7 years after bariatric surgery, with the variables of interest being loss of control over eating and related psychopathology. Postoperative loss of control over eating (with a subjectively or an objectively large amount of food) was associated with greater weight regain and robust differences in eating attitudes and behavior at longer term follow-up. Specifically, binge eaters reported gaining more since their lowest preoperative weight than did non-binge eaters. Moreover, binge eaters reported gaining weight over the 3 months before assessment, whereas non-binge eaters reported losing weight over the same period. Binge eaters reported greater concerns related to eating, shape, and weight as well as less dietary restraint, more disinhibition, and more hunger than did non-binge eaters.

In the longest term study of its kind (13–15 years after operation), Mitchell et al. (2001) compared three groups of gastric bypass patients: (1) those with no history of binge eating; (2) those who reported binge eating before surgery, but not afterward; and (3) those who reported binge eating before and after operation. Individuals who reported recurrence of BED symptoms after gastric bypass (Group 3) had regained more weight since their postoperative weight than had the other two groups. Thus the recurrence of loss of control over eating after bariatric surgery may be a marker of poorer outcome at longer term follow-up and an appropriate target for postsurgery intervention. However, we are not aware of any prospective study linking preoperative binge eating to longer term weight management. For example, one prospective study found no relationship between preoperative eating pathology, defined as binge eating or night eating, and postoperative weight outcome or vomiting at follow-up 5.5 years after operation (Powers et al., 1999). More prospective studies are needed to examine the relative impact of preoperative and postoperative psychopathology to outcomes after bariatric surgery.

Treating Psychopathology Among Bariatric Surgery Patients

Development of a lifestyle intervention for bariatric surgery patients may not only aid patients in maintenance of maximal weight loss, but also contribute to psychosocial adjustment to improved health independent of weight loss. A comprehensive lifestyle intervention for bariatric surgery patients should involve encouraging healthy eating habits, increasing physical activity, and enhancing psychosocial adjustment. A proposed model of treatment effects is shown in Figure 4.1. According to this model, a lifestyle intervention should focus on two main areas: patients' health-related behaviors and psychosocial functioning. In addition to encouraging compliance to recommendations from the health care team, target behaviors would include increasing healthy eating and physical activity and decreasing unhealthy eating and sedentary behaviors. Psychosocial targets for treatment might include interpersonal functioning, depression, and binge eating. Intervention in these two areas is expected to improve a range of outcomes by helping patients achieve and maintain maximal weight loss and enhancing their psychosocial functioning. Our research group is working toward the development of such a tailored intervention that will support bariatric surgery patients as they progress from the initial period of rapid weight loss after surgery toward longer term weight stabilization. (See chapter 8 for a complete discussion of psychosocial intervention literature.)

Summary

Bariatric surgery patients report high rates of psychopathology, especially depression, anxiety, and binge eating before the operation. Although surgery has a positive short-term impact on psychosocial functioning, these gains appear to dissipate over time as patients progress from the initial period of rapid weight loss toward longer term weight stabilization. Consistent with the literature on behavioral treatment of obesity, no robust predictors of outcomes after bariatric surgery, psychiatric or other, have been identified.

Several lines of evidence led us to hypothesize binge eating in the context of the chronic emotional instability and difficulties in interpersonal relationships characteristic of personality disorders may place patients at risk for poor outcomes after bariatric surgery. First, there is increasing recognition that personality disorders are related to adverse health outcomes in medical samples. Personality disorders have been associated with degree of weight loss after bariatric surgery (Larsen, 1990) and in obesity clinic patients (Berman, Raynes-Berman, Heymsfield, Fauci, & Ackerman, 1993). Moreover, dramatic, emotional, or erratic personality disorders

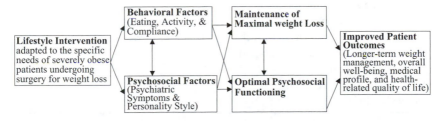

Figure. 4.1   Model of treatment.

(Cluster B), have been shown to negatively affect outcome after eating disorders treatment (Sansone & Fine, 1992). Second, individuals with Cluster B personality disorders often have problems with impulse control and can engage in binge eating, a behavior that may be associated with poorer long-term weight management after bariatric surgery (Hsu et al., 1996, 1997; Kalarchian et al., 2002). Finally, a history of trauma and abuse in childhood has been implicated in the onset of obesity (Felitti et al., 1998; Lissau & Sorensen, 1994) and eating disorders (Wonderlich et al., 2001) and is also postulated to be a risk factor for the development of personality disorders.

Prospective studies of individuals that vary in their demographic, medical, and psychiatric status are needed to identify those who are particularly vulnerable to poorer outcomes after operation. This research should include not only evaluation of clinical disorders, which may be relatively low in prevalence and a less sensitive measure for tracking changes over time, but also assessments of subthreshold symptoms, interpersonal functioning, and eating behaviors. New assessment tools are needed to study eating pathology that develops after operation. For example, de Zwaan and colleagues (see chapter 5) have adapted the Eating Disorder Examination semistructured interview for use with bariatric surgery patients. To stimulate further work, in Table 4.1, we suggest potential correlates of eating disorders among patients in the postoperative period based on our clinical experience and the research findings highlighted here. In summary, the implementation of hypothesis-driven prospective studies using measures appropriate for bariatric surgery patients will enhance our understanding of factors that predict poorer outcomes and targets for intervention.

TABLE 4.1 Possible Markers of Eating Disorders After Bariatric Surgery

1. Anxiety over eating and food aversions
2. Persistent nausea and vomiting
3. Chewing and spitting out food
4. Eating in the absence of hunger
5. Maladaptive eating behaviors, such as frequent eating episodes and excessive consumption of high-calorie liquids
6. Emotional eating
7. Loss of control over eating
8. Night eating

References

Adami, G. F., Gandolfo, P., Meneghelli, A., & Scopinaro, N. (1996). Binge eating in obesity: A longitudinal study following biliopancreatic diversion. *International Journal of Eating Disorders, 20,* 405–413.

Adami, G. F., Meneghelli, A., Bressani, A., & Scopinaro, N. (1999). Body image in obese patients before and after stable weight reduction following bariatric surgery. *Journal of Psychosomatic Research, 3,* 275–281.

Adami, G. F., Meneghelli, A., & Scopinaro, N. (1999). Night eating and binge eating disorder in obese patients. *International Journal of Eating Disorders, 25,* 335–359.

American Psychiatric Association. (1994). Diagnostic and statistical manual of mental disorders (4th ed.). Washington, DC: Author.

Atchison, M., Wade, T., Higgins, B., & Slavotinek, T. (1998). Anorexia nervosa following gastric reduction surgery for morbid obesity. *International Journal of Eating Disorders, 23,* 111–116.

Averbukh, Y., Heshka, S., El-Shoreya, H., Flancbaum, L., Geliebter, A., Kamel, S., et al. (2003). Depression score predicts weight loss following Roux-en-Y gastric bypass. *Obesity Surgery, 13,* 833–836.

Benotti, P. N., & Forse, R. A. (1995). The role of gastric surgery in the multidisciplinary management of severe obesity. *The American Journal of Surgery, 169,* 361–367.

Berman, W. H., Raynes-Berman, E., Heymsfield, S., Fauci, M., & Ackerman, S. (1993). The effect of psychiatric disorders on weight loss in obesity clinic patients. *Behavioral Medicine, 18,* 167–172.

Birketvedt, G. S., Florholmen, J., Sundsfjord, J., Osterud, B., Dinges, D., Bilker, W., et al. (1999). Behavioral and neuroendocrine characteristics of the night eating syndrome. *Journal of the American Medical Association, 282,* 657–663.

Black, D. W., Goldstein, R. B., & Mason, E. E. (1992). Prevalence of mental disorder in 88 morbidly obese bariatric clinic patients. *American Journal of Psychiatry, 149,* 227–234.

Black, D. W., Goldstein, R. B., Mason, E. E., Bell, S. E., & Blum, N. (1992). Depression and other mental disorders in the relatives of morbidly obese patients. *Journal of Affective Disorders, 25,* 91–95.

Boan, J., Kolotkin, R., Westman, E., McMahon, R., & Grant, J. (2004). Binge eating, quality of life, and physical activity improve after Roux-en-Y gastric bypass for morbid obesity. *Obesity Surgery, 14,* 341–346.

Bocchieri, L. E., Meana, M., & Fisher, B. L. (2002). A review of psychosocial outcomes of surgery for morbid obesity. *Journal of Psychosomatic Research, 52,* 155–165.

Bonne, O. B., Bashi, R., & Berry, E. M. (1996). Anorexia nervosa following gastroplasty in the male: Two cases. *International Journal of Eating Disorders, 19,* 105–108.

Brolin, R. E., Robertson, L. B., Kenler, H. A., & Cody, R. P. (1994). Weight loss and dietary intake after vertical banded gastroplasty and Roux-en-Y gastric bypass. *Annals of Surgery, 220,* 782–790.

Busetto, L., Valente, P., Pisent, C., Segato, G., de Marchi, F., & Favretti, F. (1997). Eating pattern in the first year following adjustable silicone gastric banding (ASGB) for morbid obesity. *International Journal of Obesity, 20,* 539–546.

Derogatis, L. R. (1983). *SCL-90-R administration, scoring and interpretation manual-II.* Towson, MD: Clinical Psychometric Research.

de Zwaan, M., Mitchell, J., Howell, L., Monson, N., Swan-Kremeier, L., Crosby, R., et al. (2003). Characteristics of morbidly obese patients before gastric bypass surgery. *Comprehensive Psychiatry, 44,* 428–434.

Dixon, J. B., Dixon, M. E., & O'Brien, P. E. (2003). Depression in association with severe obesity: changes with weight loss. *Archives of Internal Medicine, 163,* 2058–2065.

Doll, H. A., Petersen, S. E. K., & Stewart-Brown, S. L. (2000). Obesity and physical and emotional well-being: associations between body mass index, chronic illness, and the physical and mental components of the SF-36 questionnaire. *Obesity Research, 8,* 160–170.

Dymek, M. P., le Grange, D., Neven, K., & Alverdy, J. (2001). Quality of life and psychosocial adjustment in patients after Roux-en-Y gastric bypass: A brief report. *Obesity Surgery, 11,* 32–39.

Fairburn, C. G., & Cooper, Z. (1993). The Eating Disorder Examination. In C. G. Fairburn & T. Wilson (Eds.). *Binge eating: Nature, assessment, and treatment.* (pp. 317–360). New York: Guilford Press.

Faith, M. S., Calamaro, C. J., Dolan, M. S., & Pietrobelli, A. (2004). Mood disorders and obesity. *Current Opinion in Psychiatry, 17,* 9–13.

Felitti, V. J., Anda, R. F., Nordenberg, D., Williamson, D. F., Spitz, A. M., Edwards, V., et al. (1998). Relationships of childhood abuse and household dysfunction to many of the leading causes of death in adults. *American Journal of Preventative Medicine, 14,* 245–258.

First, M. B., Spitzer, R. L., Gibbon, M., & Williams, J. B. W. (1995). *Structured clinical interview for DSM-IV axis I & II disorders* (Version 2.0). New York: New York State Psychiatric Institute.

Ford, E. S., Moriarty, D. G., Zack, M. M., Mokdad, A. H., & Chapman, D. P. (2001). Self-reported body mass index and health-related quality of life. Findings from the behavioral risk factor surveillance system. *Obesity Research, 9,* 21–23.

Friedman, M. A., & Brownell, K. D. (1995). Psychological correlates of obesity: Moving to the next research generation. *The Psychological Bulletin, 117,* 3–20.

Glinski, J., Wetzler, S., & Goodman, E. (2001). The psychology of gastric bypass surgery. *Obesity Surgery, 11,* 581–588.

Gormally, J., Black, S., Daston, S., & Rardin, D. (1982). The assessment of binge eating severity among obese persons. *Addictive Behaviors, 7,* 47–55.

Guisado, J. A., Vaz, F. J., Lopez-Ibor, J. J., Lopez-Ibor, M. I., Del Rio, J., & Rubio, M. A. (2002). Gastric surgery and restraint from food as triggering factors of eating disorders in morbid obesity. *International Journal of Eating Disorders, 31,* 97–100.

Herpertz, S., Kielmann, R., Wolf, A. M., Langkafel, M., Senf, W., & Hebebrand, J. (2003). Does obesity surgery improve psychosocial functioning? A systematic review. *International Journal of Obesity, 27,* 1300–1314.

Higgs, M. L., Wade, T., Cescato, M., Atchison, M., Slavotinek, A., & Higgins, B. (1997). Differences between treatment seekers in an obese population: Medical intervention vs. dietary restriction. *Journal of Behavioral Medicine, 20,* 391–405.

Hsu, L. K., Benotti, P. N., Dwyer, J., Roberts, S. B., Saltzman, E., Shikora, S., et al. (1998). Nonsurgical factors that influence the outcome of bariatric surgery: a review. *Psychosomatic Medicine, 60,* 338–346.

Hsu, L. K. G., Betancourt, S., & Sullivan, S. P. (1996). Eating disturbances before and after vertical banded gastroplasty: A pilot study. *International Journal of Eating Disorders, 19,* 23–34.

Hsu, L. K. G., Mulliken, B., McDonagh, B., Krupa Das, S., Rand, W., Fairburn, C. G., et al. (2002). Binge eating disorder in extreme obesity. *International Journal of Obesity, 26,* 1398–1403.

Hsu, L. K. G., Sullivan, S. P., & Benotti, P. N. (1997). Eating disturbances and outcome of gastric bypass surgery: A pilot study. *International Journal of Eating Disorders, 21,* 385–390.

Kalarchian, M. A., Marcus, M. D., Wilson, G. T., Labouvie, E. W., Brolin, R. E., & LaMarca, L. B. (2002). Binge eating among gastric bypass patients at long-term follow-up. *Obesity Surgery, 12,* 270–275.

Kalarchian, M. A., Wilson, G. T., Brolin, R. E., & Bradley, L. (1998). Binge eating in bariatric surgery patients. *International Journal of Eating Disorders, 23,* 89–92.

Kalarchian, M. A., Wilson, G. T., Brolin, R. E., & Bradley, L. (1999). Effects of bariatric surgery on binge eating and related psychopathology. *Eating and Weight Disorders, 4,* 1–5.

Karlsson J., Sjostrom L., & Sullivan M. (1998). Swedish obese subjects (SOS)—an intervention study of obesity. Two-year follow-up of health-related quality of life (HRQL) and eating behavior after gastric surgery for severe obesity. *International Journal of Obesity, 22,* 113–126.

Kodama, K., Noda, S., Murakami, A., Azuma, Y., Takeda, N., Yamanouchi, N., et al. (1998). Depressive disorders as psychiatric complications after obesity surgery. *Psychiatry and Clinical Neurosciences, 52,* 471–476.

Larsen, F. (1990). Psychosocial function before and after gastric banding surgery for morbid obesity: A prospective psychiatric study. *Acta Psychiatrica Scandinavica, 359,* 1–57.

Latner, J. D., Wetzler, S., Goodman, E. R., & Glinski, J. (2004). Gastric bypass in a low-income, inner city population: Eating disturbances and weight loss. *Obesity Research, 12,* 956–961.

Lissau, I., & Sorensen, T. I. A. (1994). Parental neglect during childhood and increased risk of obesity in young adulthood. *Lancet, 343,* 324–327.

Macias, J. A., & Vaz Leal, F. J. (2003). Psychopathological differences between morbidly obese binge eaters and non-binge eaters after bariatric surgery. *Eating and Weight Disorders, 8*, 315–318.

Malone, M., & Alger-Mayer, S. (2004). Binge status and quality of life after gastric bypass surgery: A one-year study. *Obesity Research, 12*, 473–481.

Marcus, M. D., Wing, R. R., Ewing, L., & Kern, E. (1990). Psychiatric disorders among obese binge eaters. *International Journal of Eating Disorders, 9*, 69–77.

McHorney, C. A., Ware, J. E., & Raczek, A. E. (1993). The MOS 36-Item Short-Form Health Survey (SF-36): II Psychometric and clinical tests of validity in measuring physical and mental health constructs. *Medical Care, 31*, 247–263.

Mitchell, J. E., Lancaster, K. L., Burgard, M. A., Howell, L. M., Krahn, D. D., Crosby, R. D., et al. (2001). Long-term follow-up of patients' status after gastric bypass. *Obesity Surgery, 11*, 464–468.

Niego, S. H., Pratt, E. M., & Agras, W. S. (1997). Subjective or objective binge: Is the distinction valid? *International Journal of Eating Disorders, 22*, 291–298.

Onyike, C. U., Crum, R. M., Lee. H. B., Lyketsos, C. G., & Eaton, W. W. (2003). Is obesity associated with major depression? Results from the Third National Health and Nutrition Examination Survey. *American Journal of Epidemiology, 158*, 1139–1147.

Powers, P., Rosemurgy, A., Boyd, F., & Perez, A. (1997). Outcome of gastric restriction procedures: Weight, psychiatric diagnoses, and satisfaction. *Obesity Surgery, 7*, 471–477.

Powers, P. S., Perez, A., Boyd, F., & Rosemurgy, A. (1999). Eating pathology before and after bariatric surgery: A prospective study. *International Journal of Eating Disorders, 25*, 295–300.

Powers, P. S., Rosemurgy, A. S., Coovert, D. L., & Boyd, F. R. (1988). Psychosocial sequelae of bariatric surgery: A pilot study. *Psychosomatics, 29*, 283–288.

Rand, C. S., Macgregor, A. M., & Stunkard, A. J. (1997). The night eating syndrome in the general population and among postoperative obesity surgery patients. *International Journal of Eating Disorders, 22*, 65–69.

Roberts, R. E., Kaplan, G. A., Shema, S. J., & Strawbridge, W. J. (2000). Are the obese at greater risk for depression? *American Journal of Epidemiology, 152*, 163–170.

Robins, L. N., Helzer, J. E., Croughan, J., & Ratcliff, K. S. (1981). National Institute of Mental Health Diagnostic Interview Schedule: Its history, characteristics, and validity. *Archives of General Psychiatry, 38*, 381–389.

Sanchez-Johnsen, L., Dymek, M., Alverdy, J., & Le Grange, D. (2003). Binge eating and eating-related cognitions and behavior in ethnically diverse obese women. *Obesity Research, 11*, 1002–1009.

Sansone, R. A., & Fine, M. A. (1992). Borderline personality as a predictor of outcome in women with eating disorders. *Journal of Personality Disorders, 6*, 176–186.

Saunders, R. (2004). "Grazing": A high-risk behavior. *Obesity Surgery, 14*, 98–102.

Saunders, R., Johnson, L., & Teschner, J. (1998). Prevalence of eating disorders among bariatric surgery patients. *Eating Disorders, 6*, 309–317.

Scioscia, T. N., Bulik, C. M., Levenson, J., & Kirby, D. F. (1999). Anorexia nervosa in a 38-year-old woman 2 years after gastric bypass surgery. *Psychosomatics, 40*, 86–88.

Segal, A., Kussunoki, D., & Larino, M. A. (2004). Post-surgical refusal to eat: Anorexia nervosa, bulimia nervosa, or a new eating disorder? A case series. *Obesity Surgery, 14*, 353–360.

Solow, C., Silberfarb, P. M., & Swift, K. (1974). Psychosocial effects of intestinal bypass surgery for severe obesity. *The New England Journal of Medicine, 290*, 300–304.

Stunkard, A. J., & Allison, K. C. (2003). Two forms of disordered eating in obesity: Binge eating and night eating. *International Journal of Obesity, 27*, 1–12.

Stunkard, A. J., & Wadden, T. A. (1992). Psychological aspects of severe obesity. *American Journal of Clinical Nutrition, 55*, 524S–532S.

Sullivan, M., Karlsson, J., Sjostrom, L., Backman, L., Bengtsson, C., Bouchard, C., et al. (1993). Swedish obese subjects (SOS): An intervention study of obesity. Baseline evaluation of health and psychosocial functioning in the first 1743 subjects examined. *International Journal of Obesity and Related Metabolic Disorders, 17*, 503–512.

Valley, V., & Grace, D. M. (1987). Psychosocial risk factors in gastric surgery for obesity: Identifying guidelines for screening. *International Journal of Obesity, 11*, 105–113.

Wadden, T. A., Womble, L. G., Stunkard, A. J., & Anderson, D. A. (2002). Psychosocial consequences of obesity and weight loss. In T. A. Wadden & A. J. Stunkard (Eds.). *Handbook of obesity treatment.* (pp. 144–169). New York: Guilford Press.

Waters, G. S., Poires, W. J., Swanson, M. S., Meelheim, H. D., Flickinger, E. G., & May, H. J. (1991). Long-term studies of mental health after the Greenville gastric bypass operation for morbid obesity. *The American Journal of Surgery, 161,* 154–158.

Williamson, D. F., Thompson, T. J., Anda, R. F., Dietz, W. H., & Felitti, V. (2002). Body weight and obesity in adults and self-reported abuse in childhood. *International Journal of Obesity, 26,* 1075–1082.

Wonderlich, S. A., Crosby, R. D., Mitchell, J. E., Thompson, K. M., Redlin, J., Demuth, G., et al. (2001). Eating disturbance and sexual trauma in childhood and adulthood. *International Journal of Eating Disorders, 30,* 401–412.

Yanovski, S. Z. (2003). Binge eating disorder and obesity in 2003: Could treating an eating disorder have a positive effect on the obesity epidemic? *International Journal of Eating Disorders, 34,* S117–S120.

CHAPTER 5

Weight and Eating Changes after Bariatric Surgery

MARTINA DE ZWAAN

Whereas in Europe the vertical banded gastroplasty (VBG) and adjustable gastric banding as restrictive procedures are the most often performed operations, in the United States, the gastric bypass is the gold standard. Malabsorptive procedures are performed less frequently with the exception of biliopancreatic diversion (BPD), which is conducted primarily in Italy and is being used in the United States at some centers.

Why Do People Lose Weight After Bariatric Surgery?

Restriction and Dumping

Weight loss after bariatric surgery occurs primarily because of a reduced caloric intake. This reduction is achieved by restriction (small gastric pouch and small outlet that restricts the volume of ingestible food) and in the case of gastric bypass also by a "dumping physiology," which is believed to help patients control their sweet intake (e.g., Hsu et al., 1998).

Rapid gastric emptying, or dumping syndrome, happens when the jejunum fills too quickly with undigested food from the stomach. "Early" dumping begins during or right after a meal. Symptoms of early dumping include nausea, vomiting, bloating, diarrhea, and shortness of breath. "Late" dumping happens 1 to 3 hours after eating. Symptoms of late dumping include weakness, sweating, and dizziness. Many people have both types. The early symptoms are caused when concentrated sugar passes too rapidly from the stomach into the intestine. The body dilutes this sugar mixture by bringing fluid from body tissues into the intestine, giving a sense of fullness and causing cramping, and, occasionally, diarrhea. The loss of water from tissues can produce a temporary drop in blood pressure, with resulting weakness and faintness. The later symptoms are caused by the rapid absorption of sugar into the bloodstream, which raises the amount of blood sugar. A high level of blood sugar signals the body to produce more insulin. The excess insulin, in turn, drives blood sugar levels down. The low blood sugar (hypoglycemia) then produces the weakness, hunger, and rapid heart rate that may occur about 2 to 3 hours after eating. The patients usually avoid caloric-dense sweet foods and milk products to prevent the occurrence of these symptoms. Eating the wrong ("forbidden") nutrients causes discomfort, pain, or other highly unpleasant symptoms. To prevent these symptoms, patients avoid eating too much, eating "forbidden" foods, or not chewing the food thoroughly. Obviously, surgeons consider dumping syndrome to be a beneficial effect of gastric bypass—it seems to be important to provide quick and reliable negative feedback for intake of the "wrong" foods. In practice, most patients experience full-blown dumping only a few times and simply say that they have "lost their taste" for sweets—a possible example of conditioned taste aversion.

When dietary intake exceeds the small gastric pouch capacity, patients usually feel a strong discomfort that results in cessation of eating. The avoidance of vomiting has been proposed to be another fundamental mechanism of action on which gastric restrictive surgery is based (Pessina, Andreoli, & Vassallo, 2001; Rabner & Greenstein, 1991). However, restraint imposed by bariatric surgery on food intake fails in many patients. Maladaptive eating frequently observed after purely restrictive surgery (gastroplasty, gastric banding procedures) seems to be related to alterations in intake of liquid foods, often of high-energy content. Without dumping syndrome, this dietary change does not cause discomfort and the patients' weight might paradoxically increase. Others are unable to maintain a reduced intake and regain weight after their pouch stretches (which is a normal development over time) and restriction loosens. By increasing the frequency of intake, they may attempt to "eat out" the pouch (Hsu et al., 1998). Constant overeating might promote pouch stretching.

Consequently, not all morbidly obese patients are adequately treated with a mere restrictive procedure. The dumping syndrome that follows gastric bypass surgery (with an additional element of malabsorption) is considered to be the primary mechanism of improved weight loss after GBP as compared with purely restrictive gastroplasty. However, one study failed to demonstrate a significant relationship between dumping severity and weight loss (Mallory, Macgregor, & Rand, 1996). There is a wide range of dumping severity after GBP—some patients being exquisitely sensitive to ingested sweets, whereas others being apparently unaffected. Mallory et al. (1996) reported a frequency of 76.9% in patients 18 to 24 months after GBP and of 0% after gastroplasty. In addition, patients might have different thresholds for tolerating the symptoms.

Maldigestion and Malabsorption

The first operations performed specifically to induce weight loss were malabsorptive procedures and were conducted in the early 1950s. The prototype of malabsorptive procedures was the jejunoileal bypass (Buchwald & Buchwald, 2002). Today's most popular malabsorptive procedures are the BPD introduced by Scopinaro in 1979 and the duodenal switch. These procedures limit the length and consequently the surface area of the small intestine to create decreased digestion of normal foods and decreased absorption of digested food elements. Even though highly effective in reducing weight, malabsorptive procedures are associated with numerous side effects such as the gas-bloat syndrome, steatorrhea, electrolyte imbalance, vitamin deficiencies, liver dysfunction, and metabolic bone disease. In addition, additional surgery after BPD occurs twice as commonly as after gastric banding.

What Amount of Weight Loss Can Be Expected?

Obesity surgery should be considered in patients with a body mass index (BMI) greater than 40 kg/m^2 or between 35 and 40 kg/m^2 who fail other methods of treatment if serious obesity-related complications are present. Most samples in bariatric surgery reports are predominantly female, with a mean age of 40 years and a mean BMI of 45 to 50 kg/m^2.

The surgical approaches used to treat obesity in the United States include the vertical banded or horizontal gastroplasty, now used infrequently; gastric bypass, now used most commonly; banding procedures; and biliopancreatic diversion. All bariatric surgery techniques are increasingly performed laparoscopically. Proven benefits of laparoscopic surgery include a shorter hospital stay, quicker return to normal activity, less pain, a diminished incidence of incisional hernia, less systemic and immunologic stress, reduced adhesion formation, and a reduced incidence of ileus. In superobese patients, a combined restrictive/malabsorptive or purely malabsorptive procedure may be necessary. Several randomized studies could demonstrate that more weight is lost with gastric bypass than with gastroplasty, but the risk of complications is greater. Calcium, iron, and vitamin B_{12} supplementation is recommended in the long term. In addition, inadequate nutrient intake (e.g., protein) might make this technique hazardous (Faintuch et al., 2004). In general, weight loss of 60% to 80% of excess weight is achieved and reaches its maximum at 18 months to 2 years, with some weight regain thereafter. Unfortunately, in some surgical series up to 20% of patients ultimately regained all lost weight. To what extent surgical failures are due to the actual surgical technique or to psychological factors and eating disturbances remains unclear.

In a controlled study by Howard et al. (1995), 42 patients were randomly assigned to gastroplasty or gastric bypass and followed for up to 5 years. Gastric bypass demonstrated significantly greater weight loss that was apparent from 6 months onward. After bypass, weight loss was maintained over the follow-up period, whereas gastroplasty patients slowly regained. Hall et al. (1990) compared three techniques in a randomized study in 310 patients in Australia. After 3 years, a weight loss of more than 50% of excess weight was achieved in 17% of patients after gastrogastrostomy, 48% after VBG, and 67% after gastric bypass. Hence, gastric bypass was superior. Patients with diabetes, asthma, hypertension, or arthropathy had a greater than 50% chance of being free of medication 3 years after GBP and 10% of women younger than 40 became pregnant. However, the authors also reported "penalties" such as 11% ($n = 34$) who needed revisional surgery, 3% ($n = 8$) who had reversal of the surgery, 29% ($n = 89$) who needed obesity-related surgical procedures (trimming procedures, cholecystectomy, hernias), and 15% of GBP patients did not lose any weight.

In Europe and Australia, gastric banding procedures have been used primarily. Nonadjustable gastric banding was followed by adjustable (inflatable) gastric banding. Two uncontrolled surgical trials demonstrated that gastric banding was inferior to gastric bypass with regard to weight loss (Delin & Anderson, 1999; Hell, Miller, Moorehead, & Norman, 2000). In the study by Hell et al. (2000), 73% of the GBP patients lost 75% or more of their excess weight as opposed to only 3% of the gastric banding patients 3 to 8 years after the surgery. In a recent study with 260 patients, 36% had lost more than 50% of excess weight 3 years after gastric banding (Busetto et al., 2002). On average, the weight loss approximated a BMI loss of 10 units, from a BMI of 46.6 kg/m^2 to 36.8 kg/m^2, or a mean weight loss of about 27 kg. The authors suggest that the lower efficacy of gastric banding compared with gastric bypass with regard to weight loss needs to be balanced against the negligible rate of severe complications and the complete reversibility of the procedure.

Randomized controlled trials comparing BPD with other bariatric operations are not available. However, BPD has been performed for more than 25 years and a 70% excess weight loss is usually maintained for at least 10 years after surgery (Marinari et al., 2004).

Postoperative patients usually have more realistic expectations concerning weight loss than preoperative patients (Rabner & Greenstein, 1991). It is completely unknown if specific surgical interventions are more suitable for different groups of patients. It might also be different in different countries (e.g., the United States versus European countries) because of differences in the general diet (e.g., more fast food in the United States).

In summary, patients who undergo gastric bypass demonstrate significantly greater postoperative weight loss and are successful in maintaining their weight loss compared with patients undergoing purely restrictive surgery. However, there is a higher risk for complications after GBP and there is a need for lifelong supplement substitution to prevent iron deficiency anemia and vitamin B_{12} malabsorption.

Effects of Bariatric Surgery on Eating and Related Behaviors

Research traditionally considers change in weight and comorbidity while disregarding the role of eating behavior. Initially after surgery, patients do not have much interest in food and are focused on eating the "right things." Later, they experience a plateau or a period of less rapid weight loss and are again able to eat more.

A few studies have examined the effects of various bariatric surgery procedures on eating behavior. Most of these have relied on available questionnaires or have developed new instruments for this purpose. Pathological eating behaviors that might occur after surgery have not been categorized and there are no standardized postoperative eating behavior assessment instruments available, making cross-study comparisons problematic. It is, however, not unusual for early research in a field that many studies are of an exploratory and qualitative nature with sometimes small sample sizes. General methodological considerations for psychosocial assessment in bariatric surgery have been summarized by Bocchieri, Meana, and Fisher (2002).

It is at times difficult to draw a line between what should be considered normal eating and pathological eating after surgery, because all eating behavior will be different from presurgery and from the eating behavior of the normal population. Patients are forced to adopt an eating style that is characterized by restraint, restriction of food varieties, and ritualistic behavior around how food is eaten, such as the frequent intake of small amounts of foods and extensive chewing before swallowing. In addition, it is not known if different surgical procedures might result in different frequencies or patterns of abnormal eating behaviors.

Different eating-related behaviors will be described that have frequently been observed after bariatric surgery. Binge eating and binge eating disorder (BED) will be summarized separately because of the large number of studies about this issue. In addition, preliminary results of an ongoing follow-up study in patients after GBP will be presented.

Vomiting

Following bariatric surgery procedures with a restrictive component, patients report an increased occurrence of vomiting. Patients usually experience involuntary vomiting during the first few postoperative weeks. Vomiting usually occurs when they eat too much in relation to their pouch size or when food gets stuck in the small opening of the pouch ("plugging"), which is a painful experience. Others self-induce vomiting as a response to fullness and epigastric discomfort. Patients usually use their fingers to self-induce vomiting. They may drink water, and some just need to bend over the toilet. Others drink meat tenderizer to decrease the discomfort. Some surgeons even recommend to their patients that they induce vomiting to decrease discomfort rather than experience lengthy nausea and pain.

Powers, Perez, Boyd, and Rosemurgy (1999) reported that 5.5 years after restrictive surgery, 79% of the patients were vomiting at least occasionally and 33% were vomiting weekly. Kinzl, Traweger, Trefalt, and Biebl (2003) reported that 8 to 48 months after gastric banding, 44% vomited occasionally and 12% frequently. They noted that vomiting frequency increased with the length of time since surgery. Mitchell et al. (2001) found that 13 to 15 years after GBP, 68.8% of the patients reported continued problems with vomiting. The authors also reported an unexpectedly low level of distress caused by regular vomiting. Our own preliminary results in 48 patients at different times after GBP surgery demonstrated that self-induced vomiting was quite frequent: 93% of the patients 1 year after the surgery, 83% of the patients 1 to 2 years after the surgery, and 88% of the patients 2 to 3 years after the surgery reported at least occasional vomiting. Also, the percentage of patients reporting "plugging" did not change with the length of time since the surgery (about 80%).

Over time, patients may discover that they can vomit with ease after eating and may purposely overeat knowing it might result in vomiting, which then will prevent weight gain (Saunders, 2001). The modified anatomy in the upper gastrointestinal tract might consequently support the development of a new eating pathology. The behavior could be labeled as "semipurposeful" and might be perceived as "failed attempts to binge" (Powers, Rosemurgy, Coovert, & Boyd, 1988). It is unclear if and to what extent postoperative vomiting represents a purging behavior or if the vomiting in these patients occurs entirely unexpectedly. In addition, it might be difficult to elicit the extent to which the patients accept vomiting to not regain weight or to lose more weight. They might not be honest about it or not fully aware of the motivation. Even if the vomiting occurs spontaneously, some patients might welcome the effect that this might have on their weight. Such thoughts might serve as a cognitive reinforcement for further vomiting. In our own follow-up study, we put a lot of effort into trying to differentiate between non-weight-related vomiting, the sole purpose of which is to relieve discomfort, and weight-related vomiting that is mainly caused by fear of gaining weight or not losing weight quickly enough. We applied a modified version of the Eating Disorder Examination interview (EDE; Fairburn & Cooper, 1993), adding additional probe questions to elicit shape and weight concerns as a motivation for vomiting. However, we found only three (6.3%) patients who openly admitted to self-induced, weight-related vomiting—all of whom had had an eating disorder before the surgery. There is a definite need for more fine-grained prospective analyses of eating behavior after surgery in larger samples.

"Grazing"

Other types of problem eating behavior have also been described, including "grazing," "frequent snacking," and "nibbling" (Brolin et al., 1986; Busetto et al., 2002; Glinski, Wetzler, & Goodman, 2001; Saunders, 2004). A problem in studying these kinds of behaviors is the lack of reliable assessment instruments. They are usually assessed by self-designed questionnaires or clinical interviews. Saunders (2004) defined grazing as "a pattern of repeated episodes of consumption of smaller quantities of food over a longer period of time with accompanying feelings of loss of control." She reported that 80% of those who exhibited binge eating or grazing behavior before the surgery reported recurrent feelings of loss of control over eating starting about 6 months after surgery and many who had been binge eaters before surgery reported a shift to "grazing." In addition, 15% reported self-induced vomiting after "grazing" to avoid gaining weight. Herpertz et al. (in press) reported "grazing" in 25% of 152 females presenting for gastric banding. Busetto et al. (2002) defined "nibbling" as "eating small quantities of foods repetitively between meals, typically triggered by inactivity and/or loneliness." They reported frequent occurrence of "nibbling" in 43% of 260 presurgery patients. Brolin et al. (1986) demonstrated that "frequent snacking" preoperatively was associated with inadequate weight loss, and Rabner and Greenstein (1991) reported that more than two thirds of patients continued to snack after surgery.

Again, these findings rely on unstandardized measures and it remains unknown if the studies describe homogeneous groups of patients and if cross-study comparisons are justified. In addition, it is unclear if and to what extent such behaviors are causing distress or influencing surgery outcome.

"Sweet Eating"

Overeating on high-caloric sweet foods is possible after purely restrictive surgery (gastroplasty, gastric banding), but not after bypass surgery in which dumping occurs after ingestion of sweet foods. It has been postulated that "sweet eaters" might profit more from gastric bypass because they would consciously avoid eating sweets for fear of developing dumping syndrome, but will do poorly after gastric restrictive surgery. Sugerman, Starkey, and Birkenhauer (1987) noted that preoperative sweet eaters lost significantly less weight than non-sweet eaters with VBG 1 year after surgery. Sweet eating was defined as consuming more than 300 calories of sweet foods or beverages more than three times per week. In a second study, Sugerman et al. (1989) reported that gastric bypass resulted in more weight loss whether the patients were assigned randomly or selectively according to their sweet intake to either GBP or VBG, sweet eaters all being assigned to gastric bypass. However, they reported that weight loss after VBG was significantly improved 2 years after the surgery with selective assignment of all sweet eaters to GBP. Sweet eating was defined as consuming more than 15% of total caloric intake in the form of sweet foods or beverages.

However, there is now increasing evidence that sweet eating behavior is not predictive of weight outcome after restrictive surgical procedures (Busetto et al., 2002; Hudson, Dixon, & O'Brien, 2002; Lindroos, Lissner, & Sjöström, 1996). Preoperative and postoperative sweet eating tendencies had no influence on percent excess weight lost at 3-year follow-up (Busetto et al., 2002). Lindroos et al. (1996) even found a positive correlation between continued selection of sweet foods and weight loss in 375 subjects followed for 2 years after VBG or gastric banding in the Swedish Obesity Subjects study. In addition, two studies could demonstrate that VBG might alter postoperative eating behavior with a shift toward soft, high-calorie foods in patients who did not report sweet eating tendencies preoperatively (Brolin, Robertson, Kenler, & Cody, 1994; Mallory et al., 1996).

Consequently, there is no evidence that sweet eating behavior should be used as a preoperative selection criterion for bariatric surgery. The applied definitions of "sweet eaters" remain arbitrary and, as Lindroos et al. (1996) pointed out, 62% of all women included in the Swedish Obesity Subjects study (including normal-weight control subjects) consumed more than 15% of their calories from sweet foods, with non-sweet eaters being a minority in normal-weight subjects. Consequently, Sugerman et al. (1987, 1989) in their studies probably selected unusually health-conscious or motivated patients for the VGB procedure, thereby improving the results in this group (Herpertz, Kielmann, Wolf, Hebebrand, & Senf, 2004).

"Chewing and Spitting out Food"

A significant number of patients start chewing and spitting out food post-operatively, sometimes encouraged by the surgeons. In our study, 7% of the patients who were less then 1 year after surgery reported this behavior, as opposed to 33% 1 to 2 years and 50% 2 to 3 years after the surgery. This behavior is usually not accompanied by distress and mostly serves to avoid plugging. It is either planned (e.g., to get a taste of red meat, which they usually avoid because it easily gets stuck) or unplanned (e.g., "the one bite too much that would make me vomit").

Development of an Eating Disorder

One apparently uncommon, but unfortunate, outcome of patients under-going bariatric surgery procedures is the development of clinically signifi-cant eating disorders. There are several case reports describing patients usually in their 30s or 40s developing anorexia nervosa (Atchison, Wade, Higgins, & Slavotinek, 1998; Bonne, Bashi, & Berry, 1996; Counts, 2001; Guisado et al., 2002; Scioscia, Bulik, Levenson, & Kirby, 1999) and bulimia nervosa (Guisado, Vaz, Lopez-Ibor, & Rubio, 2001; Mitchell, 1985; Rand, Macgregor, & Hankins, 1987; Ringel, 1987; Shamblin, Sessions, & Soileau, 1984; Thompson, Weinsier, & Jacobs, 1985; Viens & Hranchuk, 1992). The exact incidence of such an outcome is unknown and this needs to be further addressed. These problems frequently occur for the first time subsequent to surgery (Guisado et al., 2001; Thompson et al., 1985; Viens & Hranschuk, 1992). Patients eat less than they would be able to, develop anorexic and bulimic attitudes, and eventually full-blown anorexia nervosa or bulimia nervosa. Patients might meet all criteria for bulimia nervosa except for "ingestion of a large amount of food," because this is simply not possible. Others might meet all criteria for anorexia nervosa except for the weight criterion because it takes many months or even years before formerly morbidly obese patients reach a body weight of "less than 85% of that expected." One explanation for the development of an eating disorder might be that individuals with a psychological vulnerability might become preoccupied with food and weight loss. Health care professionals who encounter these individuals might develop a negative attitude toward obesity surgery. They need to be cautioned that this appears to occur only in a small minority of patients who are most likely not representative of bariatric surgery patients in general.

Segal, Kinoshita Kussunoki, and Larino (2004) recently proposed a new eating disorder they called "postsurgical eating avoidance disorder," defined by a higher speed of weight loss caused by voluntary eating restriction, purging behavior, an intense fear of gaining back all the lost weight, and marked body dissatisfaction. They reported that these patients exhibited signs of malnutrition and refused treatment for their abnormal eating behavior. All five patients were women between the age of 41 and 51, 2 to 4 years after GBP surgery. The only difference from bulimia nervosa was the lack of objective binge eating episodes. However, the authors did not report on the patients' presurgery eating behavior and it remains highly unlikely that this behavior represents a distinct entity qualitatively different from bulimia nervosa.

Other Eating Behaviors and Attitudes

Patients usually experience less hunger after bariatric surgery. Many report eating at specific times rather than according to any internal stimulus, especially early on, and many foods have lower emotional valence (Delin, Watts, & Bassett, 1995; Delin, Watts, Saebel, & Anderson, 1997). Our own preliminary results in 48 patients up to 3 years after GBP surgery demonstrated that 87% were less hungry, 60% experienced less enjoyment of eating, and 68% considered food to be less important in their life compared with before surgery. Most studies found a decrease in the scores of the hunger subscales of the Three-Factor Eating Questionnaire (Stunkard & Messick, 1985) (e.g., Karlsson, Sjöström, & Sullivan, 1998; Lang, Hauser, Buddeberg, & Klaghofer, 2002).

The tendency to eat for emotional reasons appears to decline after GBP and gastric banding (Delin et al., 1997; Hörchner, Tuinebreijer, & Kelder, 2002). Also, the sensitivity to external stimuli such as smell and taste of food on eating behavior appears to decrease after surgery (Hörchner et al., 2002). Patients after GBP reported less preoccupation with food than did normal-weight comparison subjects (Rand et al., 1987). As would be expected, scores on the disinhibition subscale of the Three-Factor Eating Questionnaire usually decrease significantly after surgery (Karlsson et al., 1998; Lang et al., 2002). Not surprisingly, patients with high disinhibition scores who tend to respond to emotional disinhibitors of eating have been shown to lose less weight (Delin et al., 1995; Karlsson et al., 1998).

De Zwaan et al. (2004) applied a modified version of the EDE (Fairburn & Cooper, 1993) to 46 patients 6 months to 3 years after gastric bypass surgery. The EDE items generate four subscales: dietary restraint, eating concerns, weight concerns, and shape concerns. Many patients were still losing weight and were still in the so-called "honeymoon phase" after surgery. Even though most of the subjects were still overweight or obese, the ratings were surprisingly low and many subjects did not seem to experience even normative concerns about shape and weight. However, improvements in eating-related attitudes might begin to erode, especially as subjects reach a weight plateau or begin to regain.

Binge Eating and BED

Binge eating disorder is a widely studied eating disorder that is listed in Appendix B of the *Diagnostic and statistical manual of mental disorders*, 4th edition, as a diagnosis for further study (American Psychiatric Association, 1994). It is an example of an "eating disorder not otherwise specified." Individuals with BED report eating a large amount of food in a short period and experience a sense of loss of control. They also experience marked distress and endorse three or more of the following symptoms: eating until uncomfortably full, eating rapidly, eating large amounts of food when not hungry, eating alone from embarrassment, and feeling disgusted or guilty after overeating. The frequency of BED among obese persons applying to weight reduction programs ranges between 16% and 30% (de Zwaan, 2001). BED also appears to be common among the morbidly obese presenting for bariatric surgery; however, prevalence rates vary considerably ranging from 1.4% to 49% (Table 5.1).

Also, night eating syndrome has been assessed in bariatric surgery patients. Again, the frequency seems to be quite high, ranging from 7.9% to 26% (Adami, Meneghelli, & Scopinaro, 1999; Kuldau & Rand, 1986; Powers et al., 1999; Rand & Kuldau, 1993). In retrospective studies, nocturnal eating (getting up at night to eat) was reported in 33.3% and 42% of bariatric surgery patients preoperatively (Hsu, Betancourt, & Sullivan, 1996; Hsu, Sullivan, & Benotti, 1997).

Interestingly, the more recent studies report lower frequencies of BED compared with earlier studies. This might be due to a more stringent methodology used in the more recent studies as opposed to "first-line" studies. This methodological difference also makes cross-study comparisons difficult. About half of the studies did not diagnose their patients according to the *Diagnostic and statistical manual of mental disorders*, 4th edition, criteria, but used the presence of binge eating with or without a frequency criterion instead (Adami, Gandolfo, & Scopinaro, 1996; Busetto et al., 1996; Kalarchian, Wilson, Brolin, & Bradley, 1999; Saunders, 1999). Some studies used self-reporting instruments (Dymek, le Grange, Neven, &

TABLE 5.1 Point Prevalence of Binge Eating and Binge Eating Disorder in Presurgery and Postsurgery Patients

Authors	Sample Size	Procedure Assessment	Baseline DSM-IV BED	Baseline BED Plus Subsyndromal BED	Follow-Up BED	Follow-Up BE	Duration of Follow-Up
Adami et al., 1995	92	"Bariatric surgery," Clinical interview	46.7%	68.7%	—	—	—
Adami et al., 1996	65	BPD, Clinical interview	—	63.1%	—	9%	2 years
Busetto et al., 1996	80	Banding, Clinical interview	12.5%	—	—	—	—
Hsu et al., 1996	24	VBG, Clinical interview (retrospective)	37.5% 20.8% BN	—	20.8% 20.8% BN	—	3.5 years
Hsu et al., 1997	27	GBP, EDE (retrospective)	48.1% 1 BN	—	7.4%	—	21 months
Kalarchian et al., 1998	64	GBP, EDE	—	39% 1 be/wk/3 month 25% 2 be/wk/3 month	—	—	—
Saunders, Johnson, and Teschner, 1998	125	GBP	—	61.3% any be	—	—	—
Saunders, 1999		QEWP-R, BES		43.2% 2 be/wk; BES ≥27: 33.3%			
Powers et al., 1999	116	"Gastric restriction," BSQ	16% 10% NES	52%	—	0%	5.5 years
Kalarchian et al., 1999	50	GBP, EDE	—	44%	—	0%	4 months

Study	N	Method					
Lang, Hauser, Schlumpf, Klaghofer, and Buddeberg, 2000	79	Banding, BSQ	—	27% 1 be/wk/3 month	—	—	—
Wadden et al., 2001	122	"Bariatric surgery," QEWP-interview	27%	41.8%	—	—	—
Mitchell et al., 2001	78	GBP, EDE (retrospective)	49%	—	11.5%	—	14 years
Dymek et al., 2001	32	GBP, QEWP-R	32%	—	0%	—	6 months
Glinski et al., 2001	115	GBP, Semi-structured interview	—	10%	—	—	—
Guisado et al., 2001	40	VBG, Clinical interview	—	—	17.5% 2.5% AN, 2.5% BN ($n = 1$)	—	18 months
Lang et al., 2002	66	Banding, BSQ	—	63.6%	—	28.7%	12 months
Hsu et al., 2002	37	VBG, EDE, SCID	11%	25%	—	—	—
Busetto et al., 2002	260	Banding, Clinical interview	28.8%	—	—	—	—

(Continued)

TABLE 5.1 Point Prevalence of Binge Eating and Binge Eating Disorder in Presurgery and Postsurgery Patients (*continued*)

Authors	Sample Size	Procedure Assessment	Baseline DSM-IV BED	Baseline BED Plus Subsyndromal BED	Follow-Up BED	Follow-Up BE	Duration of Follow-Up
Kalarchian et al., 2002	99	GBP, EDE-Q	—	—	—	46%	2–7 years
de Zwaan et al., 2003	110	GBP, QEWP-R	17.3%	39.1%	—	—	—
Faria et al., 2003 Abstract	137	Clinical interview	—	35%	—	—	—
Sanchez-Johnsen, Dymek, Alverdy, and le Grange, 2003	210	GBP, Clinical interview	26.3%	—	—	—	—
Dymek-Valentine et al., 2004	168	GBP, QEWP, SCID	14% SCID 27% QEWP	30–44%	—	—	—
Larsen et al., 2004	250 cross-sect.	Banding, BES	—	BES > 17:55.9%	—	BES > 17:31.9% BES > 17:37.4%	8–24 months 25–68 months
Herpertz et al., in press	153	Banding, CIDI, SIAB	2%	21% (including grazing)	—	—	—

Note. Banding = gastric banding procedure; BE/be = binge eating; BED = binge eating disorder; BN = bulimia nervosa; BPD Gazet = biliopancreatic diversion with partial gastrectomy; BES = Binge Eating Scale; BSQ = Body Shape Questionnaire; CIDI = Composite International Diagnostic Interview; EDE(-Q) = Eating Disorder Examination (questionnaire version); GBP = gastric bypass; QEWP = Questionnaire on Eating and Weight Patterns; Restriction = restrictive type surgery; SCID = Structured Clinical Interview for DSM-IV diagnoses; SIAB = Structured Interview for Anorexia and Bulimia; VBG = vertical banded gastroplasty; wk = week.

Alverdy, 2001; Powers et al., 1999; Saunders, 1999), and others used interviews to assess binge eating. However, published studies frequently did not specify if they used a structured interview or relied on unstructured clinical interviews (Adami et al., 1996; Adami, Gandolfo, Bauer, & Scopinaro, 1995; Busetto et al., 1996; Hsu et al., 1996, 1997). Some assessments were done retrospectively, sometimes many years after surgery (Mitchell et al., 2001), and some with a rather low participation rate (Hsu et al., 1996, 1997). Retrospective assessment carries the risk of patients exaggerating the severity of prior binge eating problems. There is evidence from other areas of medicine that patients' accounts of events should be viewed with appropriate skepticism (Stunkard, Foster, Glassman, & Rosato, 1985). On the other hand, one can argue that the patients might be more honest about their original eating behavior postoperatively (Kral, 2001). The patients might be reluctant to disclose eating problems because the coverage by their health insurance company may have depended partly on the result of the psychiatric evaluation. Underreporting of eating problems to be approved for surgery has been described by others (Glinski et al., 2001).

Effect of Surgery on Binge Eating

Several research groups have studied whether binge eating and full syndromal BED might represent a relative contraindication or predict a poorer outcome in subjects undergoing various kinds of bariatric surgery procedures. When strict diagnostic criteria related to consuming a large amount of food is considered and the surgery procedure is intact, most studies have demonstrated that, in the short term, bariatric surgery has a pronounced positive effect on binge eating and associated psychopathology; it appears to be a "cure" for binge eating (Adami et al., 1999; Dymek et al., 2001, Kalarchian et al., 1999; Malone & Alger-Mayer, 2004; Powers et al., 1999). Kalarchian et al. (1999) reported that binge eating was eliminated for all of the 22 patients classified presurgically as binge eaters at 4-month follow-up. Similarly, Powers et al. (1999) reported elimination of binge eating in all subjects with presurgical BED. This is most likely explained by the fact that patients are no longer physically able to consume an objectively large amount of food after restrictive types of surgery. Given mechanical limitations resulting from bariatric surgery, outcome measures in this population will need to modify the criteria requiring an objectively large amount of food when considering the presence of binge eating and its impact on outcome. Many researchers consider a sense of loss of control as the more important criterion than whether the amount of food consumed during a binge is objectively large or not (Niego, Pratt, & Agras, 1997). Consequently, some researchers have started to define binge eating after surgery solely as a "sense of loss of control over eating" independent of the amount consumed (Hsu et al., 1996, 1997; Kalarchian et al., 1999).

As opposed to restrictive surgery procedures, subjects after BPD have a completely free eating style and can eat large meals without any limitation. There is even evidence that many subjects eat more in the long term after BPD than they did preoperatively (Scopinaro et al., 1996). Overeating and binge eating no longer lead to any weight gain. Adami, Gandolfo, Meneghelli, and Scopinaro (1996) reported that, after BPD, the prevalence of binge eating had sharply fallen, from 43% before surgery to 9.5% 2 years after surgery. This finding would support the assumption that, in many obese individuals, dieting behavior and the continuous preoccupation with food, shape, and weight leads to binge eating. Once their binge eating behavior does not lead to weight gain, but is associated with weight loss from maldigestion and malabsorption, subjects might reduce the frequency or even stop their binge eating. This finding supports the restraint hypothesis which has actually been challenged as an explanation for the pathogenesis of BED (e.g., Masheb & Grilo, 2000). The authors hypothesize that only those subjects who start or continue binge eating despite satisfactory weight loss can be considered as having a true primary eating disorder. In addition, subjects who continued binge eating did not exhibit a reduction in other eating-related psychopathology as assessed with the Three-Factor Eating Questionnaire and the Eating Disorders Inventory (EDI). More studies assessing eating behavior after nonrestrictive, primarily malabsorptive surgery procedures are clearly warranted.

Reemergence of Binge Eating

There is increasing evidence that some patients with a history of binge eating continue to experience a sense of loss of control characteristic of binge eating, and that binge eating may reemerge later during follow-up (after 2 years or more) and may be correlated with more weight regain in the long run (Hsu et al., 1996, 1997; Kalarchian et al., 2002; Lang et al., 2002; Mitchell et al., 2001; Pekkarinen, Koskela, Huikuri, & Mustajoki, 1994). In the longest follow-up to date, Mitchell et al. (2001) assessed gastric bypass patients 13 to 15 years after surgery. They found that, although 49% of patients met BED criteria before the surgery (retrospectively assessed), only 6.4% met criteria at follow-up; however, all of the binge eaters at follow-up had met BED criteria presurgery. Lang et al. (2002) reported that, 12 months after gastric banding, 24.2% continued to report binge eating, whereas only 4.5% reported the initiation of binge eating.

In our cross-sectional study in 48 post-GBP patients, we found that 14% of the patients 1 year after surgery, 28% 1 to 2 years after surgery, and 44% 2 to 3 years after surgery reported subjective binge eating episodes

(SBEs) wherein they had a feeling of having eaten too much and experienced a sense of loss of control. The frequency of SBEs during the month before the interview was highest in the patients whose operation was more than 2 years ago (11 ± 18.5, as opposed to 1 and 5.2 in patients 1 year and 1 to 2 years after the surgery). SBEs were more frequent in patients with an eating disorder before the surgery: 43% of those with BED ($n = 16$) and 100% of those with bulimia nervosa ($n = 2$) before the surgery reported at least occasional SBEs, as opposed to only 17% of those without an eating disorder before the surgery ($n = 30$). In addition, many patients reported that they sometimes do not pay enough attention while eating and consume an amount that is too large for their pouch size. However, these patients did not experience a sense of loss of control over eating, and such episodes were labeled as subjective overeating episodes. As opposed to SBEs, the percentages of patients reporting such subjective overeating episodes did not increase over time (43%, 33%, and 44%, depending on the time since the surgery). None of the patients had experienced an objective overeating or binge eating episode in which the amount of food consumed was objectively large as defined by the EDE. However, what actually constitutes a large amount of food after bariatric surgery, given the anatomical changes, is not known.

In summary, presurgical eating disturbances appear to predict postsurgical eating disturbances, most of which begin approximately 2 years after surgery. During the first postoperative phase, patients are rapidly losing weight and receive a substantial amount of positive reinforcement; people around them are complimenting and encouraging them. After their weight reaches a plateau, typically after the first year or 18 months, patients apparently lose their external sources of reinforcement, thereby consoling themselves as they did before surgery—by eating (Bocchieri et al., 2002).

Influence of Binge Eating Presurgery on Weight Postsurgery

There are conflicting results concerning the importance of presurgery binge eating for weight loss and weight loss maintenance after bariatric surgery (Table 5.2). One study demonstrated that binge eaters lost significantly less weight during the first 6 months after gastric bypass compared with non-binge eaters (Dymek et al., 2001). Similar results were reported by Hsu et al. (1997) in their 21-month follow-up study. Others found that binge eating before surgery predicted a higher frequency of vomiting after gastric banding and a fivefold higher rate of neostoma stenosis (Busetto et al., 1996).

In contrast to the results of these studies, Busetto et al. (1996, 2002), Hsu et al. (1996), and Powers et al. (1999) did not find an association between presurgical binge eating or night eating and weight loss or weight

TABLE 5.2 Influence of Binge Eating Behavior Presurgery and Postsurgery on Weight Loss/Regain After Surgery

Authors	Sample Size	Procedure	Duration Follow-Up	Pre-BE/BED Predicts Weight Loss/Regain	Post-BE/BED Correlates with Weight Loss/Regain
Rowston et al., 1992	16	BPD, Gazet	2 years	—	Yes
Pekkarinen et al., 1994	27	VBG	5.4 years	—	Yes
Busetto et al., 1996	80	GBP	12 months	No	—
Hsu et al., 1996	24	VBG	3.5 years	No	Yes
Hsu et al., 1997	27	GBP	21 months	Yes	—
Powers et al., 1999	72	Restriction	5.5 years	No	—
Dymek et al., 2001	32	GBP	6 months	Yes	—
Mitchell et al., 2001	78	GBP	14 years	—	Yes
Busetto et al., 2002	260	Banding	3 years	No	—
Kalarchian et al., 2002	99	GBP	2–7 years	—	Yes
Sabbioni et al., 2002	82	VBG	2 years	No	—
Guisado Macias and Vaz, 2003	140	VBG	18 months	—	Yes
Larsen et al., 2004	157	Banding	34 months	—	Yes

Note. Banding = gastric banding procedure; BE = binge eating; BED = binge eating disorder; BPD Gazet = biliopancreatic diversion with partial gastrectomy; GBP = gastric bypass; Restriction = restrictive type surgery; VBG = vertical banded gastroplasty.

regain. In addition, Boan, Kolotkin, Westman, McMahon, and Grant (2004) showed that patients who had higher scores on the Binge Eating Scale (Gormally, Black, Daston, & Rardin, 1982), indicating more severe binge eating, lost more weight than those with lower scores.

In summary, the relationship between presurgery binge eating and weight loss/regain does not appear to be very strong.

Correlation of Binge Eating Postsurgery and Weight Postsurgery

In an early study, Rowston et al. (1992) reported that patients who employed continued binge eating, "comfort eating," and "eating sensibly in front of others and making up in private" had a significantly less mean monthly reduction in BMI than those who did not employ these behaviors after surgery (Table 5.2). Mitchell et al. (2001) found that patients who redeveloped binge eating behaviors after gastric bypass demonstrated a greater likelihood of weight regain. Kalarchian et al. (2002) reported that almost half the subjects in their study experienced a sense of loss of control while eating, and binge eating was associated with greater weight regain and elevated scores on measures of eating pathology. Also, Hsu et al. (1996) found that patients diagnosed with an eating disorder postoperatively were more likely to exhibit weight regain before the follow-up interview. Similar results were presented by Larsen et al. (2004), who reported that patients with severe binge eating problems after gastric banding had a higher postoperative weight. As with BED, there is evidence that the reoccurrence of night eating syndrome and nocturnal eating might contribute to postsurgical weight regain (Hsu et al., 1996, 1997; Powers et al., 1999).

In summary, there seems to be a strong relationship between the (re)emergence of binge eating problems after surgery and less weight loss or more weight regain over time.

Summary

Binge eating behavior generally improves after surgery for severe obesity. However, research suggests that presurgical binge eating may place patients at higher risk for the reemergence of binge eating problems or loss of control over eating postoperatively, which is associated with poorer weight loss and greater weight regain in the long term. It must also be kept in mind, however, that patients who redevelop binge eating problems still show a satisfactory weight loss even though smaller compared with patients without binge eating problems. Consequently, BED before surgery is not a contraindication for the procedure. However, the identification and treatment of postoperative binge eating might improve long-term weight outcome in these patients. Successful long-term weight loss depends on maintaining reduced food intake even if the patients regain the ability to do otherwise.

References

Adami, G. F., Gandolfo, P., Bauer, B., & Scopinaro, N. (1995). Binge eating in massively obese patients undergoing bariatric surgery. *International Journal of Eating Disorders, 17,* 45–50.

Adami, G. F., Gandolfo, P., Meneghelli, A., & Scopinaro, N. (1996). Binge eating in obesity: A longitudinal study following biliopancreatic diversion. *International Journal of Eating Disorders, 20,* 405–413.

Adami, G. F., Gandolfo, P., & Scopinaro, N. (1996). Binge eating in obesity. *International Journal of Obesity, 20,* 793–794.

Adami, G. F., Meneghelli, A., & Scopinaro, N. (1999). Night eating and binge eating disorder in obese patients. *International Journal of Eating Disorders, 25,* 335–338.

American Psychiatric Association. (1994). *Diagnostic and statistical manual of mental disorders* (4th ed.). Washington, DC: Author.

Atchison, M., Wade, T., Higgins, B., & Slavotinek, T. (1998). Anorexia nervosa following gastric reduction surgery for obesity. *International Journal of Eating Disorders, 23,* 111–116.

Boan, J., Kolotkin, R. L., Westman, E. C., McMahon, R. L., & Grant, J. P. (2004). Binge eating, quality of life and physical activity after Roux-en-Y gastric bypass for morbid obesity. *Obesity Surgery, 14,* 341–348.

Bocchieri, L. E., Meana, M., & Fisher, B. L. (2002). A review of psychosocial outcomes of surgery for morbid obesity. *Journal of Psychosomatic Research, 52,* 155–165.

Bonne, O. B., Bashi, R., & Berry, E. (1996). Anorexia nervosa following gastroplasty in the male: Two cases. *International Journal of Eating Disorders, 19,* 105–108.

Brolin, R. E., Clemow, L. P., Kasnetz, K. A., Fynan, T. M., Silva, E. M., & Greenfield, D. P. (1986). Outcome predictors after gastroplasty for morbid obesity. *Nutrition International, 2,* 322–326.

Brolin, R. L., Robertson, L. B., Kenler, H. A., & Cody, R. P. (1994). Weight loss and dietary intake after vertical banded gastroplasty and Roux-en-Y gastric bypass. *Annals of Surgery, 220,* 782–790.

Buchwald, H., & Buchwald, J. N. (2002). Evolution of operative procedures for the management of morbid obesity 1950–2000. *Obesity Surgery, 12,* 705–717.

Busetto, L., Valente, P., Pisent, C., Segato, G., de Marchi, F., Favretti, F., et al. (1996). Eating pattern in the first year following adjustable silicone gastric banding (ASGB). *International Journal of Obesity and Related Metabolic Disorders, 20,* 539–546.

Busetto, L., Segato, G., de Marchi, F., Foletto, M., de Luca, M., Caniato, D., et al. (2002). Outcome predictors in morbidly obese recipients of an adjustable gastric band. *Obesity Surgery, 12,* 83–92.

Counts, D. (2001). An adult with Prader-Willi syndrome and anorexia nervosa: a case report. *International Journal of Eating Disorders, 30,* 231–233.

Delin, C. R., & Anderson, P. G. (1999). A preliminary comparison of the psychological impact of laparoscopic gastric banding and gastric bypass surgery for morbid obesity. *Obesity Surgery, 9,* 155–160.

Delin, C. R., Watts, J. M., & Bassett, D. L. (1995). An exploration of the outcome of gastric bypass surgery for morbid obesity: Patient characteristics and indices of success. *Obesity Surgery, 5,* 159–170.

Delin, C. R., Watts, J. M., Saebel, J. L., & Anderson, P. G. (1997). Eating behavior and the experience of hunger following gastric bypass surgery for morbid obesity. *Obesity Surgery, 7,* 405–413.

de Zwaan, M. (2001). Binge eating disorder and obesity. *International Journal of Obesity, 25,* S51–S55.

de Zwaan, M., Mitchell, J. E., Howell, L. M., Monson, N., Swan-Kremeier, L., & Crosby, R. D. (2003). Characteristics of morbidly obese patients before gastric bypass surgery. *Comprehensive Psychiatry, 44,* 428–434.

de Zwaan, M., Mitchell, J. E., Swan-Kremeier, L., McGregor, T., Howell, M. L., Roerig, J. L., et al. (2004). A comparison of different methods of assessing the features of eating disorders in post-gastric bypass patients: a pilot study. *European Eating Disorders Review, 12,* 380–386.

Dymek, M. P., le Grange, D., Neven, K., & Alverdy, J. (2001). Quality of life and psychosocial adjustment in patients after Roux-en-Y gastric bypass: A brief report. *Obesity Surgery, 11,* 32–39.

Dymek-Valentine, M., Rienecke-Hoste, R., & Alverdy, J. (2004). Assessment of binge eating disorder in morbidly obese patients evaluated for gastric bypass: SCID versus QEWP-R. *Eating and Weight Disorders, 9,* 211–216.

Faintuch, J., Matsuda, M., Cruz, M. E., Silva, M. M., Teivelis, M. P., Garrido, A. B., et al. (2004). Severe protein-calorie malnutrition after bariatric procedures. *Obesity Surgery, 14,* 175–181.

Fairburn, C. G., & Cooper, Z. (1993). The Eating Disorder Examination. In: C. G. Fairburn & G. T. Wilson (Eds.), *Binge eating: Nature, assessment and treatment.* (12th ed.). New York: Guilford.

Faria, O., Arruda, S., Leite, S., Lins, R., & Rassi, V. (2003). Prevalence of abnormal eating patterns in morbidly obese patients. *Obesity Surgery, 13,* 512.

Glinski, J., Wetzler, S., & Goodman, E. (2001). The psychology of gastric bypass surgery. *Obesity Surgery, 11,* 581–588.

Gormally, J., Black, S., Daston, S., & Rardin, D. (1982). The assessment of binge eating severity among obese persons. *Addictive Behaviors, 7,* 47–55.

Guisado, J. A., Vaz, F. J., Lopez-Ibor, J. J., Lopez-Ibor, M. I., del Rio, J., & Rubio, M. A. (2002). Gastric surgery and restraint from food as triggering factors of eating disorders in morbid obesity. *International Journal of Eating Disorders, 31,* 97–100.

Guisado, J. A., Vaz, F. J., Lopez-Ibor, J. J., & Rubio, M. A. (2001). Eating behavior in morbidly obese patients undergoing gastric surgery: Differences between obese people with and without psychiatric disorders. *Obesity Surgery, 11,* 576–580.

Guisado Macias, J. A., & Vaz Leal, F. J. (2003). Psychopathological differences between morbidly obese binge eaters and non-binge eaters after bariatric surgery. *Eating and Weight Disorders, 8,* 315–318.

Hall, J. C., Watts, J. M., O'Brian, P. E., Dunstan, R. E., Walsh, J. F., Slavotinek, A. H., & Elmslie, R. G. (1990). Gastric surgery for morbid obesity. The Adelaide study. *Annals of Surgery, 211,* 419–427.

Hell, E., Miller, K. A., Moorehead, M. K., & Norman, S. (2000). Evaluation of health status and quality of life after bariatric surgery: Comparison of standard Roux-en-Y gastric bypass, vertical banded gastroplasty and laparoscopic adjustable silicone gastric banding. *Obesity Surgery, 10,* 214–219.

Herpertz, S., Burgmer, R., Stang, A., de Zwaan, M., Wolf, A. M., Chen-Stute, A. et al. (in press). Prevalence of psychiatric disorders in normal weight and obese subjects with and without weight loss treatment in a German urban population. *Obesity Surgery.*

Herpertz, S., Kielmann, R., Wolf, A. M., Hebebrand, J., & Senf, W. (2004). Do psychosocial variables predict weight loss or mental health after obesity surgery? A systematic review. *Obesity Research, 12,* 1554–1569.

Hörchner, R., Tuinebreijer, M. W., & Kelder, P. H. (2002). Eating patterns in morbidly obese patients before and after a gastric restrictive operation. *Obesity Surgery, 12,* 108–112.

Howard, L., Malone, M., Michalek, A., Carter, J., Alger, S., & van Woert, J. (1995). Gastric bypass and vertical banded gastroplasty. *Obesity Surgery, 5,* 55–60.

Hsu, L. K., Benotti, P. N., Dwer, J., Roberts, S. B., Saltzman, E., Shikora, S., et al. (1998). Nonsurgical factors that influence the outcome of bariatric surgery: a review. *Psychosomatic Medicine, 60,* 338–346.

Hsu, L. K. G., Betancourt, S., & Sullivan, S. P. (1996). Eating disturbances before and after vertical banded gastroplasty: A pilot study. *International Journal of Eating Disorders, 19,* 23–34.

Hsu, L. K. G., Mulliken, B., McDonagh, B., Krupa Das, S., Rand, W., Fairburn, C. G., et al. (2002). Binge eating disorder in extreme obesity. *International Journal of Obesity, 26,* 1398–1493.

Hsu, L. K. G., Sullivan, S. P., & Benotti, P. N. (1997). Eating disturbances and outcome of gastric bypass surgery: A pilot study. *International Journal of Eating Disorders, 21,* 385–390.

Hudson, S. M., Dixon, J. B., & O'Brien, P. E. (2002). Sweet eating is not a predictor of outcome after Lap-Band placement. Can we finally bury the myth? *Obesity Surgery, 12,* 789–794.

Kalarchian, M. A., Marcus, M. D., Wilson, G. T., Labouvie, E. W., Brolin, R. E., & LaMarca, L. B. (2002). Binge eating among gastric bypass patients at long-term follow-up. *Obesity Surgery, 12,* 270–275.

Kalarchian, M. A., Wilson, G. T., Brolin, R. E., & Bradley, L. (1998). Binge eating in bariatric surgery patients. *International Journal of Eating Disorders, 23,* 89–92.

Kalarchian, M. A., Wilson, G. T., Brolin, R. E., & Bradley, L. (1999). Effects of bariatric surgery on binge eating and related psychopathology. *Eating and Weight Disorders, 4,* 1–5.

Karlsson, J., Sjöström, L., & Sullivan, M. (1998). Swedish obese subjects (SOS)—an intervention study of obesity. Two-year follow-up of health-related quality of life (HRQL) and eating behavior after gastric surgery for severe obesity. *International Journal of Obesity Related Metabolism Disorders, 22,* 113–126.

Kinzl, J. F., Traweger, C., Trefalt, E., & Biebl, W. (2003). Psychosocial consequences of weight loss following gastric banding for morbid obesity. *Obesity Surgery, 13,* 105–110.

Kral, J. G. (2001). Selection of patients for anti-obesity surgery. *International Journal of Obesity, 25,* S107–S112.

Kuldau, J. M., & Rand, C. S. W. (1986). The night eating syndrome and bulimia nervosa in the morbidly obese. *International Journal of Eating Disorders, 5,* 143–148.

Lang, T., Hauser, R., Buddeberg, C., & Klaghofer, R. (2002). Impact of gastric banding on eating behavior and weight. *Obesity Surgery, 12,* 100–107.

Lang, T., Hauser, R., Schlumpf, R., Klaghofer, R., & Buddeberg, C. (2000). Psychic comorbidity and quality of life in patients with morbid obesity applying for gastric banding. *Schweizer Medizinische Wochenschrift, 130,* 739–748.

Larsen, J. K., van Ramshorst B., Geenen R., Brand N., Stroebe W., & van Doornen L. J. (2004). Binge eating and its relationship to outcome after laparoscopic adjustable gastric banding. *Obesity Surgery 14,* 1111–1117.

Lindroos, A. K., Lissner, L., & Sjöström, L. (1996). Weight change in relation to intake of sugar and sweet foods before and after weight reducing gastric surgery. *International Journal of Obesity and Metabolic Disorders, 20,* 634–643.

Mallory, G. N., Macgregor, A. M., & Rand, C. S. (1996). The influence of dumping on weight loss after gastric restrictive surgery for morbid obesity. *Obesity Surgery, 6,* 474–478.

Malone, M., & Alger-Mayer, S. (2004). Binge status and quality of life after gastric bypass surgery: A one-year study. *Obesity Research, 12,* 473–481.

Marinari, G. M., Murelli, F., Camerini, G., Papadia, F., Carlini, F., Stabilini, C., et al. (2004). A 15-year evaluation of biliopancreatic diversion according to the bariatric analysis reporting outcome system (BAROS). *Obesity Surgery, 14,* 325–328.

Masheb, R. M., & Grilo, C. M. (2000). On the relation of attempting to lose weight, restraint, and binge eating in outpatients with binge-eating disorder. *Obesity Research, 8,* 638–645.

Mitchell, J. E. (1985). Bulimia with self-induced vomiting after gastric stapling. *American Journal of Psychiatry, 142,* 656.

Mitchell, J. E., Lancaster, K. L., Burgard, M. A., Howell, L. M., Krahn, D. D., Crosby, R. D., et al. (2001). Long-term follow-up of patients' status after gastric bypass. *Obesity Surgery, 11,* 464–468.

Niego, S. H., Pratt, E. M., & Agras, W. S. (1997). Subjective or objective binge: Is the distinction valid? *International Journal of Eating Disorders, 22,* 291–298.

Pekkarinen, T., Koskela, K., Huikuri, K., & Mustajoki, P. (1994). Long-term results of gastroplasty for morbid obesity: Binge-eating as a predictor for poor outcome. *Obesity Surgery, 4,* 248–255.

Pessina, A., Andreoli, M., & Vassallo, C. (2001). Adaptability and compliance of the obese patient to restrictive gastric surgery in the short term. *Obesity Surgery, 11,* 459–463.

Powers, P. S., Perez, A., Boyd, F., & Rosemurgy, A. (1999). Eating pathology before and after bariatric surgery: A prospective study. *International Journal of Eating Disorders, 25,* 293–300.

Powers, P. S., Rosemurgy, A. S., Coovert, D. L., & Boyd, F. R. (1988). Psychosocial sequelae of bariatric surgery: A pilot study. *Psychosomatics, 29,* 283–288.

Rabner, J. G., & Greenstein, R. J. (1991). Obesity surgery: expectations and reality. *International Journal of Obesity, 15,* 841–845.

Rand, C. S. W., & Kuldau, J. M. (1993). Morbid obesity: A comparison between a general population and obesity surgery patients. *International Journal of Obesity, 17,* 657–661.

Rand, C. S. W., Macgregor, A. M. C., & Hankins, G. C. (1987). Eating behavior after gastric bypass surgery for obesity. *Southern Medical Journal, 80,* 961–964.

Ringel, M. (1987). Post-gastroplasty bulimia in a 40-year-old woman. *Psychosomatics, 28,* 158–159.

Rowston, W. M., McCluskey, S. E., Gazet, J. C., Lacey, J. H., Franks, G., & Lynch, D. (1992). Eating behaviour, physical symptoms and psychological factors associated with weight reduction following the Scopinaro Operation as modified by Gazet. *Obesity Surgery, 2,* 355–360.

Sabbioni, M. E. E., Dickson, M. H., Eychmuller, S., Franke, D., Goetz, S., Hurny, C., et al. (2002). Intermediate results of health related quality of life after vertical banded gastroplasty. *International Journal of Obesity, 26,* 277–280.

Sanchez-Johnsen, L. A., Dymek, M., Alverdy, J., & le Grange, D. (2003). Binge eating and eating-related cognitions and behavior in ethnically diverse obese women. *Obesity Research, 11,* 1002–1009.

Saunders, R. (1999). Binge eating disorders in gastric bypass patients before surgery. *Obesity Surgery, 9,* 72–76.

Saunders, R. (2001). Compulsive eating and gastric bypass surgery: What does hunger have to do with it? *Obesity Surgery, 11,* 757–761.

Saunders, R. (2004). "Grazing": A high-risk behavior. *Obesity Surgery, 14,* 98–102.

Saunders, R., Johnson, L., & Teschner, J. (1998). Prevalence of eating disorders among bariatric surgery patients. *Eating Disorders, 6,* 309–317.

Scioscia, T. N., Bulik, C. M., Levenson, J., & Kirby, D. F. (1999). Anorexia nervosa in a 38-year-old woman 2 years after gastric bypass surgery. *Psychosomatics, 40,* 86–88.

Scopinaro, N., Gianetta, E., Adami, G. F., Friedman, D., Traverso, E., Marinari, G. M., et al. (1996). Biliopancreatic diversion of obesity at eighteen years. *Surgery, 119,* 261–268.

Segal, A., Kinoshita Kussunoki, D., & Larino, M. A. (2004). Post-surgical refusal to eat: anorexia nervosa, bulimia nervosa or a new eating disorder? A case series. *Obesity Surgery, 14,* 353–356.

Shamblin, J. R., Sessions, J. W., & Soileau, M. K. (1984). Vertical staple gastroplasty: Experience with 100 patients. *Southern Medical Journal, 77,* 33–37.

Stunkard, A., Foster, G., Glassman, J., & Rosato, E. (1985). Retrospective exaggeration of symptoms: Vomiting after gastric surgery for obesity. *Psychosomatic Medicine, 47,* 150–155.

Stunkard, A., & Messik, S. (1985). The Three-Factor Eating Questionnaire to measure dietary restraint, disinhibition, and hunger. *Journal of Psychosomatic Research, 29,* 71–83.

Sugerman, H. J., Londrey, G. I., Kellum, J. M., Wolf, L., Liszka, T., Engle, K. M., et al. (1989). Weight loss with vertical banded gastroplasty and Roux-en-Y gastric bypass for morbid obesity with selective versus random assignment. *American Journal of Surgery, 157,* 93–102.

Sugerman, H. J., Starkey, J. V., & Birkenhauer, R. (1987). A randomized prospective trial of gastric bypass versus vertical banded gastroplasty for morbid obesity and their effects on sweets versus non-sweets eaters. *Annals of Surgery, 205,* 613–624.

Thompson, J. K., Weinsier, R. L., & Jacobs, B. (1985). Self-induced vomiting and subclinical bulimia following gastroplasty surgery for morbid obesity: A case description and report of a multi-component cognitive-behavioral treatment strategy. *International Journal of Eating Disorders, 4,* 609–615.

Viens, M. J., & Hranchuk, K. (1992). The treatment of bulimia nervosa following surgery using stimulus control procedure: A case study. *Journal of Behavioral Therapy and Experimental Psychiatry, 23,* 313–317.

Wadden, T. A., Sarwe, D. B., Womble, L. G., Foster, G. D., McGuckin, B. G., & Schimmel, A. (2001). Psychosocial aspects of obesity and obesity surgery. *The Surgical Clinics of North America, 81,* 1001–1024.

CHAPTER 6

Psychosocial Outcome of Bariatric Surgery

LORRAINE A. SWAN-KREMEIER

The most common impetus for many patients to pursue bariatric surgery is to achieve improvement in medical complications related to obesity. As has been reviewed, weight loss after bariatric surgery clearly results in substantial benefits in achieving reductions or eliminating various medical complications of obesity such as high blood pressure, high cholesterol, osteoarthritis, and type II diabetes. However, to fully appreciate a patient's motivation and decision to undergo bariatric surgery, one must also be cognizant of the nonmedical consequences of obesity on an individual's functioning, lifestyle, and quality of life. Numerous psychosocial factors affect an individual's decision to pursue surgery. These factors are also important in considering a patient's response to surgery and ultimately their prognosis. This chapter will review the research on changes in psychosocial functioning after bariatric surgery as well as psychosocial variables known to have predictive effects on outcome.

Comorbid Psychopathology

Psychiatric comorbidity is common in patients seeking bariatric surgery. A history of Axis I disorders have been found to occur in 27% to 42% of patients seeking surgery (Gentry, Halverson, & Heisler, 1984; Gertler & Ramsey-Stewart, 1986), and rates are substantially higher when considering subthreshold diagnoses (Gertler & Ramsey-Stewart, 1986). Research indicates that adjustment disorders, affective disorders, anxiety disorders, and eating disorders are the most common psychiatric comorbidities in these patients. A history of adjustment disorders (15%), followed by anxiety disorders (14%) and affective disorders (8%) were the most common psychiatric conditions in a sample of 90 patients accepted for bariatric surgery in a study conducted by Larsen (1990). Powers, Boyd, Blair, Stevens, and Rosemurgy (1992) reported that 34% of the patients in their study met criteria for an affective disorder, 9% for an anxiety disorder, 8% for a substance abuse disorder, 4% for posttraumatic stress disorder, and 4% for an eating disorder. In all, 62 different Axis I disorders were represented. A subsequent study (Powers, Rosemurgy, Boyd & Perez, 1997) found similar prevalence rates.

Increased rates of Axis II disorders are also prevalent in this population. Larsen (1990) found a prevalence rate of presurgical Axis II disorders in 22% of his sample, with a "mixed" personality pattern the most common, followed by histrionic and dependent personality disorders. Powers et al. (1992) cited similar results. Twenty percent of patients in their study met criteria for a personality disorder, most commonly dependent personality disorder, followed by personality disorder not otherwise specified. Using a clinical interview and the Minnesota Multiphasic Personality Inventory-2, Glinski, Wetzler, and Goodman (2001) diagnosed personality disorders in 36% of their sample, most diagnosed with personality disorder not otherwise specified.

The increased prevalence of psychiatric comorbidity among bariatric surgery patients must be considered within the context of the stigmatization of and discrimination against the obese in society today. It is understandable that depression and social anxiety would occur in obese individuals who live in our society. The pursuit of a surgical weight loss procedure to improve potential psychiatric consequences of obesity is also understandable.

Research has been conducted investigating the impact of bariatric surgery (and subsequent weight loss) on psychopathology. A review of this research indicates an overall positive psychiatric outcome for most bariatric surgery patients. Several studies found that depressive symptomatology was improved after surgery (Gentry et al., 1984; Gertler & Ramsey-Stewart, 1986; Larsen, 1990; Powers, Rosemurgy, Boyd, & Perez, 1997). Similar improvements in anxiety symptoms after surgery have been documented (Hafner, Rogers, & Watts, 1990; Larsen, 1990). Some studies point out the dose-dependent nature of improvements in psychopathology: the more weight lost, the greater the improvements.

In contrast, significant reductions in the prevalence of personality disorders are not usually seen. Larsen (1990) reported that although rates of Axis I disorders were significantly reduced after surgery, there was little change in Axis II disorders. However, some changes in personality traits have been detected. Larsen and Torgersen (1989) found a significant reduction in traits of self-doubt, insecurity, sensitivity, dependence, compliance, and emotional instability (as measured by the Basic Character Inventory) postsurgically. In contrast, obsessive traits, parsimony, and orderliness were significantly increased. Chandarana, Conlon, Holliday, Deslippe, and Field (1990) reported a reduction in schizoid, avoidant, and passive aggressive subscale scores on the Millon Clinical Multiaxial Inventory.

Despite apparent improvements in several areas of psychopathology after surgery, there is evidence that these improvements may begin to erode over time and the bariatric surgery patient may be at risk for a reemergence or onset of psychiatric symptomatology. In their study of psychiatric issues in bariatric surgery, Powers et al. (1992) reported that 17% of patients experienced significant psychiatric symptoms postsurgically that required hospitalization. Mitchell et al. (2001) found that 29% of their sample experienced an episode of major depression postsurgically and 24.4% experienced problems with specific phobias. A worsening of psychiatric status is also suggested in the suicide rates for bariatric surgery patients. In their 13- to 15-year follow-up study of bariatric surgery patients, Mitchell et al. (2001) reported psychiatrically related deaths (suicide and gastrointestinal bleeding associated with chronic alcoholism) in 2 of 86 patients. Based on their review of the research, Hsu et al. (1998) concluded that "suicide is a major cause of death after bariatric surgery," although differences in sample demographics and follow-up interval preclude a direct correlation between bariatric surgery and suicidality.

Because bariatric surgery has become an increasingly viable and common treatment for obesity, interest has grown regarding what factors predict a positive versus negative surgical outcome. Given the significant presence of psychopathology in bariatric surgery patients, some research has begun to explore the impact of psychiatric comorbidity on surgical outcome. Definitive conclusions regarding outcome have been difficult to derive because of the great variability in methodology, surgical procedures, and outcome variables examined. Surgical outcome is most commonly measured by amount of excess weight lost (%EWL); however, some studies have considered other variables including medical complications, psychiatric status, psychosocial functioning, eating patterns, and quality of life. It is likely that these areas are highly intercorrelated and that outcome is multidimensional (Kral, 2001).

The majority of research conducted in this area has not found that presurgical psychiatric status negatively impacts bariatric surgery outcome when weight loss is used as the outcome measure (Barrash, Rodriguez, Scott, Mason, & Sines, 1987; Clark et al., 2003; Gentry et al., 1984; Hafner et al., 1990; Halmi, Long, Stunkard, & Mason, 1980; Hsu, Betancourt, & Sullivan, 1996; Powers et al., 1997; Powers, Rosemurgy, Coovert, & Boyd, 1988; Rowston et al., 1992; Saltzstein & Gutmann, 1980; Schrader et al., 1990; Valley & Grace, 1987). However, as noted previously, there is great variability across studies related to independent variables and surgical procedures, making it difficult to draw definitive conclusions.

Schrader et al. (1990) investigated whether psychosocial factors, including psychiatric history, contributed to weight loss after three different bariatric surgery procedures (gastroplasty, gastric bypass, and gastrogastrostomy). Patients were interviewed before surgery and weight was measured at 6, 12, 24, and 36 months postoperatively. A history of a psychiatric disorder was not predictive of weight loss or compliance with recommendations; however, psychiatric history was not clearly defined. Hafner et al. (1990) hypothesized that presurgical psychopathology would predict outcome of "gastric restriction surgery." Their results did not support their hypothesis and the presence of presurgical psychiatric symptoms did not predict weight loss. Hsu et al. (1996) reported similar findings in a sample of patients who had undergone vertical banded gastroplasty (VBG), in that presurgical psychiatric conditions did not appear to affect weight loss.

Although the presence of psychopathology presurgically does not appear to negatively affect weight loss outcome, there is some evidence that the severity of psychopathology may. Barrash et al. (1987) found that increased severity or the symptomatic nature of psychiatric symptoms (as measured by the Minnesota Multiphasic Personality Inventory) were associated with poorer weight loss in a sample of women who underwent VBG. Direct, linear relationships between symptom severity and weight loss were not found; however, types of psychopathology such as emotional lability, self-injurious behaviors, impaired interpersonal functioning, suspiciousness, self-defeating behaviors, and familial psychiatric history were associated with poorer weight loss.

Additional research has investigated the impact of psychopathology on other variables of outcome. Results suggest that although a history of psychopathology may not affect %EWL, it does affect patients' postsurgical experience and functioning in important ways. Valley and Grace (1987) found that presurgical psychiatric status, symptom severity as measured by the Minnesota Multiphasic Personality Inventory, negative life events, and lack of social support failed to predict weight loss in a sample of patients undergoing horizontal reinforced gastroplasty. However, a history of psychiatric hospitalizations and lack of social support did predict increased medical complications and decreased satisfaction with surgical outcome. Based on the correlation between severity of psychopathology and the presence and severity of medical complications, the authors hypothesized that these patients may have used food as a source of coping with negative emotional states before surgery, which resulted in poor compliance with dietary recommendations and subsequent medical complications. Similarly, Saltzstein and Gutmann (1980) found that increased psychopathology correlated with postoperative medical complications and psychological complications. Powers et al. (1988) found that a diagnosis of depression or anxiety presurgically was associated with postsurgical complications, including medical complications, eating disturbances, psychosexual adjustment difficulties, and impaired social functioning.

Eating-Specific Psychopathology

Understanding eating pathology is particularly important in working with obese patients pursuing bariatric surgery. Binge eating is likely the most common eating disturbance seen in obese patients. It has been estimated that 25% to 43% of obese patients participating in weight loss programs engage in binge eating (Adami, Gandolfo, Bauer, & Scopinaro, 1995).

Several studies have investigated the prevalence of binge eating in bariatric surgery patients. Results highlight the significance and pervasiveness of this form of eating pathology. Kalarchian, Wilson, Brolin, and Bradley (1998) reported the presence of binge eating on at least a once-per-week basis in 39% of a sample of patients pursuing bariatric surgery. Almost half of the patients in a long-term follow-up study met criteria for binge eating disorder (BED) presurgically in another study (Mitchell et al., 2001). Powers, Perez, Boyd, and Rosemurgy (1999) reported a prevalence rate of binge eating in 52%, 19% of whom met full criteria for BED. The work of Hsu and others (Hsu et al., 1996; Hsu, Sullivan, & Benotti, 1997) found that more than 50% of patients in two separate cohorts met criteria for BED or bulimia nervosa.

Powers et al. (1999) found the presence of night eating syndrome in 10% of their sample of bariatric surgery patients. Hsu et al. (1996) found night eating syndrome in 42% of their sample. "Grazing" also appears to be a significant problem in this population (Saunders, Johnson, & Teschner, 1998).

Binge eating as defined in the *Diagnostic and statistical manual for mental disorders*, 4th edition (American Psychiatric Association, 1994) is virtually impossible after bariatric surgery given the surgical restriction of stomach capacity. Most studies report significant reductions, if not elimination of binge eating after surgery. When the strict diagnostic criterion related to consuming an objectively large amount of food is considered, bariatric surgery could be viewed as a "cure" for BED. For example, Kalarchian, Wilson, Brolin, and Bradley (1999) found that binge eating (as defined by consuming an objectively large amount of food in a discrete period) was eliminated at 4-month follow-up in all 22 patients who were classified as binge eaters presurgically. Binge eating was also completely eliminated in a study conducted by Powers et al. (1999). However, it is important to consider that hallmarks of binge eating, most importantly a sense of loss of control, can persist or return after surgery (Kalarchian et al., 1999). Kalarchian et al. (2002) conducted a long-term follow-up study with gastric bypass patients 2 to 7 years after surgery. Forty-six percent of subjects experienced a recurrent sense of loss of control while eating postsurgically. These subjects had regained significantly more weight; reported greater concerns regarding eating, weight, and shape; and experienced greater hunger, less cognitive restraint, and more disinhibition over eating than those who did not experience a sense of loss of control while eating. Hsu et al. (1996) found that 20.8% of a sample of VBG patients reported an experience of loss of control while eating. In a separate sample Hsu, et al. (1997) found that 25.9% of patients met criteria for BED when the criterion of requiring an objectively large amount of food was modified.

Recent research has investigated whether presurgical binge eating is associated with poor weight loss outcome (Hsu et al., 1996, 1997; Mitchell et al., 2001; Pekkarinen, Koskela, Hulkuri, & Mustajoki, 1994; Powers et al., 1999). Investigators have also been interested in other aberrant eating behaviors such as night eating syndrome and grazing. Pekkarinen et al. (1994) found that, whereas preoperative BED did not affect weight loss after VBG in the first year, patients with a history of BED demonstrated significantly more weight regain at 2 years after surgery. Mitchell et al. (2001) found that patients who experienced a reemergence of binge eating after gastric bypass surgery had a greater likelihood of weight regain. Similarly Kalarchian et al. (2002) found that almost half the subjects in their study experienced loss of control while eating, which was associated with greater weight regain and elevated scores on measures of other eating pathology. In contrast, Powers et al. (1999) did not find an association between presurgical binge eating or night eating and weight loss or weight regain. The topic of eating changes and binge eating after surgery is dealt with more fully in chapter 5.

Quality of Life

A less researched, but vitally important consideration is the impact of obesity on an individual's quality of life (QOL). Quality of life relates to an individual's experience of satisfaction and happiness related to physical, psychological, emotional, social, and spiritual aspects of life (Livingston & Fink, 2003). Health-related quality of life (HRQOL) refers to the impact of health or medical conditions on general life functioning (Dymek, le Grange, Neven, & Alverdy, 2002). The most frequently used measure of HRQOL in research is the Medical Outcomes Study Short-Form 36 Health Status Survey (SF-36), which is a self-report survey that assesses eight areas of QOL including physical functioning, role limitations from health problems, social functioning, bodily pain, general mental health, role limitations from emotional problems, vitality, and general health perception (Ware, Snow, Kosinski, & Gandek, 1993). The Impact of Weight on QOL Questionnaire is a self-report instrument specifically designed to assess the impact of obesity on QOL in areas of health, social functioning, work, physical mobility, self-esteem, sexual life, activities of daily living, and comfort with food (Kolotkin, Crosby, Kosloski, & Williams, 2001).

The majority of obese individuals demonstrate decreased QOL as a result of obesity (Wadden et al., 2001) and weight loss alone can significantly improve QOL in a number of areas. Fontaine, Barofsky, Bartlett, Franchkowiak, & Andersen (2004) reported improvements on SF-36 scales of physical functioning, role limitations from physical problems, general health, vitality, and mental health scales immediately after participation in a 13-week weight loss program. This is certainly not surprising given not only the physical and medical consequences of obesity, but also the toll that weight-related discrimination takes on an individual's self-esteem and interpersonal functioning. Recent research has begun to specifically explore the impact of weight loss on QOL in bariatric surgery patients.

Dymek et al. (2002) conducted a controlled cross-sectional study examining HRQOL in four groups of gastric bypass patients (presurgery, several weeks after surgery, and 6 and 12 months postsurgically). Significant differences in HRQOL were found as early as 2 to 4 weeks after gastric bypass surgery. Specifically, patients demonstrated differences in appraisal of general health, self-esteem, vitality, and physical functioning as measured by the SF-36 or Impact of Weight on QOL Questionnaire. By 6 months after surgery, subjects demonstrated significant improvements in weight loss, medical comorbidities, and QOL and reported "normal" values for HRQOL. In an earlier study (Dymek, le Grange, Neven, & Alverdy, 2001), this group prospectively examined the impact of gastric bypass surgery on QOL and psychosocial adjustment. Results again indicated improvements very early after gastric bypass surgery. Improvements in QOL were demonstrated in a linear fashion in accordance with weight loss. Mitchell et al. (2001) also examined the impact of gastric bypass surgery on QOL in their 13- to 15-year follow-up study. The majority of surgical patients reported improved physical and mental QOL at long-term follow-up approaching normative levels.

The aforementioned studies have assessed QOL after gastric bypass surgery; however, similar improvements have been found in patients undergoing VBG. Tolonen and Victorzon (2003) found significant improvements in QOL after VBG in a sample of 52 patients. Horchner and Tulnebreijer (1999) found significant improvements in QOL, particularly suggestive of greater physical mobility and independence 1 year after VBG. Wyss, Laurent-Jaccard, Burckhardt, Jayet, and Gazzola (1995) conducted a long-term follow-up of VBG patients. Although patients demonstrated improvements in QOL, multiple side effects including vomiting, esophagitis, prolonged eating time, and restriction in choice of food were thought to affect long-term QOL outcome for some patients.

Given the increased gastrointestinal complications of gastric bypass surgery (i.e., vomiting, plugging, and dumping), it has been speculated that improvements in HRQOL would be lower for these patients. Arcila et al. (2002) conducted a prospective study comparing QOL in surgical (VBG and gastric bypass) and nonsurgical obese subjects at a minimum of 1-year follow-up. Surgical subjects reported significantly greater physical and mental well-being. Although it was speculated that gastric bypass surgery patients would demonstrate lower scores on a QOL measure than VBG patients because of the higher incidence of gastrointestinal complications (i.e., vomiting, plugging, and dumping), this was not the case.

Recent research has begun to explore whether QOL varies in regard to the presence of binge eating pathology. De Zwann et al. (2002) compared HRQOL in patients with and without BED previous to gastric bypass surgery. All presurgical patients demonstrated poorer HRQOL compared with SF-36 US norms, particularly on physical domains. Patients with BED demonstrated significantly lower scores on vitality, social functioning, role limitations from emotional problems, and role limitations from physical problems than patients without BED. The authors concluded that BED appears to have a pronounced impact on HRQOL beyond that of obesity.

Other studies investigated the impact of BED on HRQOL after bariatric surgery. Malone and Alger-Mayer (2004) evaluated the impact on QOL after gastric bypass surgery according to presurgical binge eating severity. One hundred and nine patients were categorized into non-binge eating, moderate binge eating, and severe binge eating groups. There were no significant differences between groups on SF-36 physical composite scores; however, mental composite scores were significantly lower for patients in the severe binge eating group. Severe binge eaters demonstrated significantly greater impairment in role limitations from emotional problems, mental health, and vitality presurgically. Similar to results of the de Zwaan (2002) study, there appeared to be a compounded effect of binge eating and obesity in that moderate binge eaters had a poorer perception of their health than non- or severe binge eaters. Severe binge eaters demonstrated the most significant improvements in depression, binge eating, and HRQOL after surgery when compared with moderate and non-binge eaters after surgery. The authors reported similar outcomes related to improved depression, binge eating, and HRQOL regardless of presurgical binge eating status or severity. Although those patients with the most severe binge eating presurgically demonstrated the most severe depression and impact of obesity on HRQOL, they also demonstrated the greatest improvements after surgery. Dymek et al. (2001) found that BED did not affect outcome on depression or QOL measures.

Self-Esteem

Comparable to the medical consequences of obesity is the impact of obesity on self-esteem. In a culture espousing thinness as the body ideal, obese individuals are subjected to stigmatization and discrimination, both overt and covert. Hopes of improving self-esteem are often at the forefront of reasons for considering bariatric surgery. Although the studies have been highly variable in methodology and thus difficult to compare, results of research in the area of self-esteem and bariatric surgery in general demonstrate considerable improvements in self-esteem, self-image, and self-confidence after surgery.

In their work with gastric bypass patients in a support group, Glinski et al. (2001) found that bariatric surgery does improve self-esteem through weight loss. They postulated that the association between self-esteem and obesity is "not necessarily unidirectional," in that not only does obesity contribute to low self-esteem, but negative self-esteem can contribute to obesity. Maladaptive eating behavior in response to feelings of inadequacy, as if a form of self-punishment, was described in their patients.

Few studies have specifically examined self-esteem outcomes of bariatric surgery; however, many studies include measures of self-esteem. Rowston et al. (1992) conducted a prospective study with 16 patients undergoing bariatric surgery. Several indices of self-esteem were found to significantly improve over the 2 years after surgery, including sense of attractiveness, assertiveness, and liking oneself. Bull and Legorreta (1991) found improved self-esteem and decreased feelings of inadequacy and inferiority with weight loss. In a study conducted by Rand, Macgregor, and Hankins (1987) the majority of subjects reported a greater sense of self-confidence. One study (van Gemert, Severeijns, Greve, Groenman, & Soeters, 1998) found a significant association between self-esteem and weight loss. Patients with lower self-esteem presurgically lost more weight after surgery.

In contrast to the research finding significant improvements in self-confidence and self-esteem after bariatric surgery, one study (Gentry et al., 1984) did not find changes in a measure of self-esteem. However, increased self-confidence and satisfaction with life after surgery were found.

Body Image

The positive impact of weight loss after surgery on self-esteem appears primarily related to improvements in body image. Although anecdotally it is clear that bariatric surgery patients experience substantial improvements in body image, few systematic investigations have been conducted. This is surprising given that body disparagement is often a significant impetus to pursuing bariatric surgery. Thirty-two percent of subjects in a study conducted by Libeton, Dixon, Laurie, and O'Brien (2004) cited dissatisfaction with appearance and embarrassment regarding weight and shape as the primary motivation for seeking bariatric surgery, second only to health concerns and medical conditions.

In an early study conducted by Halmi, Stunkard, and Mason (1980), 70% of participants reported severe body disparagement previous to surgery; less than 4% reported such severe negative body image postsurgically. Almost half of the subjects reported the absence of body disparagement. Halmi et al. (1980) also examined "mirror avoidance," an element of body disparagement in which one dislikes observing themselves in the mirror and may avoid doing so to a great degree. Half of the subjects admitted to mirror avoidance presurgically. The majority of these subjects (84%) reported significant improvement in this behavior after surgery.

Seventy-six percent of subjects in a study conducted by Gentry et al. (1984) reported being very dissatisfied with body image before surgery. Twenty-four percent reported being very dissatisfied with their body after surgery, and there was an increase in subjects reporting being satisfied or "neutral." Despite these changes, Gentry et al. (1984) concluded that body image, in general, remained poor for this group.

Of note in the Gentry et al. (1984) and Halmi et al. (1980) studies is that these reported changes occurred within 6 months of surgery, suggesting that definitive improvements in body image occur before maximum weight loss occurs (Stunkard, Stinnett, & Smoller, 1986). Some research results (Leon, Eckert, Teed, & Buchwald, 1979) indicate that body image improves exponentially with weight loss. Others suggest that, although some elements of body image improve with weight loss after surgery, other elements remain problematic. For example, Kinzl, Traweger, Trefalt, and Biebl (2003) found that more than half of their subjects demonstrated a severe fear of regaining weight.

Attempts have been made to investigate which patients may be at risk for continued body disparagement and dissatisfaction despite significant weight loss after bariatric surgery. Stunkard et al. (1986) viewed body disparagement as an emotional disturbance of obesity particular to individuals whose onset of obesity was in childhood. Adami et al. (1998) explored this hypothesis in their investigation of the impact of weight and weight loss on body image. Severely obese patients and patients who had achieved normal weight after bariatric surgery were compared on a self-report measure of body image. Patients were further compared as to whether obesity began in childhood or adulthood. Results indicate that the age of onset of obesity was a critical determinant of changes in body image after bariatric surgery. After weight loss, the body image of individuals with adult-onset obesity did not differ from that of never-obese controls. In contrast, those with early-onset obesity were significantly less satisfied with their weight and shape than were those with adult-onset obesity and normal-weight controls, despite significant weight loss. In support of Stunkard et al. (1986), the authors argued that body image develops and is internalized during childhood and adolescence and individuals with early-onset obesity are at risk for retaining the internalized negative body image independent of weight loss.

Adami, Meneghelli, Bressani, and Scopinaro (1999) examined the impact of weight loss on body image in a sample of 30 patients previous to undergoing biliopancreatic diversion and 3 years postsurgically. Body dissatisfaction, fear of fatness, and feelings of physical attractiveness all improved significantly from baseline to 3-year follow-up and were similar to normal-weight controls. In contrast, surgery patients continued to demonstrate greater preoccupation and concern with weight and shape, fear of weight gain, and body disparagement than normal weight controls. Results suggest that some aspects of body image respond well to weight loss, whereas others may be independent of body weight and thus more resistant to change.

Some studies have attempted to investigate the impact of negative body image on bariatric surgery outcome. Hotter et al. (2003) attempted to delineate variables associated with bariatric surgery success or failure. Their study compared patients considered to have a good versus poor outcome on variables of health status, emotional state, weight loss, postoperative course, and responses on self-report instruments of body perception and body image at 1-year follow-up. There were no significant preoperative differences in body perception or body image between groups on measures completed retrospectively. However, there were significant differences between groups after surgery. Subjects considered to have a positive outcome demonstrated improvements on all measures showing normalization of body dissatisfaction. In contrast, subjects considered to have a poor outcome, regardless of weight loss, experienced ongoing impaired body image and body disparagement.

Guisado et al. (2002) included a measure of body dissatisfaction in their study examining differences in psychopathological status and interpersonal relationships related to extent of weight loss 18 months after VBG. One hundred subjects who had undergone VBG were divided into two groups according to %EWL. Greater weight loss was strongly correlated with less body dissatisfaction.

Although body image and body disparagement are largely improved in bariatric surgery patients, it is common for patients to experience a reemergence of body dissatisfaction in the context of extreme weight loss. Significant weight loss frequently results in excess skin on one's abdomen, face, arms, and thighs. At times, excess skin can cause irritation, soreness, and infection. For others, excess skin constitutes a source of distress and feelings of fatness that lead to ongoing avoidance of activities requiring body exposure (e.g., swimming, wearing shorts). The impact of excess skin after weight loss in bariatric surgery patients is infrequently mentioned and rarely studied (Bocchieri, Meana, & Fisher, 2002). Kinzl et al. (2003) reported that 70% of patients considered excess skin a negative consequence of surgery. Interestingly, it was the patients who had lost significantly more weight more rapidly who were most dissatisfied with their bodies, primarily related to the excess skin. The authors cautioned against the encouragement of too rapid and excessive weight loss.

Intimate Relationships and Sexual Functioning

It has been speculated that weight loss and subsequent enhancement of self-esteem and decreased social avoidance may negatively affect an individual's intimate relationships. Although questions regarding sexual functioning and partnership are frequently included in studies examining psychosocial outcomes of bariatric surgery, there are few studies that examine these issues specifically. The research in the area has not fully supported the intuitive belief that bariatric surgery negatively affects intimate relationships. A recent summary of the literature in this area (Herpertz et al., 2003) highlights the overall positive impact of weight loss postsurgically on partnership and sexuality.

Kinzl et al. (2001) conducted a study investigating the impact of bariatric surgery on sexual attitudes and partnership in an all-female sample. A semistructured interview assessing partnership satisfaction, frequency and quality of sexual behavior, obesity-related sexual limitations, body image perception, and changes in intimate relationship functioning and sexuality was administered preoperatively and 1 year postoperatively. Seventeen percent admitted to seeking surgery in hopes of enhancing sexual functioning and sexuality. Preoperatively, less than half (44%) of patients assessed sexual relationships as satisfying and reported regular sexual contact, and more than half reported sexual related problems (i.e., avoidance, low frequency, physical limitations). Postoperatively, 63% reported increased enjoyment in sexual relations, whereas 12% reported a decrease in sexual enjoyment. Most patients reported no change or improved quality of their intimate relationships after surgery. Only 10% reported a negative impact of surgery on their partnership. This study found that enhancement of sexual functioning was related to improvements in self-esteem, assessment of oneself as sexually attractive, and decreased physical limitations, whereas deterioration in sexual functioning was related to ongoing body dissatisfaction, increased discord in their relationships, or possible decreased sexual desire secondary to nutritional deficiencies.

Camps, Zervos, Goode, & Rosemurgy (1996) investigated the impact of VBG on body image and sexual QOL through assessment of both patients' and partners' perceptions. Of the 28 patients, 14% admitted that hopes of improving sexual functioning played a role in the decision to have surgery. At least 1 year after surgery, 50% of patients reported increased frequency and quality of sexual relations, with 75% of their partners in agreement. Almost one fourth of patients reported new problems in sexual functioning after surgery, typically related to complications of wound healing. The majority of patients (63%) reported feelings of unattractiveness before surgery, whereas the majority of their partners (73%) disagreed. Improvements in body image, reflected in greater feelings of attractiveness and demonstrated behaviorally in undressing in front of their partners more frequently, were reported in 63% of the patients. Again, partners tended to have more positive perceptions, 94% reporting their partner as more attractive.

Hafner et al. (1990) specifically investigated husbands' adjustment to their wives' weight loss. In this study, husbands' psychosocial adjustment before their wives' surgery was considered normal; however, marital dissatisfaction was significantly higher compared with controls. Twelve months after surgery, husbands reported increased marital dissatisfaction and increased discomfort with assertiveness. Results suggest that as wives became more assertive in the context of weight loss, husbands became less assertive and experienced increased dissatisfaction in their marital relationship.

These findings are important in considering the value of partners' support after bariatric surgery. Valley and Grace (1987) identified lack of social support as a predictor of postoperative psychological complications. Results indicated that the presence of life stress, including familial discord during the first postoperative year, was associated with medical complications and less satisfaction with surgery. The authors speculate that social support may serve as a buffer for stressors involved in adaptation after surgery.

Occupational Functioning

An aspect of QOL infrequently studied in the bariatric surgery literature is the impact of obesity on one's ability to perform occupational responsibilities. The multitude of medical complications resulting from obesity clearly affects an individual's mobility and the ease with which he or she functions. The consequences of obesity-related complications (i.e., sleep apnea, heart disease, osteoarthritis) affect attendance patterns and employment leave. For some with severe obesity, employment may not be possible. Despite the intuitive connection between obesity and occupational problems, few studies have specifically examined occupational outcomes of bariatric surgery.

Narbro et al. (1999) conducted a prospective investigation of sick leave and disability pension use in bariatric surgery patients. Days of sick leave and days of receiving disability pension for bariatric patients were compared with obese controls. No difference between groups was found presurgically. In the first postoperative year, surgical patients had 50% more days of sick leave or disability pension compared with controls, primarily resulting from postoperative recuperation. However, in the second and third postoperative years, bariatric surgery patients had significantly less (10%–14% less) use of sick leave and disability pension. Although not statistically significant, surgically treated patients used 8% less leave and disability pay. The reduction in sick leave and disability pension was particularly striking for patients aged 47–60.

As part of the same large-scale study, Naslund and Agren (1991) investigated the social and economic effects of bariatric surgery. Bariatric surgery patients were again compared with obese controls on indices of physical, economical, social, and psychological consequences of obesity 1 to 7 years after surgery. Bariatric surgery patients demonstrated higher rates of employment, worked more hours, and subsequently had a higher income than nonsurgical controls. Surgical patients were also more physically and socially active, reported a better sex life, required less medical care, and took fewer sick days. Given the higher rates of employment and decreased use of sick leave and disability resulting in fewer dollars spent, the authors highlighted the cost-effectiveness of bariatric surgery.

Summary

Bariatric surgery has become an increasingly viable option for the treatment of obesity for many individuals. Despite advancements in surgical procedures that have increased the safety, efficacy, and availability of bariatric surgery, remarkably little is known about what factors influence surgical outcome, particularly psychosocial outcomes. Until recently, little attention has been paid to the psychosocial aspects of obesity or bariatric surgery. Recent research has been beneficial in highlighting the multitude of medical, physical, emotional, psychological, and social consequences of obesity. Results have provided a clearer understanding of the multifaceted impact of bariatric surgery on a patient's life. However, variations in surgical procedures, methodology, outcome measures, and rigor across studies make it difficult to draw definitive conclusions from the research that has been conducted. Additional research is needed using standardized instruments and methodology toward delineating predictor variables and guiding interventions aimed at promoting a successful bariatric surgery outcome.

References

Adami, G. F., Gandolfo, P., Bauer, B., & Scopinaro, N. (1995). Binge eating in massively obese patients undergoing bariatric surgery. *International Journal of Eating Disorders, 17,* 45–50.

Adami, G. F., Gandolfo, P., Campostano, A., Meneghelli, A., Ravera, G., & Scopinaro, N. (1998). Body image and body weight in obese patients. *International Journal of Eating Disorders, 24,* 299–306.

Adami, G. F., Meneghelli, A., Bressani, A., & Scopinaro, N. (1999). Body image in obese patients before and after stable weight reduction following bariatric surgery. *Journal of Psychosomatic Research, 46,* 275–281.

American Psychiatric Association (1994). *Diagnostic and statistical manual of mental disorders* (4th ed.). Washington, DC: Author.

Arcila, D., Velazquez, D., Gamino, R., Sierra, M., Salin-Pascual, R., Gonzalez-Barranco, J., et al. (2002). Quality of life in bariatric surgery. *Obesity Surgery, 12,* 661–665.

Barrash, J., Rodriguez, E., Scott, D. H., Mason, E. E., & Sines, J. O. (1987). The utility of MMPI subtypes for the prediction of weight loss after bariatric surgery. Minnesota Multiphasic Personality Inventory. *International Journal of Obesity, 11,* 115–128.

Bocchieri, L. E., Meana, M., & Fisher, B. L. (2002). A review of psychosocial outcomes of surgery for morbid obesity. *Journal of Psychosomatic Research, 52,* 155–165.

Bull, R. H., & Legorreta, G. (1991). Outcome of gastric surgery for morbid obesity: Weight changes and personality traits. *Psychotherapie, Psychosomatik, medizinische Psychologie, 56,* 146–156

Camps, M. A., Zervos, E., Goode, S., & Rosemurgy, A. S. (1996). Impact of bariatric surgery on body image perception and sexuality in morbidly obese patients and their partners. *Obesity Surgery, 6,* 356–360.

Chandarana, P. C., Conlon, P., Holliday, R. L., Deslippe, T., & Field, V. A. (1990). A prospective study of psychosocial aspects of gastric stapling surgery. *Psychiatric Journal of the University of Ottawa, 15,* 32–35.

Clark, M. M., Balsiger, B. M., Sletten, C. D., Dahlman, K. L., Ames, G., Williams, D. E., et al. (2003). Psychosocial factors and 2-year outcome following bariatric surgery for weight loss. *Obesity Surgery, 13,* 739–745.

de Zwaan, M., Mitchell, J. E., Howell, L. M., Monson, N., Swan-Kremeier, L., Kolotkin, R. L., et al. (2002). Two measures of health-related quality of life in morbid obesity. *Obesity Research, 10,* 1143–1151.

Dymek, M. P., le Grange, D., Neven, K., & Alverdy, J. (2002). Quality of life after gastric bypass surgery: a cross-sectional study. *Obesity Research, 10,* 1135–1142.

Dymek, M. P., le Grange, D., Neven, K., & Alverdy, J. (2001). Quality of life and psychosocial adjustment in patients after Roux-en-Y gastric bypass: A brief report. *Obesity Surgery, 11,* 32–39.

Fontaine, D. R., Barofsky, I., Bartlett, S. J., Franchkowiak, S. C., & Andersen, R. E. (2004). Weight loss and health-related quality of life: results at 1-year follow-up. *Eating Behaviors 5,* 85–88.

Gentry, K., Halverson, J. D., & Heisler, S. (1984). Psychologic assessment of morbidly obese patients undergoing gastric bypass: A comparison of preoperative and postoperative adjustment. *Surgery, 95,* 215–220.

Gertler, R., & Ramsey-Stewart, G. (1986). Pre-operative psychiatric assessment of patients presenting for gastric bariatric surgery (surgical control of morbid obesity). *Australian New Zealand Journal of Surgery, 56,* 157–161.

Glinski, J., Wetzler, S., & Goodman, E. (2001). The psychology of gastric bypass surgery. *Obesity Surgery, 11,* 581–588.

Guisado, J. A., Vaz, F. J., Alarcon, J., Lopez-Ibor, J. J., Rubio, M. A., & Gaite, L. (2002). Psychopathological status and interpersonal functioning following weight loss in morbidly obese patients undergoing bariatric surgery. *Obesity Surgery, 12,* 835–840.

Hafner, R. J., Rogers, J., & Watts, J. M. (1990). Psychological status before and after gastric restriction as predictors of weight loss in the morbidly obese. *Journal of Psychosomatic Research, 34,* 295–302.

Halmi, K. A., Long, M., Stunkard, A. J., & Mason, E. (1980). Psychiatric diagnosis of morbidly obese gastric bypass patients. *American Journal of Psychiatry, 137,* 470–472.

Halmi, K. A., Stunkard, A. J., & Mason, E. E. (1980). Emotional responses to weight reduction by three methods: Gastric bypass, jejunoileal bypass, diet. *The American Journal of Clinical Nutrition, 33,* 446–451.

Herpertz, A., Kielmann, R., Wolf, A. M., Langkafel, M,, Senf, W., & Hebebrand, J. (2003). Does obesity surgery improve psychosocial functioning? A systematic review. *International Journal of Obesity, 27,* 1300–1314.

Horchner, R., & Tulnebreijer, W. (1999). Improvement of physical functioning of morbidly obese patients who have undergone a Lap-Band operation: 1-year study. *Obesity Surgery, 9,* 399–402.

Hotter, A., Mangweth, B., Kemmler, G., Fiala, M., Kinzl, J., & Biebl, W. (2003). Therapeutic outcome of adjustable gastric banding in morbid obese patients. *Eating and Weight Disorders, 8,* 218–224.

Hsu, L. K. G., Benotti, P. N., Dwyer, J., Roberts, S. B., Saltzman, E., Shikora, S., et al. (1998). Nonsurgical factors that influence the outcome of bariatric surgery: A review. *Psychosomatic Medicine, 60,* 338–346.

Hsu, L. K. G., Betancourt, S., & Sullivan, S. P. (1996). Eating disturbances before and after vertical banded gastroplasty: A pilot study. *International Journal of Eating Disorders 19,* 23–34.

Hsu, L. K. G., Sullivan, S. P., & Benotti, P. N. (1997). Eating disturbances and outcome of gastric bypass surgery: A pilot study. *International Journal of Eating Disorders, 21,* 385.

Kalarchian, M. A., Marcus, M. D., Wilson, G. T., Labouvie, E. W., Brolin, R. E., & LaMarca, L. B. (2002). Binge eating among gastric bypass patients at long-term follow-up. *Obesity Surgery, 12,* 270–275.

Kalarchian, M. A., Wilson, G. T., Brolin, R. E., & Bradley, L. (1999). Effects of bariatric surgery on binge eating and related pathology. *Eating and Weight Disorders, 4,* 1–5.

Kalarchian, M. A., Wilson, G. T., Brolin, R. E., & Bradley, L. (1998). Binge eating in bariatric surgery patients. *International Journal of Eating Disorders, 2,* 89–92.

Kinzl, J. F., Traweger, C., Trefalt, E., & Biebl, W. (2003). Psychosocial consequences of weight loss following gastric banding for morbid obesity. *Obesity Surgery, 13,* 105–110.

Kinzl, J. F., Trefalt, E., Fiala, M., Hotter, A., Biebl, W., & Aigner, F. (2001). Partnership, sexuality, and sexual disorders in morbidly obese women: Consequences of weight loss after gastric banding. *Obesity Surgery, 11,* 455–458.

Kolotkin, R. L., Crosby, R. D., Kosloski, K. D., & Williams, G. R. (2001). Development of a brief measure to assess quality of life in obesity. *Obesity Research, 9,* 102–111.

Kral, J. G. (2001). Selection of patients for anti-obesity surgery. *International Journal of Obesity, 25*(Suppl. 1), S107–S112.

Larsen, F. (1990). Psychosocial function before and after gastric banding surgery for morbid obesity. A prospective psychiatric study. *Acta Psychiatric Scandinavian Supplement, 359,* 1–57.

Larsen, F., & Torgersen, S. (1989). Personality changes after gastric banding surgery for morbid obesity: A prospective study. *Journal of Psychosomatic Research, 33,* 323–34.

Leon, G. R., Eckert, E. D., Teed, D., & Buchwald, H. (1979). Changes in body image and other psychological factors after intestinal bypass surgery for massive obesity. *Journal of Behavioral Medicine, 2,* 39–55.

Libeton, M., Dixon, J. B., Laurie, C., & O'Brien, P. E. (2004). Patient motivation for bariatric surgery: Characteristics and impact on outcomes. *Obesity Surgery, 14,* 392–398.

Livingston, E. H., & Fink, A. S. (2003). Quality of life: Cost and future of bariatric surgery. *Archives of Surgery, 138,* 383–387.

Malone, M., & Alger-Mayer, S. (2004). Binge status and quality of life after gastric bypass surgery: A one-year study. *Obesity Research, 12,* 473–481.

Mitchell, J. E., Lancaster, K. L., Burgard, M. A., Howell, L. M., Krahn, D. D., Crosby, R., et al. (2001). Long-term follow-up of patients' status after gastric bypass. *Obesity Surgery, 11,* 464–468.

Narbro, K., Agren, G., Jonsson, E., Larsson, B., Naslund, I., Wedel, H., et al. (1999). Sick leave and disability pension before and after treatment for obesity: A report from the Swedish Obese Subjects (SOS) study. *International Journal of Obesity, 23,* 619–624.

Naslund, I., & Agren, G. (1991). Social and economic effects of bariatric surgery. *Obesity Surgery, 1,* 137–140.

Pekkarinen, T., Koskela, K., Hulkuri, K., & Mustajoki, P. (1994). Long-term results of gastroplasty for morbid obesity: binge-eating as a predictor of poor outcome. *Obesity Surgery, 4,* 248–255.

Powers, P. S., Boyd, F., Blair, C. R., Stevens, B., & Rosemurgy, A. (1992). Psychiatric issues in bariatric surgery. *Obesity Surgery, 2,* 315–325.

Powers, P. S., Perez, A., Boyd, F., & Rosemurgy, A. (1999). Eating pathology before and after bariatric surgery: A prospective study. *International Journal of Eating Disorders, 25,* 293–300.

Powers, P. S., Rosemurgy, A., Boyd, F., & Perez, A. (1997). Outcome of gastric restriction procedures: Weight, psychiatric diagnoses and satisfaction. *Obesity Surgery, 7,* 471–477.

Powers, P. S., Rosemurgy, A. S., Coovert, D. L., & Boyd, F. R. (1988). Psychosocial sequelae of bariatric surgery: A pilot study. *Psychosomatics, 29,* 283–288.

Rand, C. S. W., Macgregor, A. M. C., & Hankins, G. C. (1987). Eating behavior after gastric bypass surgery for obesity. *Southern Medical Journal, 80,* 961–964.

Rowston, W. M., McCluskey, S. E., Gazet, J. C., Lacey, J. H., Franks, G., & Lynch, D. (1992). Eating behaviour, physical symptoms and psychological factors associated with weight reduction following the Scopinaro Operation as modified by Gazet. *Obesity Surgery, 2,* 355–360.

Saltzstein, E. C., & Gutmann, M. C. (1980). Gastric bypass for morbid obesity: Preoperative and postoperative psychological evaluation of patients. *Archives of Surgery, 115*, 21–28.

Saunders, R., Johnson, L., & Teschner, J. (1998). Prevalence of eating disorders among bariatric surgery patients. *International Journal of Eating Disorders, 6*, 309–317.

Schrader, G., Stefanovic, S., Gibbs, A., Elmslie, R,, Higgins, B., & Slavotinek, A. (1990). Do psychosocial factors predict weight loss following gastric surgery for obesity? *Australian and New Zealand Journal of Psychiatry, 24*, 496–499.

Stunkard, A. J., Stinnett, J. L., & Smoller, J. W. (1986). Psychological and social aspects of the surgical treatment of obesity. *American Journal of Psychiatry, 143*, 417–429.

Tolonen, F., & Victorzon, M. (2003). Quality of life following laparoscopic adjustable gastric banding—the Swedish band and the Moorehead-Ardelt questionnaire. *Obesity Surgery, 13*, 424–426

Valley, V., & Grace, D. M. (1987). Psychosocial risk factors in gastric surgery for obesity: Identifying guidelines for screening. *International Journal of Obesity, 11*, 105–113.

van Gemert, W. G., Severeijns, R. M., Greve, J. W. M., Groenman, N., & Soeters, P. B. (1998). Psychological functioning of morbidly obese patients after surgical treatment. *International Journal of Obesity, 22*, 393–398.

Wadden, T A., Sarwer, D. B., Womble, L. G., Foster, F. D., McGuckin B. G., & Schimmel, A. (2001). Psychosocial aspects of obesity and obesity surgery. *Obesity Surgery, 81*, 1001–1024.

Ware, J., Snow, K., Kosinski M., & Gandek, B. (1993). *SF-36 health survey: Manual and interpretation guide.* Boston, MA: The Health Institute, New England Medical Center.

Wyss, C., Laurent-Jaccard, A., Burckhardt, P., Jayet, A., & Gazzola, L. (1995). Long-term results on quality of life of surgical treatment of obesity with vertical banded gastroplasty. *Obesity Surgery, 5*, 387–392.

CHAPTER 7

Nutritional Problems after Bariatric Surgery

JONATHAN FLOM

John Halverson wrote "the cost of excellent weight loss is metabolic risk" (1987). When considering elective surgery, one must weigh the potential benefits against the possible risks. Surgical risks can be divided into two categories. The first category consists of common surgical complications such as wound infections. The second category consists of those risks that are specific to the procedure. Procedure-specific risks often result from the anatomic and physiological changes created by the surgery. A common example of this is cholecystectomy, or removal of the gall bladder. Although the patient may be relieved of painful attacks of biliary colic, he or she may find that they can no longer tolerate highly fatty meals. The very purpose of bariatric surgery is to alter the gastrointestinal tract in such a way that caloric absorption falls well below the threshold needed to maintain one's weight. This benefit comes with the risk of developing clinically apparent nutritional deficiencies. In this chapter, we will look at the various nutritional problems that have been reported in bariatric surgery patients.

Types of Procedures

Many variations of bariatric surgery have been developed, but for the purpose of considering nutritional problems, the procedures fall into two categories (Elliot, 2003). The first are those procedures that are exclusively restrictive in nature. Examples of exclusively restrictive procedures include vertical banded gastroplasty and lap banding. These procedures produce weight loss by limiting food intake via a smaller gastric pouch, but they leave the gastrointestinal tract beyond the stomach intact, and ingested food passes through the remaining tract. The second category of bariatric surgeries includes those that induce malabsorption, which also may include restriction. Examples of malabsorptive procedures include Roux-en-Y gastric bypass and biliopancreatic diversion (see chapter 1). These procedures alter the functional anatomy of the remaining gastrointestinal tract so that after the food leaves the stomach or restricted gastric pouch, it bypasses portions of the small intestine and thus is exposed to less of the absorptive surface. Some procedures are also designed to decrease the amount of exposure to digestive enzymes.

Protein–Calorie Malnutrition

The increasing popularity of bariatric surgery has led some to express concerns that the procedures may cause excessive protein–calorie malnutrition, which would result in disproportionate loss of muscle tissue. Several studies have shown that this is generally not the case, including the study by Avinoah, Ovnat, and Charuzi (1992) that followed a group of patients after Roux-en-Y gastric bypass.

In purely restrictive procedures, patients can develop excessive protein–calorie malnutrition if they fail to modify their diets and eating behaviors, resulting in frequent postprandial vomiting. Because the surgery generally creates a gastric pouch with a capacity of 50 ml or less, patients who are unable to eat smaller portions over longer periods will experience nausea and vomiting. Some dietitians recommend a blended diet for bariatric surgery patients before discharge to demonstrate the consistency they need to achieve in limiting intake and in chewing their food (Bukoff & Carlson, 1981). Because the outlet of the gastric pouch is generally 10 to 12 mm, if the patient does not thoroughly chew food before it is swallowed, the outlet can become obstructed, which can also result in nausea and vomiting. Following restrictive procedures, patients can potentially develop vitamin or mineral deficiencies from markedly impaired intake combined with lack of supplementation. This becomes especially problematic when intake is further compromised by frequent vomiting.

Patients who undergo procedures that combine restriction with an element of malabsorption have the risks discussed previously, but also have an increased risk of nutritional deficiencies secondary to the anatomical changes created by the surgery, which will be discussed in the following sections.

Thiamine

Thiamine (vitamin B_1) is a water-soluble vitamin contained largely in the muscle, heart, liver, kidneys, and brain. The body contains a total supply of approximately 30 mg; this supply has a biologic half life of about 15 days. As a result, patients can develop clinical symptoms of thiamine deficiency in less than 3 weeks on a thiamine-deficient diet. Thiamine is important in carbohydrate metabolism as a coenzyme for transketolase, and also plays a role in nerve conduction and in ion transport. When an excess of carbohydrates in the diet relative to thiamine occurs, the development of thiamine deficiency states such as Wernicke's encephalopathy can occur. Patients with acute Wernicke's encephalopathy generally present with the classic clinical triad of inattentiveness, ataxia, and ophthalmoplegia. Thiamine deficiency has been found to lead to decreased levels of thiamine-dependent enzymes and a series of adverse metabolic effects can occur including decreased levels of intracellular energy and accumulation of glutamate (Toth & Voll, 2001). Serum thiamine levels are unreliable for the diagnosis of Wernicke's encephalopathy because of low sensitivity and specificity. Thiamine deficiency leads to an elevation in the red blood cell transketolase, which can be assayed.

There are numerous case reports of Wernicke's encephalopathy in patients after bariatric surgery (Albina, Stone, Bates, & Felder, 1988; Chaves, Feintuch, Kahwage & Alencar, 2002; Halverson, 1992; Loh et al., 2004; Sola et al., 2003; Toth & Voll, 2001). Most of these have occurred in patients who developed persistent nausea and vomiting, preventing them from ingesting food and their vitamin supplements.

Treatment for Wernicke's encephalopathy includes 100 to 200 mg of thiamine intravenously daily. Magnesium, a cofactor for transketolase, should be given as magnesium sulfate with thiamine to correct thiamine resistance and the frequently accompanying hypomagnesemia (Toth & Voll, 2001). Most, but not all, reports indicate that the patients recovered fully with proper thiamine replacement.

Folate

Folate is an essential water-soluble vitamin. It acts as a coenzyme in the production of DNA, RNA, and amino acids. Folate deficiency can lead to problems with cell division and protein synthesis. These effects are most apparent in rapidly dividing tissues. Deficiency can result in macrocytic anemia and, in pregnancy, fetal neural tube defects. Folate can be measured directly from the serum. As with thiamine, individuals can develop deficiency after as little as 3 weeks on a folate-restricted diet. Folate is thought to be absorbed in the initial third of the small intestine, though it is capable of being absorbed from the entire length of the small bowel. Folate absorption is strongly pH-dependent. Decreased gastric acidity can cause malabsorption of folate by raising the pH in the proximal small intestine. (Mallory & Macgregor, 1991). In addition to folate absorbed in the small intestine, it is thought that the bacterial flora of the large intestine may produce significant amounts of folate that may be absorbed.

Following reports of folate deficiency occurring in as many as 65% of patients after bariatric surgery, Mallory & MacGregor (1991) examined folate levels in 1,067 patients who were candidates for gastric bypass procedures. They found that preoperatively the patients had a 6% rate of folate deficiency. After surgery, with proper vitamin supplementation, the incidence of folate deficiency was 1%.

The vitamins used in this study contained 400 mcg of folate, although others recommend 800 to 1000 mcg daily, especially for pregnant women.

Vitamin B_{12}

Vitamin B_{12}, or cobalamin, is a water-soluble vitamin stored in the liver. It acts as a cofactor in two enzymatic reactions. One, with folic acid, involves nucleic acid production, and the other is related to amino acid and fatty acid breakdown. Deficiency can lead to potentially irreversible demyelination of central and peripheral nerve tissue and macrocytic anemia. Nervous tissue damage is seen at less severe levels of deficiency than are required for macrocytic anemia to occur.

Vitamin B_{12} deficiency after Roux-en-Y gastric bypass is partially caused by decreased intake. There is also diminished gastric acid, which is needed for the release of protein-bound B_{12}. Additionally, loss of intrinsic factor can result in markedly decreased absorption.

Yale, Gohdes, and Schilling (1993) examined B_{12} levels in two series of patients, about half of whom had undergone gastric bypass and half of whom had undergone vertical banded gastroplasty. They found low B_{12} levels in 33% of gastric bypass patients at 1 year, compared with less than 5% in the gastroplasty group. They also looked at B_{12} absorption and found significant impairment in the gastric bypass group's ability to absorb B_{12}. Interestingly, they found that B_{12} in a boiled solution was better absorbed than that in the raw solution.

Three hundred and fifty micrograms of B_{12} administered sublingually daily is sufficient to prevent deficiency. Intramuscular injections may be necessary in some patients.

Iron

Iron is an essential nutrient involved in oxygen transport and various enzymatic reactions. Body stores of iron are concentrated in the bone marrow, liver, and spleen and can be estimated from serum ferritin levels. Iron deficiency leads to microcytic anemia.

Deficiency in bariatric patients can take years to develop. It usually results from decreased intake, especially of red meats, which can be difficult for bariatric patients to tolerate (Avinoah et al., 1992). In addition to the reduction in iron intake, there is also a reduction in gastric acid, which is needed to convert iron from the ferrous to the ferric form, which is the form more readily absorbed. Absorption in the duodenum is also compromised.

It is estimated that somewhere between 33% and 50% of patients will develop iron deficiency after a Roux-en-Y gastric bypass. Recommended replacement levels range from 40 mg to 65 mg per day.

Calcium

Calcium is the most common element in the body, with the bone tissues acting as a storage reservoir. Calcium is important for bone structure, electrophysiology, intracellular regulation, and in enzymatic reactions. The estimated rates of calcium deficiency vary from none to common. Halverson (1987) reports that as many as one third of patients may develop osteomalacia during weight loss, which may spontaneously heal in the majority of patients during stabilization. Because calcium is lost from the storage pool in the bone tissue, serum calcium levels remain normal even with ongoing losses. Such losses will lead to increases in parathyroid hormone. Supplementation with 1,200 mg to 1,500 mg of calcium citrate, which does not require acid for absorption, is generally sufficient.

Vitamin A

Vitamin A is a fat-soluble vitamin that is primarily stored in the liver. It plays a role in vision, gene expression, and differentiation of epithelial cells. Deficiency can lead to night blindness, scarring of the cornea, and skin problems. Halverson (1987) reports that there have been cases of night blindness in bariatric patients, and recommends supplementation with 25,000 to 50,000 units of vitamin A each day.

Summary

Although the nature of bariatric surgery places its recipients at increased risk for nutritional deficiencies, these appear to be avoidable with proper supplementation. As Mallory and Macgregor (1991, p. 70) stated, "in a bariatric surgical practice in which patients are encouraged, reminded and even badgered into taking postoperative vitamin/mineral supplements, the occurrence of folate deficiency should be a rarity."

The occasional cases in which clinically relevant deficiencies occur seem to be patients who develop recurrent nausea and vomiting. Patients need to be educated that if this condition develops, they need to be carefully monitored for signs of thiamine deficiency with immediate intravenuous replacement. If one deficiency is noted, the possibility of other deficiencies should be strongly suspected, because patients noncompliant with any part of their postsurgical regimen may be noncompliant with other aspects as well.

The multidisciplinary team that follows patients after bariatric surgery must include both a dietitian and a physician. These members of the team can evaluate the patient's diet and nutritional status and provide intervention as necessary. Communication among all members of the team is also crucial.

References

Albina, J. E., Stone, W. M., Bates, M., & Felder, M. E. (1988). Catastrophic weight loss after vertical banded gastroplasty: Malnutrition and neurologic alterations. *Journal of Parenteral and Enteral Nutrition, 12,* 619–620.

Avinoah, E., Ovnat, A., & Charuzi, I. (1992). Nutritional status 7 years after Roux-en-Y gastric bypass surgery. *Surgery, 111,* 137–142.

Bukoff, M., & Carlson, S. (1981). Diet modifications and behavioral changes for bariatric gastric surgery. *Journal of the American Dietetic Association, 78,* 158–161.

Chaves, L. C., Feintuch, J., Kahwage, S., & Alencar, T. A. (2002). A cluster of polyneuropathy and Wernicke-Korsakoff syndrome in a bariatric unit. *Obesity Surgery, 12,* 328–334.

Elliot, K. (2003). Nutritional considerations after bariatric surgery. *Critical Care Nursing Quarterly, 26,* 133–138.

Halverson, J. D. (1987). Vitamin and mineral deficiencies following obesity surgery. *Gastroenterology Clinics of North America, 16,* 307–315.

Halverson, J. D. (1992). Metabolic risk of obesity surgery and long-term follow-up. *American Journal of Clinical Nutrition, 55,* 602S–605S.

Loh, Y., Watson, W. D., Verma, A., Chang, S. T., Stocker, D. J., & Labutta, R. J. (2004). Acute Wernicke's encephalopathy following bariatric surgery: Clinical course and MRI correlation. *Obesity Surgery, 14,* 129–132.

Mallory, G., & Macgregor, A. (1991). Folate status following gastric bypass surgery (the great folate mystery). *Obesity Surgery, 1,* 69–72.

Sola, E., Morillas, C., Garzon, S., Ferrer, J. M., Martin, J., & Hernandez-Mijares, A. (2003). Rapid onset of Wernicke's encephalopathy following gastric restrictive surgery. *Obesity Surgery, 13,* 661–662.

Toth, C., & Voll, C. (2001). Wernicke's encephalopathy following gastroplasty for morbid obesity. *The Canadian Journal of Neurological Sciences, 28,* 89–92.

Yale, C. E., Gohdes, P. N., & Schilling, R. F. (1993). Cobalamin absorption and hematologic status after two types of gastric surgery for obesity. *American Journal of Hematology, 42,* 63–66.

CHAPTER 8

Psychological Management after Bariatric Surgery

TRICIA COOK MYERS

In the rapidly expanding field of weight loss surgery, it is extremely rare to find a multidisciplinary approach to bariatric patient care that includes not only the surgeon and a dietitian, but involvement by a mental health professional as well. In fact, mental health professionals such as psychologists, social workers, and counselors have typically had little to no involvement in the management of patients undergoing gastric bypass surgery. In some instances, insurance companies may require a psychological assessment before approving coverage for the surgery or the surgeon may have significant enough concerns about emotional stability to refer a patient to a mental health professional for a presurgical evaluation. Otherwise, psychosocial issues are often not addressed.

When mental health professionals are involved, it is typically in the role of a consultant outside of the treatment team who sees the patient for a one-time assessment in order to determine if the patient is inappropriate for bariatric surgery. Exclusionary criteria are few and for most individuals this assessment, although reportedly anxiety-provoking, is cursory, with the majority of people going on to receive approval for the surgery. Even when concerns arise that may affect the psychiatric suitability of the patient, the surgical team sometimes overrides these and performs the procedure. In addition, patient compliance with any presurgical assessment recommendations is questionable, unless following the recommendations is a necessary precursor to approval. However, usually there is no follow-up by the surgical team, insurance company, or assessing psychologist to ensure follow-through with nonrequired recommendations.

To some degree, these failures are due to the ambiguous nature of the presurgical psychological assessment as well as the mental health professional's peripheral role on the treatment team. Although psychiatric comorbidity such as binge eating disorder, depression, and personality disorders are relatively common among individuals presenting for bariatric surgery, there is little to no evidence that psychiatric difficulties are more common in the obese than nonobese (Halmi, Long, Stunkard, & Mason, 1980). Also, there are no clear guidelines in the research literature, let alone the clinical arena, as to which patients should undergo a presurgical evaluation, which mental health professionals should perform the assessment, or what measures should be used. These inconsistencies make it difficult to compare results or make predictions about what pathologies should delay or even preclude the surgery.

At the same time, there is variability in the success of bariatric surgery with approximately 20% of patients considered to be surgical failures because of insufficient weight loss (Benotti & Forse, 1995). However, aside from the variability associated with the type of procedure (Hall et al., 1990; Sugerman, Starkey, & Birkenhauer, 1987), very little information is known about why some patients lose more weight than others. Inadequate coping strategies have been implicated by some (Delin & Watts, 1995). In terms of medical complications, there is some evidence that psychiatric comorbidity may be associated with an increased risk of postsurgical medical complications. Powers and colleagues found an association between raised Beck Depression Inventory scores or other Axis I disorders and medical as well as psychiatric difficulties after the surgery (Powers, Rosemurgy, Coovert, & Boyd, 1988). A study by Valley and Grace (1987) showed that patients who had a higher number of inpatient psychiatric admissions before the surgery were more likely to experience medical complications and report increased distress and dissatisfaction 1 year after the surgery. However, there is a paucity of information about the impact of various specific psychiatric difficulties on surgical outcome.

Although surgery and resulting weight loss are generally thought to lead to significant improvements in Axis I disorders such as depression, anxiety, and binge eating disorder, there is little improvement in Axis II disorders. Personality disorders are considered to be pervasive and persistent, and as evidence has shown, in general can have a negative influence on medical outcome. These individuals require more expensive and complicated treatment resources and tend to respond less well to medical interventions (Ruegg & Frances, 1995). Further, personality disorders tend to be more common in patients seeking weight loss surgery than in controls and may be associated with less weight loss in patients presenting to obesity clinics (Berman, Raynes Berman, Heymsfield, Fauci, & Ackerman, 1993).

Premorbid disordered eating has also been thought to influence the outcome of bariatric surgery. Binge eating disorder in particular has been associated with increased occurrence of medical complications and weight regain. Binge eating tends to improve immediately after surgery because of limited stomach capacity; however, a recurrence in this pattern is noted about 2 years after surgery (Hsu, Betancourt, & Sullivan, 1996; Hsu, Sullivan, & Benotti, 1997). Although the stomach pouch is still restricted in size, some patients begin to experience a loss of control over eating with associated weight gain at that time. Of note, most leading researchers now believe that binge eating disorder can be diagnosed after bariatric surgery in the absence of eating a large amount of food. The distress and behavioral disturbance after these "adjusted" binge episodes is of significant concern. Kalarchian and colleagues (2000) demonstrated that those patients who were binge eating 2 to 7 years after surgery displayed more hunger and disinhibition and less dietary restraint as well as more significant weight, shape, and eating concerns than those who were not binge eating.

For these reasons, it seems important to expand the role of the mental health professional in the surgical treatment of obesity. Although there is a role for the mental health professional in the assessment of the patient before surgery, an equally or even more important undertaking may be to assist the patient with his or her unique needs throughout short- and long-term recovery from obesity. The problems, needs, and interventions, while at times overlapping, are specific to each of these transitional phases and will be reviewed in detail later in this chapter. First, it is important to review the available literature on psychological treatments after bariatric surgery.

Literature Review

Very few empirical data are available on psychological interventions after bariatric surgery with only one published controlled treatment trial after surgery, to our knowledge. Those in clinical practice who work with bariatric patients know that psychological problems do sometimes occur; however, there is a stigma and also a strong sense of failure that often prevents patients from seeking professional treatment in a timely fashion, if at all. When patients do seek help from a mental health professional, there are no guidelines on what approach should be taken. In addition, if professionals know that bariatric patients are likely to encounter certain difficulties or that certain subsets of the bariatric population are at risk, wouldn't preventive versus tertiary intervention be a wiser course of action? Research on these burgeoning topics is currently under way with early promising results.

For starters, attempts have been made preoperatively to improve surgical success via psychological means. In one study, a preparatory program ($n = 11$) was compared with standard care ($n = 14$) (Horchner & Tuinebreijer, 1999). The preparatory program included information specific to the surgical procedure, sensations associated with the procedure (e.g., nausea from stomach probe, taste of contrast fluid, fullness after small amounts of food), and aspects of the experience that the patient could positively influence. The authors found that although there were no significant between-group differences, the patients who received the preparatory program reported less postoperative pain, vomiting, and use of analgesia, and required a shorter duration of nursing care. However, the study lacked adequate power to detect significant differences and is in need of replication.

Kinzel, Trefalt, Fiala, and Biebl (2002) discussed their clinical post-bariatric protocol at a university hospital in Austria. All patients were informed of the available psychotherapeutic opportunities, including a monthly support group open to patients before and after surgery; a monthly support group open to patients who have had the surgery; small-group psychotherapy held every other week for 12 to 36 months to address eating difficulties, coping strategies, and adjustment issues; and individual therapy for those with significant depression, anxiety, or history of trauma. Self-esteem, reactions from significant others, physical complaints, risk of developing an eating disorder, and alternative means of dealing with negative emotions were thought to be primary issues of concern to discuss in each of these formats. The authors noted that a successful surgical outcome was related to ongoing contact with a therapist. In their experience, more patients were willing to seek support postoperatively with less than 5% willing to participate before surgery. However, they estimate that only about 25% of patients used these services at any point.

Other groups have evaluated the effectiveness of support groups. Hildebrandt (1998) mailed surveys to about 1,000 patients who had previously received weight loss surgery. Results were based on 102 responses and showed that the amount of weight lost over time was significantly correlated to the number of group meetings that the patient attended. When patients who never attended a meeting ($n = 33$) were compared with those who did attend at least one meeting ($n = 69$), there were no significant differences, leading the author to theorize that attendance at one or two meetings was not sufficient enough to reap any benefits. Instead, weight loss may be dependent on regular participation. Group participation did not significantly alter mood or weight regain and there were no differences in reported problems between groups.

In another study, 128 patients who underwent laparoscopic adjustable gastric banding in Italy were categorized as "normal," "hysteric," or "depressed" based on Minnesota Multiphasic Personality Inventory profiles (Nicolai, Ippoliti, & Petrelli, 2002). Individualized psychotherapeutic programs were devised for each; however, only 11 of 51 "normals," 18 of 48 "hysterics," and 15 of 29 "depressed" were compliant with attendance. Results showed that significant improvements were noted at 1-year follow-up on the Minnesota Multiphasic Personality Inventory profiles of those who participated in a psychotherapeutic program but not those who failed to follow through with treatment. In addition, those who followed the psychotherapeutic program required fewer laparoscopic adjustable gastric banding calibrations and less inflation than the noncompliant group.

A study from Italy tested the benefits of brief strategic therapy (BST) on the outcome of laparoscopic adjustable gastric banding for at-risk individuals such as those with binge eating disorder, sweet eating, nibbling, patients younger than 20 years of age, and those with a history of depression (Caniato & Skorjanec, 2002). BST is a solution-oriented therapy that aims to break the cyclical reaction pattern responsible for maintenance of a problem. It is time-limited, typically consisting of 10 or fewer sessions, and focuses on changing the patient's perception of his or her experience rather than on altering the actual experience. Patients who received BST preoperatively ($n = 152$) and those who received standard care ($n = 385$) were compared on various outcome measures including weight loss, health status, and improvements in quality of life and self-perception on the Moorehead-Ardelt Quality of Life Questionnaire. Patients were categorized according to excess weight loss. At 1-year follow-up, BST (46% excess weight loss) was superior to no treatment (40% excess weight loss) in regard to weight loss. Results were similar at 2-year follow-up, but did not reach statistical significance. Quality of life was improved overall. The authors concluded that although selection of patients for surgery is important, some vulnerable patients such as those with binge eating or nibbling fare quite well when treated presurgically with supportive therapy.

Behavioral interventions have also been used to increase the benefits of bariatric surgery, in large part from the drastic behavioral changes required of those who undergo the operation. In addition, it was thought that behavioral treatments may be helpful to those patients who fail to experience improvements in psychological functioning simply as a result of surgery. Before undergoing the operation, patients in one trial were randomly assigned to receive minimal treatment ($n = 15$) or a behavioral intervention ($n = 17$) (Tucker, Samo, Rand, & Woodward, 1991). Subjects in both conditions were educated presurgically about required changes in eating. In addition, patients in the behavioral intervention were mailed 12 psychoeducational packets about eating and lifestyle changes and participated in monthly consultations during the 6 months after surgery. The authors found that, although the addition of a behavioral intervention to bariatric surgery did not result in statistically different weight loss between groups, it did lead to improved postoperative functioning. Specifically, patients who received the behavioral treatment reported better marital/family satisfaction and participated in more physical activity than controls. These same patients also consumed less dietary fat and, unfortunately, less protein than controls. These findings highlight the need for more extensive dietary intervention as both groups displayed inadequate nutrition. There were no significant between-group differences on emotional health ratings, daily caloric intake, frequency of vomiting, or stomach pain.

Saunders (2001) also developed a group intervention for bariatric patients with full or subthreshold binge eating disorder, considered to be high risk for problems about 2 years after surgery, but has not made statistical results available. Titled the "Compulsive Eater's Program for Gastric Bypass Patients," patients started the cognitive-behavioral group 2 to 6 months after surgery and met on a weekly basis for 12 weeks. Subsequently, participants could also attend a monthly aftercare group or engage in individual therapy. Patients were surveyed by the author and reported that they frequently did not know when they were full, ate in response to emotional states, frequently grazed on food, felt that their eating was out of control, and continued to have psychosocial difficulties or develop new eating disorder symptoms. Reportedly, the intervention had a positive impact on the patients' understanding and awareness of their problems. It also helped them develop alternative coping strategies and means of self-nurturance. Ideally, Saunders (2001) feels that this type of intervention should be offered presurgery to those with disturbed eating patterns.

More recently, Kalarchian and Marcus (2003) reviewed the literature on bariatric surgical outcome and its association with psychological factors. In particular, they point out that the presence of binge eating disorder is correlated with worse outcome. They advocate for an expanded role of the cognitive-behavioral psychologist and recommend that a mental health professional be involved in patient care before surgery, after surgery, and in the long-term maintenance of outcome. The authors lay out recommendations for each of these phases in a clear and concise manner. Recently, Kalarchian has been awarded a federally funded career development award to study their proposal in more detail.

A federally funded Bariatric Surgery Clinical Research Consortium is getting under way. The National Institute of Diabetes and Digestive and Kidney Diseases is funding this consortium of six experienced bariatric surgery sites to perform the largest study of its kind looking at medical and behavioral correlates and outcome variables associated with weight loss surgery. The participating sites are Columbia University, New York, NY; East Carolina University, Greenville, NC; Neuropsychiatric Research Institute, Fargo, ND; University of California Davis Medical Center, Davis; University of Pittsburgh, Pittsburgh, PA; and the University of Washington, Seattle. The consortium will work collaboratively to gather extensive physical and psychological information to help expand our knowledge of the bariatric population and ultimately to improve outcome.

Psychological Interventions

There are various stages that a bariatric patient progresses through in his or her weight loss. Each of these stages is associated with particular needs and concerns and therefore interventions should be matched appropriately. Although the focus of this chapter is on the psychological management of bariatric patients after surgery, the patient's presentation before surgery is also appropriate to discuss here because there are some interventions, if delivered before surgery, that may significantly impact later outcome in a positive manner.

Therefore, the following four stages have been identified: (1) presurgery, (2) postsurgery: physical adjustment, (3) postsurgery: psychosocial adjustment, and (4) long-term maintenance. Arbitrary timelines for each stage have been identified and will be discussed in detail in the following sections. It is important to note that not all patients experience these common difficulties, nor do all patients progress through the stages at the same pace. Some may get "stuck" and require additional assistance, whereas others will experience few obstacles. Additionally, each patient will perceive the course of events in his or her own unique way. Described are the author's thoughts as guided by the literature on how best to approach and structure the psychological management of the bariatric patient. Support groups will be discussed individually as they are appropriate during all stages of progress.

Support Groups

There is an obvious need for support groups. Typically, such groups are inclusive of patients considering bariatric surgery as well as those who have already had the procedure performed. The surgical team frequently refers standard bariatric patients to these meetings. Often free of charge and located in the surgical clinic, these meetings offer an opportunity to discuss concerns, difficulties, and highlights with other individuals who can relate to the physical and psychological manifestations of obesity and obesity surgery. Most often these groups are held on a monthly, sometimes weekly, basis. In well-established bariatric surgery practices, support groups are often facilitated by a member of the surgical team such as a nurse or coordinator. In some instances, a psychologist, social worker, or counselor may facilitate the group as an integral part of his or her role on the surgical team. In other situations, a local mental health professional may recognize the need and set up a support group for bariatric patients in the community.

Several articles have been written by experienced clinicians (e.g., Algazi, 2000; Marcus & Elkins, 2004) on how to structure these groups and certainly there is no "right" way; however, a good support group should contain several components. If at all possible, groups should be supervised by a professional trained in group dynamics. Although groups can be a powerful experience for participants when they exert a positive influence, at times group focus can get off track and potentially be harmful. A skilled mental health professional will be better equipped to keep group members on task and appropriate, allowing no one member to dominate.

Algazi (2000) lays out the essential features of a support group in narrative form. First, compliance and success, no matter how small, should be praised and supported. Second, support groups should offer education about required behavioral changes after surgery. They should also identify potential problems and work toward the development of appropriate forms of self-nurturance. Support groups should also afford a safe environment and an opportunity to process the challenges associated with surgical weight loss in the presence of others with similar experiences. Algazi also feels that this should be a place where significant others and close family members can be invited to better understand what the patient is going through and gain awareness into their own issues and concerns about the patient's dramatic weight loss. Last, individuals who are considering the surgery should be made to feel welcome and offered the opportunity to learn more from those who have already experienced it.

Presurgery

Before surgery, patients are actively considering having the procedure performed and, although apprehensive, are eager to experience the rapid weight loss and give up their dieting battles. Some arrive via a physician referral, whereas others have researched the procedure on their own. Many patients have already concluded that they want the surgery; however, some remain unsure. Bariatric patients have varying degrees of knowledge and their expectations about outcome may or may not be realistic. Most look forward to the freedom that the surgery will provide.

In addition to a thorough assessment, the process of which was discussed comprehensively in chapter 2, the mental health professional can also offer significant other contributions during this time of preparation. For those patients who are unsure or who have very little knowledge about the dramatic changes that will take place postoperatively, the clinician can take a nonjudgmental approach to exploration of these issues. Motivational interviewing, as originally described and used by Miller and Rollnick (1991) with a substance abuse population, is an appropriate method to use with these patients. The cognitive-behavioral approach of problem solving can be used to plan for foreseeable difficulties such as child care or time away from work. Expectations should also be discussed in detail. Most obese patients remain obese after the surgical procedure, even though quality of life improves dramatically. Therefore, the majority of patients may never reach their "ideal" weight and, if expecting to do so, may be more prone to experience depression and disillusionment. Presurgical interventions should explore unreasonable or unattainable goals and help the patient arrive at more moderate ideals.

In addition, mental health professionals with a behavioral background are in an ideal position to work with patients who have not yet tried less invasive means of weight loss. Setting realistic and attainable goals, the use of stimulus control, and alternative behaviors could all be beneficial. Fortunately, some insurance companies have recently begun to cover psychological services for health-related problems without a *Diagnostic and statistical manual of mental disorders*, 4th edition, Axis I diagnosis, offering patients the possibility of treatment that they might not otherwise receive. Mental health services should also be used before surgery for those patients with exclusionary conditions such as substance abuse or dependence, as well as uncontrolled psychiatric conditions such as depression or anxiety that may not entirely preclude a patient from surgery but could complicate matters down the road. Substance dependence issues should always be addressed before surgery takes place.

Although the research suggests that obese patients do not have higher rates of psychopathology than normal-weight peers, there are clear-cut differences between obese patients with and without binge eating disorder. Obese patients with binge eating disorder display greater psychopathology, report more dissatisfaction with body image, and psychologically function at a lower level (Telch & Agras, 1994). In addition, it is believed that the yo-yo pattern of dieting that most obese people engage in, vacillating between restriction and overeating, can leave the individual vulnerable to significant eating disturbances after surgery. Hsu et al. (1996) reported that the presence of binge eating before surgery was associated with weight regain after surgery.

As mentioned previously, a significant proportion of bariatric patients engage in binge eating or other significant eating disorder pathology (Kalarchian et al., 2000). Because these eating difficulties frequently reemerge during long-term maintenance and lead to weight regain, it seems reasonable to identify and treat this subset of patients before surgery. Cognitive behavioral approaches to the treatment of binge eating disorder exist and have shown good effectiveness in controlled trials (Marcus, Wing, & Fairburn, 1995; Peterson et al., 1998; Telch, Agras, Rossiter, Wilfley, & Kenardy, 1990; Wilfley et al., 1993). However, the delivery of these approaches before bariatric surgery has not yet been examined, so it is unclear what benefits in outcome will occur. Bariatric surgery itself results in cessation of binge eating in a strict sense, yet some patients do begin to report a loss of control over eating about 2 years after surgery. Therefore, it does seem reasonable to offer this intervention presurgically in an attempt to educate patients before the difficulties reoccur. If not delivered before surgery, cognitive behavioral approaches to binge eating could routinely be delivered during the psychosocial adjustment phase. An alternative would be to provide interventions if and when these difficulties reemerge postoperatively.

Typically, these treatments consist of approximately 15 sessions in a group-based format. Participants are asked to self-monitor foods and liquids consumed and to record thoughts that influence their mood and eating throughout the day. A regular pattern of eating is recommended, consisting of three meals and about two snacks each day. Many obese individuals skip early meals and tend to overeat later in the day after coming home from work. Underestimation of food consumption is also common, so much attention needs to be devoted to review of the patient's food logs. A regular pattern of exercise is also prescribed with the clinician careful to work with the patient on setting attainable goals. Additionally, patients are encouraged to engage in alternative behaviors during vulnerable times to distract themselves from any urges that might occur. It is best if alternative behaviors are incompatible with eating (e.g., knitting versus watching television).

Binge eating disorder is also commonly associated with a distorted pattern of thinking that contributes to overeating and low mood. Cognitive restructuring can be used to address problematic thoughts such as, "I've already eaten two cookies so I might as well go ahead and eat all dozen," or "I failed because I didn't lose 5 pounds this week." Using the cognitive restructuring process, patients are asked first to become aware of problematic thoughts, examine the evidence that supports those thoughts, the evidence that does not support those thoughts, and use the evidence to arrive at a reasoned conclusion.

It is also important to address the problems frequently associated with binge eating disorder such as body image disturbances, impulsivity, stress management, assertiveness, and problem solving. Finally, treatment for binge eating disorder should incorporate relapse prevention techniques including education about the difference between a lapse and relapse as well as a formal, written relapse prevention plan.

Postsurgery Adjustment

Immediately after the surgery, during the first 6 months or so, patients tend to focus on their physical recovery and most seem to enter a honeymoon phase of rapid weight loss and elated mood. An unfortunate few experience significant difficulties at this point that are primarily managed in the medical realm by the surgeon and affiliated staff. Fatigue, inadequate nutritional intake, occasional vomiting, plugging or diarrhea, and dysphoria may become a focus for some and may persist past the 6-month adjustment stage. However, for most, the physical adjustment stage is characterized by improved self-esteem and mood, ongoing weight loss, adjustment to behavioral limitations, and a return to normal activities. Even those who experienced disturbed eating patterns before surgery—such as binge eating disorder, night eating, or grazing—tend to do well during this period. It is not until the long-term maintenance stage that these difficulties tend to become problematic again.

It is rare for a mental health clinician to become involved in patient care during this stage. This is not to say that these professionals have nothing to offer. On the contrary, they could be instrumental with issues of compliance. Bariatric patients are required to make significant alterations to their patterns of eating and may at times experience food cravings, lack of hunger sensations, or anxiety about vomiting or plugging, among a variety of other issues. Typically, patients will meet with the surgeon and a dietitian on a consistent basis during this time. However, some patients report that their needs are not entirely met. The well-informed mental health clinician can work closely with the rest of the treatment team to problem solve difficulties and reinforce progress. In particular, patients should continue to complete food logs with a focus each session on a thorough review of how close they are to achieving a regular protein- and calcium-dense pattern of eating.

Kalarchian and Marcus (2003) point out that the cognitive-behavioral therapist can aid the bariatric patient in the difficult task of adjusting to the physical manifestations of surgery. Specifically, the mental health professional can help increase compliance with the behaviors of thoroughly chewing each mouthful, eating slowly, and ceasing eating as soon as sensations of fullness occur. It has been shown that failure to comply with these recommendations can lead to an early and unnecessary weight loss plateau (Halverson & Koehler, 1981).

Exercise is another important behavior that will help promote weight loss and improved energy level and mood. However, patients often have difficulty going from a sedentary to a more active lifestyle. Behavioral strategies may also be helpful during this stage to promote compliance with recommendations in this regard. A common pitfall in regard to exercise routines is that patients (and sometimes team members) can expect too much too soon. It is helpful to get an idea of the patient's current level of physical conditioning and set goals accordingly. If a patient has been engaging in no programmed exercise, it is certainly unrealistic to expect him or her to jog 30 minutes each day for the next week. Instead, initial goals should be more consistent with current levels of functioning and activity. Other helpful strategies include scheduling a time to exercise and increasing accountability with the addition of an exercise buddy, self-monitoring, or more frequent sessions. For some patients, it may also be helpful to set up a formal behavioral contract with a family member that clearly spells out what reinforcement will be received if the goal is accomplished.

In addition, some bariatric patients who experience frequent plugging, vomiting, or dumping syndrome may begin to develop significant anticipatory anxiety. Solid food may be avoided altogether or the patient may feel comfortable eating only a very select variety of food items at a time when nutrition is extremely important. Other patients may begin to avoid eating in public situations or in front of others. Still others may begin to experience increased episodes of vomiting and stomach discomfort after eating. When medical causes have been ruled out, it is appropriate for the mental health professional to offer cognitive behavioral interventions for this type of anxiety. Specifically, desensitization and exposure and response prevention should be used as well as supportive therapy.

The psychosocial adjustment stage tends to occur 6 to 18 months after the operation. Patients tend to enter this stage after their body has healed from the operation, they have made serious attempts to comply with the surgeon's and dietitian's recommendations, and they have already lost a significant amount of weight. Most patients will continue to feel good about their progress; however, a substantial subset will begin to become more aware of changes to their psychosocial environment, not all of which are well received. Patients may begin to experience conflict with their spouse or significant other brought about by changes in the patient's level of assertiveness or social activity. On the other hand, some patients may begin to feel disillusioned when weight loss does not prove to be the answer to all of their problems.

Psychological well-being during this stage can be tenuous for some; especially those who suffered with depression, anxiety, or binge eating disorder before bariatric surgery. Because these psychiatric disorders tend to reemerge approximately 2 years after the operation (Hsu et al., 1998; Hsu et al., 1997; Pories & MacDonald, 1993), this stage offers an underused opportunity to offer a secondary intervention program.

At-risk patients could be offered intermittent evaluations and supportive care by a mental health professional to monitor for these disorders or to provide psychoeducation about the early signs and symptoms of these difficulties. These appointments can occur on a monthly basis for individuals who are progressing well. This way, detection can occur as soon as possible and the patient can begin more intensive, specific treatment in an effort to curtail the extent of his or her distress and dysfunction. Various theoretical orientations can provide a framework to approach these problems with cognitive-behavioral and interpersonal strategies especially well-suited. Patients who are experiencing difficulties would likely benefit from increased frequency of appointments. Psychotropic medication could also be introduced at this point if deemed necessary.

Even though the majority of bariatric patients go on to enjoy improved social and occupational opportunities, these improvements, although positive, can be quite stressful. Patients may have trouble adjusting to changes in friendships as a result of diverging activity levels or lack of acceptance of the changes brought about by the surgery. Some patients begin to notice significant marital or relational strain during this phase. This may be particularly true for those individuals who report a less positive relationship with their significant other before surgery. In addition, patients with certain personality styles may be more likely to experience marital discord after the operation (Rand, Kuldau, & Robbins, 1982). However, it has been hypothesized that the elevated divorce rates may in fact be a positive sign. It seems possible that mood and self-confidence may improve significantly enough as a result of weight loss that the patient begins to feel that he or she deserves better treatment or is willing to take a chance and leave a bad relationship.

In other cases, the patient's significant other may become fearful and anxious that their loved one will leave. In fact, there is some evidence that wives who have had bariatric surgery do find their husbands significantly less sociable and interesting (Hafner, 1991). The significant other may or may not have been supportive of the surgery in the first place and may be uncomfortable with the changes in personality brought about by the weight loss. For example, Hafner (1991) found that although husbands wished their wives were more sociable before surgery; after surgery, they wished them to be less outgoing. In these cases, the patient and his or her family would likely benefit from joint counseling to address changes in the relationship. In some cases it may be best to refer the couple for marital counseling with another therapist to avoid any appearance of an alliance with the bariatric patient. The patient should still attend individual appointments with the original mental health professional in order to continue ongoing detection and intervention.

Long-Term Maintenance

Long-term maintenance is a stage characterized by ongoing adjustment and weight normalization. At this point, the surgical team usually has only peripheral, if any, involvement in the care of the patient. The typical patient will be very pleased with his or her weight loss, yet many will be hoping for or actively working toward even greater decreases in weight. Unfortunately, many patients will experience an increase in body weight during this stage, for reasons that are not well understood. It is possible that a technical failure may be to blame; however, changes in dietary intake as patients learn what they can and cannot eat are likely largely responsible (Cook & Edwards, 1999). On average, most will regain approximately 10% of their lowest achieved weight after surgery, which can be quite distressing for some, even though surgeons usually prepare their patients for the likelihood of this event. This weight regain can be exacerbated by noncompliance with dietary or other recommendations. At this point, the newness of the surgical outcome has worn off and some patients may begin to slip back into old habits. For example, patients may start to ingest calorie-dense food items through increased liquid consumption or "grazing" patterns of eating (Brolin, Robertson, Kenler, & Cody, 1994).

Also, a significant minority of patients will become increasingly dissatisfied with their body, in particular the loose, excess skin left behind after the dramatic weight loss. Some will seriously consider plastic surgery. Another significant subset who were previously depressed, anxious, or binge eating will begin to reexperience these difficulties. Some will seek professional help, although many will try to persevere on their own. Professional interventions should target distorted patterns of thought, avoidance, or excessive checking behaviors, as well as the importance of appearance on self-esteem. It may also be helpful to focus on the non-appearance–related qualities that contribute to self-esteem as well as list aspects of appearance that the patient feels more positively or at least neutral about. It may be beneficial to incorporate self-help materials such as Cash's (1997) *The Body Image Workbook* to better target negative body image, always keeping in mind the specific issues a bariatric patient is likely to encounter.

During this stage, the mental health professional can aid these patients through continued individual therapy to address ongoing difficulties. In addition, the therapist should continue to work with the patient to sustain weight loss and improve general psychosocial functioning. Behavioral modification techniques can be used to identify and alter maladaptive dietary changes that have come about in the years since the surgery so that a premature weight plateau can be avoided. Kalarchian and Marcus (2003) argue that a "comprehensive" approach to treatment during this stage should focus on three main components: healthy eating habits, increased physical activity, and disordered eating.

An unfortunate side effect of this weight regain is a decreased level of satisfaction. Research has shown that patient satisfaction with the changes in their lives was higher at 1 year after surgery than at 7 years after surgery (van de Weijgert, Ruseler, & Elte, 1999). Patients often see their lowest weight achieved postsurgery as the benchmark of success. Anything more than that can be perceived as a failure.

Quality of life is of paramount importance and should also be a focus of interventions during this time. Although the surgical team tends to focus on weight loss and, to some extent, on *Diagnostic and Statistical Manual of Mental Disorders* comorbidities as the primary outcome measures, others have recommended that outcome also be judged on more general quality of life issues such as physical, social, and sexual satisfaction (Wolf, Falcone, Kortner, & Kuhlmann, 2000). With this in mind, the mental health professional should take a collaborative role in terms of identifying inappropriate excesses or deficits and making referrals to skilled providers such as exercise physiologists or dietitians as appropriate. Cognitive restructuring exercises and behavioral strategies to address compliance with core issues during this stage would also likely be helpful.

Last, it may also be helpful to incorporate components of traditional relapse prevention. With the aid and support of the mental health professional, the bariatric patient should be encouraged to compose a formal, written plan to prepare for potential difficulties in the future. This plan should list the recommendations and components of treatment that the patient found to be most beneficial and should also identify specific times or activities during which the patient feels most vulnerable to difficulties. The relapse prevention plan should also include a detailed plan for dealing with these vulnerable situations and a list of warning signs that serve to forewarn the individual that difficulties may lay ahead. The patient should also include all relevant materials received over the course of recovery from the surgical team, dietitian, or other treating providers so that this important information can easily be accessed if the person begins to experience difficulties.

Summary

Research continues to support bariatric surgery as the most effective means of weight loss for obese individuals. As a result, variants of weight loss surgery are becoming more and more commonplace across the world, with surgeons taking up subspecialties in this area. However, the surgery is not without its limitations. The expansion of the bariatric field is occurring at such a rate that empirical evidence is not always available to guide supportive and specialty interventions. Not only are surgeons unsure about what steps should be taken with patients who experience psychological difficulties unrelated to the technical aspects of the procedure, but mental health professionals are often unaware of what approach is best.

Up to this point, the role of the mental health professional has been limited in scope, typically confined to a cursory presurgical evaluation. Yet, as this chapter demonstrates, mental health professionals have much to offer in terms of the ongoing adjustment of bariatric patients to physical and psychosocial changes as well as maintenance of weight loss. Behavioral and cognitive-behavioral interventions in particular seem to be ideally suited to this population and the common presenting concerns. These approaches also suggest that in addition to weight loss, there may be equally important outcome variables such as psychosocial and physical functioning when determining the success of bariatric surgery.

Ideally, the mental health professional should be an integral part of the surgical treatment team. As more general surgeons take up bariatric practices, patients are often referred to mental health professionals in the community for both assessment and treatment needs. This is not optimum. Communication between the mental health professional and surgeon is impaired by the physical distance and possibly by different perceptions and beliefs. Follow-up is also complicated with this arrangement. Although this setup can work for those surgeons who do not have ready access to a mental health team member, it may be beneficial to work primarily with one or two professionals who can become very familiar with the unique needs and commonly encountered difficulties of the bariatric population. Patient care will likely be notably improved with the incorporation of a mental health professional on the surgical team.

No matter if the therapist is a member of the surgical team or not, the mental health professional should take a supportive, nonjudgmental approach to the identification and treatment of each patient's individual concerns. Careful consideration and attention should also be given to ongoing communication with the remainder of the surgical team. Common difficulties include reemergence of mood disorders, binge eating disorder, and weight regain. With appropriate treatment, research suggests that all of these problems may be avoided or minimized with improved quality of life.

References

Algazi, L. P (2000). Transactions in a support group meeting: A case study. *Obesity Surgery, 10*, 186–191.

Benotti, P. N., & Forse, R. A. (1995). The role of gastric surgery in the multidisciplinary management of severe obesity. The *American Journal of Surgery, 169*, 361–367.

Berman, W. H., Raynes Berman, E., Heymsfield, S., Fauci, M., & Ackerman, S. (1993). The effect of psychiatric disorders on weight loss in obesity clinic patients. *Behavioral Medicine, 18*, 167–172.

Brolin, R. E., Robertson, L. B., Kenler, H. A., & Cody, R. P. (1994). Weight loss and dietary intake after vertical banded gastroplasty and Roux-en-Y gastric bypass. *Annals of Surgery, 220*, 782–790.

Caniato, D., & Skorjanec, B. (2002). The role of brief strategic therapy on the outcome of gastric banding. *Obesity Surgery, 12*, 666–671.

Cash, T. F. (1997). *The body image workbook: An 8-step program for learning to like your looks.* Oakland, CA: New Harbinger Publications, Inc.

Cook, C. M., & Edwards, C. E. (1999). Success habits of long-term gastric bypass patients. *Obesity Surgery, 9*, 80–82.

Delin, C. R., & Watts, J. (1995). Success in surgical intervention for morbid obesity: Is weight loss enough? *Obesity Surgery, 5*, 189–191.

Hafner, R. J. (1991). Morbid obesity: Effects on the marital system of weight loss after gastric restriction. *Psychotherapy Psychosomatics, 56*, 162–166.

Hall, J. C., Watts, J. M., O'Brien, P. E., Dunstan, R. E., Walsh, J. F., Slavotinek, A. H., et al. (1990). Gastric surgery for morbid obesity. The Adelaide Study. *Annals of Surgery, 211*, 419–427.

Halmi, K. A., Long, M., Stunkard, A. J., & Mason, E. (1980). Psychiatric diagnosis of morbidly obese gastric bypass patients. *American Journal of Psychiatry, 137*, 470–471.

Halverson, J. D., & Koehler, R. E. (1981). Gastric bypass: Analysis of weight loss and factors determining success. *Surgery* 90:, 446–455.

Hildebrandt, S. E. (1998). Effects of participation in bariatric support group after Roux-en-Y gastric bypass. *Obesity Surgery, 8*, 535–542.

Horchner, R., & Tuinebreijer, W. (1999). Preoperative preparatory program has no effect on morbidly obese patients undergoing a Lap-Band operation. *Obesity Surgery, 9,* 250–257.

Hsu, L. K., Benotti, P. N., Roberts, S. B., Saltzman, E., Shikory, S., Rolls, B. J., et al. (1998). Nonsurgical factors that influence the outcome of bariatric surgery: a review. *Psychosomatic Medicine, 60,* 338–346.

Hsu, L. K. G., Betancourt, S., & Sullivan, S. P. (1996). Eating disturbances before and after vertical banded gastroplasty: A pilot study. *International Journal of Eating Disorders, 19,* 23–34.

Hsu, L. K. G., Sullivan, S. P., & Benotti, P. N. (1997). Eating disturbances and outcome of gastric bypass surgery: A pilot study. *International Journal of Eating Disorders, 21,* 385–390.

Kalarchian, M. A., & Marcus, M. D. (2003). Management of the bariatric surgery patient: Is there a role for the cognitive behavior therapist? *Cognitive & Behavioral Practice, 10,* 112–119.

Kalarchian, M. A., Marcus, M. D., Wilson, G. T., Labouvie, E., Brolin, R. E., & La Marca, L. (2000). Binge eating among gastric bypass patients at long-term follow-up. *Obesity Surgery, 12,* 270–275.

Kinzel, J. F., Trefalt, E., Fiala, M., & Biebl, W. (2002). Psychotherapeutic treatment of morbidly obese patients after gastric banding. *Obesity Surgery, 12,* 292–294.

Marcus, J. D., & Elkins, G. R. (2004). Development of a model for a structured support group for patients following bariatric surgery. Obesity Surgery, 14, 103–106.

Marcus, M. D., Wing, R. R., & Fairburn, C. G. (1995). Cognitive treatment of binge eating versus behavioral weight control in the treatment of binge eating disorder. *Annals of Behavior Medicine, 17,* S090.

Miller, W. R., & Rollnick, S. (1991). *Motivational interviewing: Preparing people to change addictive behavior.* New York: The Guilford Press.

Nicolai, A., Ippoliti, C., & Petrelli, M. D. (2002). Laparoscopic adjustable gastric banding: Essential role of psychological support. *Obesity Surgery, 12,* 857–863.

Peterson, C. B., Mitchell, J. E., Engbloom, S., Nugent, S., Mussell, M. P., Crow, S. J., et al. (1998). Binge eating disorder with and without a history of purging symptoms. *International Journal of Eating Disorders, 24,* 251–257.

Pories, W. J., & MacDonald, K. G. (1993). The surgical treatment of morbid obesity. *Current Opinions in General Surgery,* 195–202.

Powers, P. S., Rosemurgy, A. S., Coovert, D. L., & Boyd, F. R. (1988). Psychosocial sequelae of bariatric surgery: A pilot study. *Psychosomatics, 29,* 283–288.

Rand, C. S., Kuldau, J. M., & Robbins, L. (1982). Surgery for obesity and marriage quality. *Journal of the American Medical Association, 24,* 1419–1422.

Ruegg, R., & Frances, A. (1995). New research in personality disorders. *Journal of Personality Disorders, 9,* 1–48.

Saunders, R. (2001). Compulsive eating and gastric bypass surgery: What does hunger have to do with it? *Obesity Surgery, 11,* 757–761.

Sugerman, H. J., Starkey, J. V., & Birkenhauer, R. (1987). A randomized prospective trial of gastric bypass versus vertical banded gastroplasty for morbid obesity and their effects on sweets versus non-sweets eaters. *Annals of Surgery, 205,* 613–624.

Telch, C. F., & Agras, W. S. (1994). Obesity, binge eating, and psychopathology. *International Journal of Eating Disorders, 15,* 53–62.

Telch, C. F., Agras, W. S., Rossiter, E. M., Wilfley, D., & Kenardy, J. (1990). Group cognitive-behavioral treatment for the nonpurging bulimic: An initial evaluation. *Journal of Consulting and Clinical Psychology, 58,* 629–635.

Tucker, J. A., Samo, J. A., Rand, C. S. W., & Woodward, E. R. (1991). Behavioral interventions to promote adaptive eating behavior and lifestyle changes following surgery for obesity: Results of a 2-year outcome evaluation. *International Journal of Eating Disorders, 10,* 689–698.

Valley, V., & Grace, D. M. (1987). Psychosocial risk factors in gastric surgery for obesity: Identifying guidelines for screening. *International Journal of Obesity, 11,* 105–113.

Van de Weijgert, E. J. H. M., Ruseler, C. H., & Elte, J. W. F. (1999). Long-term follow-up after gastric surgery for morbid obesity: Preoperative weight loss improves the long-term control of morbid obesity after vertical banded gastroplasty. *Obesity Surgery, 9,* 426–432.

Wilfley, D. E., Agras, W. S., Telch, C. F., Rossiter, E. M., Schneider, J. A., Cole, A. G., et al., (1993). Group cognitive-behavioral therapy and group interpersonal psychotherapy for the non-purging bulimic individual: A controlled comparison. *Journal of Consulting and Clinical Psychology, 61,* 296–305.

Wolf, A. M., Falcone, A. R., Kortner, B., & Kuhlmann, H. W. (2000). BAROS: An effective system to evaluate the results of patients after bariatric surgery. *10,* 445–450.

CHAPTER 9

Surgical Revisions and Surgery with Adolescents

ANITA P. COURCOULAS, MELISSA A. KALARCHIAN,
AND MARSHA D. MARCUS

The purpose of this chapter is to review two special topics in bariatric surgery: revisionary surgery for obesity and the role of bariatric surgery for children and adolescents. Both revision patients and children are special surgical populations that have been the subject of increasing attention and interest with the increase in severe obesity and growth of bariatric surgery. With the increasing prevalence of obesity in the United States and worldwide, and the increasing number of patients undergoing gastric surgery for severe obesity, a substantial number of patients will be considered for second and possibly even third revisionary surgical procedures for the treatment of obesity and its complications. The entire spectrum of revisionary surgery will be covered in this chapter, including indications to reoperate, the presurgical workup—including psychological assessment, surgical procedural options, and results and complications after surgery. In addition, with obesity as the most common nutritional disorder among children and adolescents (Dietz, 1998), the role of surgery among severely obese children and adolescents will be addressed in some detail. Much of the interest in surgery for young patients is attributable to the increase in severe obesity and the development of complications such as diabetes and hypertension, which were rarely seen in children in the past. Offering surgical options for weight loss to adolescents is a slowly growing and still controversial area in bariatric surgery.

Revisionary Bariatric Surgery

Revisionary bariatric surgery is a growing field owing to the increasing incidence of initial obesity surgery procedures. Both the indications and safety and efficacy of these "redo" procedures remain controversial (Benotti & Forse, 1996). The true incidence of revisionary procedures is not well documented. What is known from the available published data is that the incidence of secondary procedures performed varies with the type of initial procedure. Many (25% or more) of those patients who underwent an initial jejunoileal bypass (JIB) come to revision, mostly for metabolic and nutritional problems. Approximately 5% to 13% of bilio-pancreatic diversion and other severely malabsorptive procedures will come to revision also mostly for metabolic reasons. Of those patients who have undergone vertical banded gastroplasty (VBG), up to 36% or more will require some type of revision, and of those undergoing Roux-en-Y gastric bypass (RYGB), between 5% and 23% will come to revisionary surgery (Benotti & Forse, 1996; MacLean, Rhode, & Forse, 1990). As yet undetermined numbers of laparoscopic band patients may seek removal and conversion to another procedure because of failure to achieve adequate weight loss or problems requiring band removal. In one recent series, the overall need for band removal and revision because of these listed causes exceeded 50% (DeMaria, 2001).

There are two broad indications for revisionary obesity procedures: inadequate weight loss and complications or side effects as a result of the initial surgery (Table 9.1). In most series, the most common indication for reoperative bariatric surgery is failure to lose and maintain adequate weight loss (Behrns, Smith, Kelly, & Sarr, 1993; Benotti & Forse, 1996; Courcoulas, del Pino, Udekwu, Raftopoulos, & Luketich, 2004). Among those patients with inadequate weight loss, some had good initial weight loss in the first 18 months after the primary operation and then slowly regained a significant percent of weight, whereas others never lost the initial expected 60% to 80% of their excess body weight. This group of patients is also remarkably heterogeneous with respect to their anatomy at the time of revision. Many have disrupted staple lines with gastro-gastric fistulae, whereas others have major gastric pouch enlargement. On the other end of the spectrum, poor pouch emptying from stomal stenosis may lead patients to increase the consumption of high-calorie soft "snack" foods that pass through a small pouch and opening relatively easily, but which leads to weight gain. Some laparoscopic banding patients can

TABLE 9.1 Indications for Revisionary Surgery

Inadequate weight loss:
- Staple line disruption
- Major pouch enlargement
- Stomal enlargement
- Laparoscopic band slippage
- Inadequate weight loss with intact surgical anatomy

Complications or side effects from initial surgery:
- Gastric outlet stenosis or obstruction
- Refractory gastroesophageal reflux
- Nonhealing marginal (stomal) ulceration
- Refractory dumping syndrome
- Metabolic complications
- Protein–calorie malnutrition

experience band slippage and inadequate weight loss, and many other patients seeking secondary surgery can present with intact anatomy from the first operation. Side effects or complications from the original surgery can also lead to the need for revision. These problems include gastric outlet stenosis or frank obstruction, refractory gastroesophageal reflux, nonhealing stomal ulceration, or refractory symptomatic dumping syndrome. Protein–calorie malnutrition and other metabolic complications are also disabling side effects of the more malabsorptive procedures that can require further surgery.

The completion of an algorithm to evaluate a presurgical patient either seeking or referred for revisionary surgery is the most important part of the decision-making process toward a potential second surgery. There are three main contributing factors to this algorithm: the surgical details of the original procedure and the delineation of the remaining anatomy, the current and historical lifestyle adaptations, and the contributing psychological factors. It is essential to define the history of postsurgical weight loss, define current eating and exercise behaviors, identify possible psychological contributing factors and previously undiagnosed eating disorders, and define the surgical anatomy and patient risk profile. The suggested detailed presurgical workup is presented in Table 9.2. Possible predictors of successful secondary surgery and a guide to selecting the best possible candidates for revisionary surgery will be addressed at the conclusion of this section.

The surgical approaches to revisionary surgery vary by initial procedure and the technical details are beyond the scope of this text, so we will simply summarize the approach by procedure. Patients with a history of

TABLE 9.2 Presurgical Assessment for Revisionary Surgery

Postsurgical weight loss history:
- 6, 12, and 18 months
- Time and rate of weight regain
- Assess changes in food variety (e.g., liquid calories, soft snacks)
- Ability to tolerate meats and breads?

Gastrointestinal review of systems:
- Symptoms of nausea, vomiting, diarrhea, and constipation

Complete nutritional and activity evaluation:
- Weekly food logs
- Frequency of high-calorie liquids and soft snacks
- Exercise patterns, regularity, and frequency

Psychological evaluation and assessment:
- Binge eating disorder, night eating syndrome
- Clinical depression or anxiety
- Substance abuse or addiction
- Major, recent life stressors
- Social support

Define surgical anatomy with upper gastrointestinal series, upper endoscopy, and review of operative notes:
- Estimated gastric pouch size
- Staple line integrity
- Outlet caliber between pouch and intestine
- Length of common channel, bypass

Assess patient's surgical risk:
- Age
- Body mass index (BMI)
- Comorbid medical conditions
- Blood chemistries, stress test, etc.

JIB usually present with symptoms of severe diarrhea, cramping, foul-smelling stools, polyarthropathy, and even liver and renal failure. All symptomatic and most asymptomatic patients should undergo JIB take-down with ultimate conversion to a procedure with a restrictive component such as a RYGB, in two stages, to allow for the adaptation of the formerly bypassed long segment of small intestine. Most metabolic complications can be remediated by this approach, but some patients are dissatisfied with their resultant lifestyle because of the marked, forced change in eating habits induced by the restrictive component of the revisionary procedure. Extremely malabsorptive procedures such as biliopancreatic diversion are most often revised secondary to protein–calorie malnutrition and diarrhea, and the conversion procedure of choice is to lengthen the common channel for better nutrient absorption or limb lengthening with additional gastric pouch restriction. Experience gained from the failure of some laparoscopic band placements include problems with band erosion, slippage, infection, and cuff leakage. Most, if not all, band failures are treated with removal and conversion to a gastric bypass. Previous gastric bypass (RYGB) procedures can be revised if there is a staple line disruption causing pouch enlargement with gastro-gastric fistula; narrowing or obstruction of the gastrojejunal opening causing vomiting, reflux, or malnutrition, and diarrhea and malabsorption from a short common channel; or a short Roux limb contributing to poor weight loss. Each of these technical problems can by addressed by specific procedural approaches.

Because of the evolution of surgical therapy for obesity, many operative procedures have been performed and then abandoned due to high failure rates and complications. One of the most common secondary procedures encountered in clinical practice is revision of the now outdated VBG. Problems encountered with the VBG are major pouch enlargement, because the gastric pouch is quite distensible; staple line failures resulting in pouch disruption; outlet stenosis; and refractory reflux. Most of these patients will undergo conversion to a RYGB with the resulting pouch restriction, dumping, and malabsorptive components.

Assessing the results of revisionary surgery is difficult because much of the literature summarizes a population of heterogeneous patients with different indications for operation, variable procedures, and results at variable time points. In our recent work, we found preoperative upper gastrointestinal studies to be helpful in predicting successful revision of VBG to gastric bypass (Courcoulas et al., 2005). In a group of 43 patients who underwent revisionary surgery, the findings of an abnormal upper gastrointestinal x-ray (staple line failure, pouch enlargement, reflux, or stricture) predicted successful weight loss outcome in 94% of patients. In recent work by others (Cordera, Mai, Thompson, & Sarr, 2004), 54 patients followed for nearly 7 years showed safe and effective conversion of VBG to RYGB with sustained weight loss, improved quality of life, reversal of medical problems, and high patient satisfaction. In the Benotti and Forse study (1996), 63 patients underwent conversion to RYGB from variable primary procedures with no mortalities, a 41% morbidity rate, and a 16% serious complication rate. In this group, the patients who were originally superobese, with body mass indexes greater than 50, experienced significantly overall better weight loss than their lighter counterparts after secondary surgery. Weight loss results after revisionary surgery are variable at around 50% excess weight loss (Linner & Drew, 1992; Yale, 1989). In most of these case series, the secondary surgery patients experienced less excess weight loss than successful primary surgery subjects (60%–80% excess). One hypothesis for this discrepancy is that the physiologic changes from the second surgery are not as dramatic, or that revisionary candidates are less ideal patients for lifestyle modification following the onset of the "tool" of bariatric surgery. These ideas and others warrant further in-depth metabolic and behavioral studies of revisionary surgical patients.

The complications from secondary surgery include all those known for primary surgery as well as some others. In almost all cases, a revisionary procedure is a longer and more technically complicated and challenging operation that leads to higher morbidity and even higher mortality than initial operations. Several case series report morbidity and mortality rates as high as 50% and 13%, respectively (Cates et al., 1990; Linner & Drew, 1992; Schwarz, Strodel, Simpson, & Griffen, 1988). Most surgeons experience and quote a lower mortality rate of 1% to 2% and a serious complication rate of approximately 5% to 17%—rates that are two times higher than initial surgery risks. Secondary surgery results in many more surgical adhesions (scar tissue), because most procedures being revised today follow primary open surgery. In addition, the blood supply to the gastric pouch is frequently disrupted in some way from the first procedure, which can lead to a problem with healing, leakage, and serious infection. Operative times are prolonged because of the surgical complexity and adhesions that predispose patients to deep venous thrombosis and possible life-threatening pulmonary emboli. Both intestinal leakage and pulmonary emboli are the most serious, life-threatening complications encountered after obesity surgery and occur more frequently after revisionary surgery. Failure to lose adequate weight after a second surgery, if defined as failure to lose 50% excess weight, is also possible in as many as 35% of revisionary patients (Benotti & Forse, 1996).

It is clear that these are procedures with significantly elevated surgical risks and somewhat less favorable weight loss benefits. Nevertheless, they should be considered in well-informed, good-risk patients with anatomic abnormalities or complications from initial surgery. Proper patient selection may be the most important determining factor at the time of revisionary surgery. From limited experience and available literature, several possible predictors of a successful, long-term revisionary surgical outcome can be proposed. These include adequate weight loss at the time of initial surgery, identification of an anatomic abnormality that is correctable by a second surgery, the lack of an eating disorder syndrome, the presence of psychological and behavioral support systems, and a history of successful lifestyle modification. Candidates for revisionary surgery should be made aware that recurrent, refractory pathologic eating behaviors are a major contributing factor to weight loss failure after all bariatric surgical procedures and are especially disabling in those patients without structural or anatomic problems such as staple line failures or pouch or stomal enlargement (Benotti & Forse, 1996). For these patients, a behavioral and psychological support and education program should be in place prior to the revisionary surgery.

Bariatric Surgery for Adolescents

Obesity is the most prevalent nutritional disease of children and adolescents in the United States today (Dietz, 1998). Approximately 11% of adolescents in the United States are obese. The most marked increase in obesity prevalence has occurred among children (Troiano & Flegal, 1998). Significant obesity-related comorbidities such as diabetes, hypertension, the metabolic syndrome, and others are now occurring in obese children and adolescents (Weiss et al., 2004). There is persistence of obesity into adulthood with nearly 80% of severely obese children becoming obese adults with the resultant long-term medical and psychosocial consequences. This section of the special topics chapter will provide a detailed overview of the topic of bariatric surgery for adolescents with particular focus on the presurgical workup, options for surgical intervention, and future directions in this controversial area.

Children or adolescents with a body mass index greater than the 95th percentile for children of the same age and gender should be considered obese. The term *adolescent* refers to a child between 12 and 17 years and the terms *children* and *adolescents* will be used interchangeably.

The etiology of childhood obesity is multifactorial. There is strong evidence implicating genetic, biological, behavioral, and environmental influences as causal factors. The estimates of the heritability of relative weight range from 35% to 75%. If genes set biological limits for metabolism and other weight-related mechanisms, behavior and environment influence variation within these limits. The increasing prevalence of obesity in the United States is widely attributed to a decrease in physical activity and increased sedentary activities, along with increased caloric and fat intake. Social factors and childhood adversity may also play a role as contributing factors to obesity as neglected children are more likely to become obese as adults (Lissau & Sorenson, 1994; Williamson, Thompson, Anda, Deitz, & Felitti, 2002). Among adults seeking obesity surgery, there is a fourfold increased prevalence of a history of childhood sexual abuse (Ray, Nickels, Sayeed, & Sax 2003).

The profound consequences of childhood and adolescent obesity can be categorized into those that have immediate implications in children and those with long-term effects into adulthood (Yanovski, 2001). Table 9.3 shows the adverse psychological, socioeconomic, and health effects of childhood obesity. No organ system is unaffected by childhood obesity, and the persistence of obesity into adulthood is among the most serious consequences of pediatric obesity.

TABLE 9.3 Consequences and Risks of Pediatric Obesity

Psychosocial:
- Adverse effects on socialization
- Effects of discrimination
- Lower self-esteem

Socioeconomic:
- Negative effect on later socioeconomic status
- Fewer years of advanced education completed
- Lower rates of marriage in women
- Higher rates of poverty in women

Adverse health effects:
- Orthopedic
- Cardiovascular
  - Hypertension
  - Later atherosclerosis
- Gastroenterologic
  - Fatty liver disease
  - Gallstone disease
- Endocrine and metabolic
  - Insulin resistance
  - Diabetes
  - Polycystic ovary syndrome
  - Dyslipidemia
  - Diminished growth hormone secretion
- Pulmonary
  - Asthma
  - Sleep disordered breathing
  - Sleep apnea
- Neurological
  - Pseudotumor cerebri

Persistence of childhood obesity into adulthood

Early mortality

In the adult population, there are three main forms of treatment for obesity: behavioral, pharmacologic, and surgical, but among children behavioral therapy has been the cornerstone of treatment programs because the role for pharmacology is limited and the results of surgery are being evaluated. Family-based behavioral treatment programs that include moderate caloric restriction and promotion of physical activity have been found to have a favorable impact on children's weight in highly motivated populations (Epstein, Roemmich, & Raynor, 2001; Yanovski, 2001). Outside of clinical trials, there are no pharmacologic agents approved for use in patients younger than 16 years of age (Yanovski & Yanovski, 2002). Medications that are currently undergoing pediatric clinical trials include orlistat, sibutramine, and metformin. Surgical options are restricted to severely overweight adolescents, in the absence of endocrine disorders, who have achieved puberty and growth landmarks and who have failed more conservative therapy. The rationale for considering surgical options for adolescents rests on the success of such therapy in adults with excellent long-term weight loss results, reversal of medical complications, low morbidity and mortality, and improved quality of life (Higa, Ho, & Boone, 2001). Furthermore, bariatric surgery is increasingly being performed on adolescents with clinically severe obesity and recent experience suggests that it is both safe and effective (Garcia, Langford, & Inge, 2003; Strauss, Bradley, & Brolin, 2001).

The history of the surgical treatment of morbid obesity in children and adolescents dates back to the 1970s, when surgeons used jejunoileal bypass in four morbidly obese teenagers (Randolph & Weintraub, 1974). The surgery group from Iowa (Anderson, Soper, & Scott, 1980; Soper, Mason, Printen, & Zellweger, 1975) then followed with a report of 25 and updated it with 41 young patients who were successfully treated by gastric bypass or gastroplasty. They did note significantly less weight loss in the small subset of these patients with Prader-Willi syndrome. A Swiss group reported a case series of three patients with Prader-Willi syndrome, characterized by compulsive hyperphagia, treated with biliopancreatic diversion with some modest effect on weight loss that allowed for the lifting of coercive dietary measures otherwise required for nonsurgical treatment (Laurent-Jaccard, Hofstetter, Saegesser, & Chapuis, 1991). Greenstein and Rabner (1995) treated 18 morbidly obese patients younger than 21 years of age with VBG and found acceptable weight loss results when accompanied by intensive dietary counseling and increased exercise activity. An intragastric balloon was placed in five adolescents with morbid obesity with resulting temporary weight loss in the first 3 months followed by weight regain, leading the authors to conclude that intragastric balloons are not indicated in the treatment of severe obesity (Vandenplas, Bollen, Delanghe, Vandemaele, & De Schepper, 1998).

Patient selection for bariatric surgery is critical to the success of the procedure and the long-term outcomes. This selection becomes even more important in the adolescent population because an operation will dramatically and permanently change the gastrointestinal anatomy and lifestyle habits at an early age. Behavior modification, dietary changes, lifestyle modifications, and supplement compliance are necessary for long-term safety and weight loss success with this "tool" for weight management. For these reasons and some others, the presurgical evaluation and education for bariatric surgery in children must be extensive. This includes a detailed assessment of height, weight, dietary history, physical activity, and family interactions. Surgically related psychological assessments are aimed at diagnosing and treating underlying depression and other psychiatric and psychosocial symptoms such as low self-esteem. A thorough evaluation for eating disorders including binge eating and purging should be obtained along with an assessment of readiness for change. Psychological readiness may predict better short- and long-term outcomes, whereas binge eating may be associated with poorer long-term weight loss and other outcomes (Kalarchian & Marcus, 2004). There are no other well-characterized or definitive screening criteria to identify prospective "ideal" pediatric candidates for surgery at this time.

Both endocrine disorders and genetic syndromes should be considered and excluded in the differential diagnosis (Table 9.4) (Yanovski, 2001). Medical treatment of associated comorbid conditions such as diabetes, hypertension, and sleep apnea should be optimized.

The preoperative education program should be multidisciplinary, well-structured, and geared to both the patient and the patient's family. Family-based behavioral intervention after surgery is a necessary adjunct

---

TABLE 9.4 Endocrine and Genetic Syndromes

Endocrine Disorders:
- Cushing syndrome
- Hypothyroidism
- Hyperinsulinemia (Beckwith Widemann syndrome)
- Growth hormone deficiency
- Leptin deficiency or resistance

Genetic Syndromes:
- Turner syndrome—1 in 2,500 live births
- Prader-Willi syndrome—1 in 25,000 live births
- Other genetic multisystem syndromes—much less prevalent

to the treatment of obesity with surgery. In this educational process, the application of the principles of adolescent growth, development and compliance is essential to avoid adverse outcomes after surgery (Garcia et al., 2003). Bariatric surgery should be part of a multidisciplinary approach in the care of the adolescent patient that includes a nutritionist, anesthesiologist, psychologist or psychiatrist, internist or pediatrician, and surgeon— all of whom are dedicated to the care of young patients in a specialized and experienced program setting.

There are no formally established guidelines for the application of bariatric surgical procedures in adolescents (Inge et al., 2004). No long-term prospective studies or outcome analyses of bariatric surgery in the adolescent population exist. Nevertheless, data are evolving from the adult experience and case series of selected adolescent patients that support the consideration of several bariatric operations in selected adolescents in the setting of an experienced surgical weight loss program. Surgical options include laparoscopic banding, laparoscopic and open gastric bypass, and possibly biliopancreatic diversion in Prader-Willi syndrome patients (Dolan, Creighton, Hopkins, & Fielding, 2003; Garcia et al., 2003; Marinari, 2001; Strauss et al., 2001). Laparoscopic banding has been performed in small groups of younger patients with very low complication rates and nearly 60% excess weight loss results at 2-year follow-up (Dolan et al., 2003). It appears to be safe and effective in the short term, and is appealing because of the ease of placement, adjustability, and lack of intestinal restructuring. It is not clear what the long-term consequences and weight loss will show. More long-term, prospective studies are first needed in adults and then children to determine the equivalent safety and efficacy of the band to the bypass.

Gastric bypass has so far proven to be safe and effective in small series of pediatric patients with low morbidity, no mortality, and few unanticipated side effects (Garcia et al., 2003; Strauss et al., 2001). The excellent results with gastric bypass in adults argue for its preferential use in the younger population, but more long-term prospective trials are needed. The potential for serious nutritional deficiencies with the more malabsorptive procedures may argue against their use in younger patients, but there may be a role for biliopancreatic diversion in Prader-Willi syndrome patients (Laurent-Jaccard et al., 1991; Marinari, 2001).

The complications of the surgical treatment of obesity in children include the same short- and long-term problems seen in adults. Early complications include bowel obstruction, bleeding, blood clots, and persistent nausea. Late problems can be experienced, such as gallstones, hernias, vitamin and iron deficiencies, and weight loss failures. To date, in the small series published, there have not been any unanticipated side effects after surgery that are specific to adolescents (Strauss et al., 2001).

The role of bariatric surgery in adolescents is growing slowly, but is still controversial. Those who argue against surgery as an option for children express concerns for growth and development and long-term physiological consequences, and changes including dumping, anemia, vitamin and mineral deficiencies, and possible poor compliance with necessary supplementation. There are issues of compliance with diet and exercise instruction and lifelong lifestyle modification that are necessary for long-term success after surgery. There are concerns about any possible effect on future procreation and issues of proper informed, surgical consent that should involve both parents and patient. Many of these concerns can be addressed by proper patient- and family-centered education along with lifelong medical and nutritional surveillance in the setting of a multidisciplinary surgical weight loss program.

The arguments that support surgery as an alternative for treating severe obesity in children center on the growing, serious health consequences of obesity in childhood. These include diabetes, hypertension, early cardiovascular disease, sleep apnea, fatty liver disease, and many other serious medical conditions that are being recognized with increasing frequency in the younger population. The persistence of these problems along with severe obesity into adulthood increases the disease burden and eventual mortality (Must et al., 1999; Stevens et al., 1998). The outcomes with gastric bypass in the United States have established it as the gold standard procedure for sustained surgically induced weight loss and medical problem amelioration in adults with concomitant low mortality and morbidity (Higa, Boone, & Ho, 2000). There is evolving evidence and promise that this adult surgical experience can be replicated in carefully selected younger patients. In addition, the development of the laparoscopic approach to surgery along with overall improved safety of surgery allows for the extension of surgical treatment to severely obese adolescents.

Summary

Bariatric surgery remains a viable last resort option for a selected number of severely obese adolescents for whom other comprehensive, family-based dietary and behavioral approaches to weight loss have been unsuccessful. Future directions indicate the need for long-term, prospective outcome analyses of bariatric surgery in younger patients. The importance of family support as an adjunct to surgery in the context of a family-based behavioral weight control program should not be underestimated. As with the adult population, the surgical program should be part of a multidisciplinary approach to the care of the adolescent patient. Lifelong medical and nutritional surveillance after surgery are required, especially during later pregnancy. Obesity surgery should not be undertaken without a long-term commitment on the part of the patients, parents, and physicians.

References

Anderson, A. E., Soper, R. T., & Scott, D. H. (1980). Gastric bypass for morbid obesity in children and adolescents. *Journal of Pediatric Surgery, 15,* 876–881.

Behrns, K. E., Smith, C. D., Kelly, K. A., & Sarr, M. G. (1993). Reoperative bariatric surgery: Lessons learned to improve patient selection and results. *Annals of Surgery, 218,* 646–653.

Benotti, P. N., & Forse, R. A. (1996). Safety and long-term efficacy of revisional surgery in severe obesity. *The American Journal of Surgery, 172,* 232–235.

Cates, J. A., Drenick, E. J., Abedin, M. Z., Doty, J. E., Saunders, K. D., & Roslyn, J. J. (1990). Reoperative surgery for the morbidly obese. *Archives of Surgery, 125,* 1400–1404.

Cordera, F., Mai, J. L., Thompson, G. B., & Sarr, M. G. (2004). Unsatisfactory weight loss after vertical banded gastroplasty: Is conversion to Roux-en-Y gastric bypass successful? *Central Surgical Association;* in press.

Courcoulas, A. P., del Pino, D. M., Udekwu, A. O., Raftopoulos, I. S., & Luketich, J. D. (2005). Upper gastrointestinal contrast studies predict outcome after revision of vertical banded gastroplasty to gastric bypass. *Surgery for Obesity and Related Diseases;* in review.

Dietz, W. H. (1998). Health consequences of obesity in youth: Childhood predictors of adult disease. *Pediatrics,* 1101, 518–525.

Dolan, K., Creighton, L., Hopkins, G., & Fielding, G. (2003). Laparoscopic gastric banding in morbidly obese adolescents. *Obesity Surgery, 13,* 101–104.

Epstein, L. H., Roemmich, J. N., & Raynor, H. A. (2001). Behavioral therapy in the treatment of pediatric obesity. *Pediatric Clinics of North America, 48,* 981–993.

Garcia, V. F., Langford, L., & Inge, T. H. (2003). Application of laparoscopy for bariatric surgery in adolescents. *Current Opinion in Pediatrics, 15,* 248–255.

Greenstein, R. J., & Rabner, J. G. (1995). Is adolescent gastric-restrictive antiobesity surgery warranted? *Obesity Surgery, 5,* 138–144.

Higa, K. D., Boone, K. B., & Ho, T. (2000). Complications of the laparoscopic Roux-en-Y gastric bypass: 1,040 patients—What have we learned? *Obesity Surgery, 10,* 509–513.

Higa, K. D., Ho, T., Boone, K. B. (2001). Laparoscopic Roux-en-Y gastric bypass: Technique and 3-year follow-up. *Journal of Laparoendoscopic & Advanced Surgical Techniques,* 11:377–382.

Inge, T. H., Krebs, N. F., Garcia, V. F., Skelton, J. A., Guice, K. S., Strauss, R. S., et al. (2004). Bariatric surgery for severely overweight adolescents: concerns and recommendations. *Pediatrics,* 114, 217–223.

Kalarchian, M. A., & Marcus, M. D. (in press). Management of the bariatric surgery patient: Is there a role for the cognitive behavior therapist? *Cognitive and Behavioral Practice.*

Laurent-Jaccard, A. L., Hofstetter, J. R., Saegesser, F., & Chapuis, G. (1991). Long-term results of treatment of Prader-Willi syndrome by Scopinaro's biliopancreatic diversion. Study of three cases and the effect of dextrofenfluramine on the postoperative evolution. *Obesity Surgery, 1,* 83–87.

Linner, J. H., & Drew, R. L. (1992). Reoperative surgery—indications, efficacy, and long-term follow-up. *American Journal of Clinical Nutrition, 55,* 606S–610S.

Lissau, I., & Sorenson, T. (1994). Parental neglect during childhood and increased risk of obesity in young adulthood. *Lancet, 343,* 324–327.

MacLean, L. D., Rhode, B. M., & Forse, R. A. (1990). Late results of vertical banded gastroplasty for morbid and super obesity. *Surgery, 107,* 20–27.

Marinari, G. M. (2001). Outcome of biliopancreatic diversion in subjects with Prader-Willi syndrome. *Obesity Surgery, 11,* 491–495.

Must, A., Spadano, J., Coakley, E. H., Field, A. E., Colditz, G., Dietz, W. H. (1999). The disease burden associated with overweight and obesity. *Journal of the American Medical Association, 282,* 1523–1529.

Ray, E., Nickels, M., Sayeed, S., & Sax, H. (2003). Predicting success after gastric bypass: The role of psychosocial and behavioral factors. *Surgery, 134,* 555–564.

Stevens, J., Cai, J., Pamuk, E. R., Williamson, D. F., Thun, M. J., & Wood, J. L. (1998). The effect of age on the association between body mass index and mortality. *The New England Journal of Medicine, 338,* 1–7.

Strauss, R. S., Bradley, L. J., & Brolin, R. E. (2001). Gastric bypass surgery in adolescents with morbid obesity. *The Journal of Pediatrics, 138,* 499–504.

Troiano, R. P., & Flegal, K. M. (1998). Overweight children and adolescents: Description, epidemiology, and demographics. *Pediatrics, 101,* 497–504.

Vandenplas, Y., Bollen, B., Delanghe, K., Vandemaele, K., & De Schepper, J. (1998). Intragastric balloons for morbid obesity in adolescents. *Journal of Pediatric Gastroenterology and Nutrition, 26,* 598.

Weiss, R., Dziura, J., Burgert, T. S., Tamborlane, W. V., Taksali, S. E., Yeckel, C. W., et al. (2004). Obesity and the metabolic syndrome in children and adolescents. *The New England Journal of Medicine, 350,* 2362–2374.

Williamson, D., Thompson, T., Anda, R., Deitz, W., & Felitti, V. (2002). Body weight and obesity in adults and self-reported abuse in childhood. *International Journal of Obesity, 26,* 1075–1082.

Yale, C. E. (1989). Conversion surgery for morbid obesity: Complications and long-term weight control. *Surgery, 106,* 474–480.

Yanovski, J. A. (2001). Pediatric obesity. *Endocrine & Metabolic Disorders, 2,* 371–383.

Yanovski, S. Z., & Yanovski, J. A. (2002). Drug therapy: Obesity. *New England Journal of Medicine, 346,* 591–602.

Glossary

Adhesion—bands of surgically induced scar tissue

Alimentary—that part of the intestine that carries food substances

Bariatric—from the Greek root "baros," meaning burden or weight

Biliopancreatic—combined gallbladder (bile) and endocrine (pancreas) secretions that allow for the absorption of fats and carbohydrates

Common channel—the length of small intestine that follows the connection of the food stream with the digestive juices that allows for absorption of nutrients

Distal—term indicating the more distant or farther distance from a specified beginning point

Dumping syndrome—a clinical syndrome induced when a large bolus of carbohydrates is introduced rapidly into the small intestine, causing increased heart rate, sweating, and abdominal cramps

Duodenum—the first of three parts or segments of the small intestine that immediately follows the stomach

Greater curvature—the inferior border of the stomach

Hernia—a rupture or opening of the abdominal wall or an abnormal intra-abdominal opening that can cause bowels to become blocked or obstructed

Ileum—the third part of the small intestine that immediately connects to the colon

Jejunum—the second or middle part of the small intestine that is preceded by the duodenum and followed by the ileum

Laparoscope—a tubular camera device that is inserted into the abdomen to visualize structures and facilitate surgery

Lesser curvature—the superior border of the stomach

Malabsorption—a clinical condition in which certain nutrients, vitamins, and minerals are poorly, if at all, absorbed by the intestines

Marginal ulcer—an ulcer that forms at a surgical connection between the stomach and the small intestine

Protein calorie malnutrition—a state of severe malnutrition induced by poor absorption of calories and nutrients

Proximal—term indicating the closer distance from a specified beginning point

Roux-en-Y—surgical term for reconstruction of the stomach to the small intestine with the bile and pancreatic juices attached as a Y-like configuration, from the French, "route configured in a Y-shape"

Stoma—surgically created opening from intestine to intestine or from an intestinal structure to the abdominal wall

Subtotal gastrectomy—surgical removal of two thirds of the stomach

Index